Heathrow's
Terminal 5

HEATHROW'S TERMINAL 5

History in the Making

Sharon Doherty

ThinQ Differently

John Wiley & Sons, Ltd

Other Wiley Editorial Offices

John Wiley & Sons Inc., 111 River Street, Hoboken, NJ 07030, USA

Jossey-Bass, 989 Market Street, San Francisco, CA 94103-1741, USA

Wiley-VCH Verlag GmbH, Boschstr. 12, D-69469 Weinheim, Germany

John Wiley & Sons Australia Ltd, 42 McDougall Street, Milton, Queensland 4064, Australia

John Wiley & Sons (Asia) Pte Ltd, 2 Clementi Loop #02-01, Jin Xing Distripark, Singapore
129809

John Wiley & Sons Canada Ltd, 6045 Freemont Blvd, Mississauga, Ontario, L5R 4J3, Canada

Wiley also publishes its books in a variety of electronic formats. Some content that appears
in print may not be available in electronic books.

Library of Congress Cataloging-in-Publication Data

Doherty, Sharon.
   Heathrow's terminal 5 : history in the making / Sharon Doherty.
      p. cm.
   Includes bibliographical references and index.
   ISBN 978-0-470-75435-1 (cloth)
   1. Airport terminals – England – London – Design and construction – History – 21st
century. 2. Heathrow Airport (London, England) I. Title.
   TL726.6.G72L6624 2008
   690′.539094218 – dc22

                                        2008009583

British Library Cataloguing in Publication Data

A catalogue record for this book is available from the British Library

ISBN   978-0-470-75435-1

Typeset in 11.5/15pt Bembo by Laserwords Private Limited, Chennai, India

CONTENTS

FOREWORD

Sir John Egan

*T*here are some stories in business that are worth telling and some that are worth learning from. Heathrow's Terminal 5, over 20 years in the making, falls into both categories in my opinion. It has all the ingredients of what makes business unpredictable, challenging and ultimately extremely rewarding.

As I reflect on T5, I remember the over 10-year-long frustrations of dealing with the pitfalls and politics of UK planning regulations, the balance to be struck between the need for world-class infrastructure for London and yet the need for responsible expansion, while trying to get the right regulatory settlement to be able to afford to build T5. Both Sir Mike Hodgkinson, my successor, and I battled through these challenges for over a decade. All of this was before we even started to think about the building of T5, which in its own right threatened to place a significant burden on the company. One billion pounds overspent and a year late were the predictions, if we followed the industry norm. A tightly regulated BAA could afford neither.

Coming from the car industry, I had been astonished by the waste and poor practice that I found in the construction industry in the 1990s, an industry of time and cost overruns that was killing over 130 people a year. As I chaired the Rethinking Construction government-sponsored thinktank, it became clear to me that the role of the client had to be fundamentally different. We needed to think differently about risk management and about long-term relationships with profitable suppliers, who worked with us to change the approach to the use of computer-based design, design for manufacture, supply chain management and safe and efficient processes, thus getting the best out of a well-trained workforce.

I certainly didn't have all the answers, but the commitment to a ground-breaking contract – the T5 Agreement, in which BAA held most of the risk – set a principle for the way of working. The right leadership, ongoing client involvement and a focus on getting integrated teams to perform to a world-class standard has meant that the UK construction industry has delivered a rare success story. I take my hat off to Mike Clasper and the senior T5 team, in particular, who really had to hold their nerve during construction as the theory of the T5 Agreement was tested. Delivering a £4.3 billion project that integrates with the rest of Heathrow airport on time and on budget is a great achievement.

The most rewarding part of T5 is the first-class passenger experience that will act as a fitting legacy to all who have been involved. I visited T5 a little while ago. It is an iconic piece of infrastructure, which is a tribute to the best of the world's design and engineering. The look and feel is bright and modern, with intuitive way finding, great views and retail options that will make it a pleasure to pass through at pace or with time to dwell.

I look back on my engagement with the teams and the project with pride, and look forward to using T5 as a passenger.

NOTE FROM THE AUTHOR

I took three months off work to write this book, and what I thought would be a leisurely, cathartic experience ended up being a seven-day-a-week, 3000-words-a-day challenge to hit the publishing deadline, so even in the writing T5 was demanding. I felt compelled to tell the Terminal 5 story from an insider's perspective, to share what really happened over so many years. I wanted to try to capture a moment in time when 50 000 people from 20 000 companies came together and achieved a common goal: to open T5 on time and on budget, and to start to put some of the glamour back into flying at Heathrow.

This is my first mega project, but for so many involved in designing, building and opening large infrastructures it is easy to see why it gets under your skin. Regardless of the time or cost overruns that so many complex projects encounter, the thrill of seeing the work you have been involved in for years of your life stand the test of time, be used and admired by so many, is something that instils much pride and a determination to do the best work you can do.

During my five years involved in T5 as the HR and organizational effectiveness director, I had the opportunity to talk and listen to thousands of people, and over a hundred of them again in some detail to write this book. While my job was to help step-change how things were done in big, complex projects in terms of people and organization, I was always impressed with the project-management and engineering capability that enabled 8000 people at any one time, from so many companies, to coordinate so much in a timely and safe manner, delivering roads, rail, buildings and systems on a site the size of Hyde Park.

In my conversations it was always interesting that so many of the people I spoke to described T5 as 'the best job they had ever been involved in'. That was normally followed by things they would do differently, so I think they were being pretty frank. These were comments from senior people, but also the men and women who worked on the tools. For so many the theme was the same: BAA had created an environment that actually allowed them to focus on being the best they could as project managers, design leaders, engineers or supervisors, rather than spending time second guessing the commercial impact on their company of every change or challenge.

This book is dedicated to the people who were involved in T5, some who gave a few weeks, but many who gave five, ten and in some cases over twenty years to see T5 opened successfully. I would also like to acknowledge the openness of senior BAA staff and suppliers, who trod a fine line in sharing learning without damaging company reputations.

Finally, it is fitting that most of the author's proceeds from this book go to a local T5 charity. This was a book to which so many people contributed. For five years the T5 charity committee worked and raised over £300 000 for the local community and they have asked that the proceeds go to one of the charities T5 supported: the local Fordway Centre, a school that helps children aged 5–11 who are presented with BESD; behavioural, emotional and social difficulties.

Lots of things didn't go to plan on T5. There were challenges, plan Bs and heated conversations along the way. But my overwhelming memory will be one of a really committed team of senior people, from many companies, who pulled in the same direction, made the difficult decisions and stood by the consequences. A team of people who worked really hard, 24/7 at times, but who enjoyed working together. Leaders for whom T5 was personal, not a job, but a project in which the stakes were high and most days were matched by the same degree of determination to succeed.

PART 1

THE T5 CONTEXT

*T*here are five parts to this book to help you navigate the T5 context, story, critical success factors and the verdict on the overall approach, followed by appendices:

Part 1 positions the aviation, retail and construction industry context in which decisions to develop T5 were taken.

Part 2 looks at each of the phases of the T5 journey: planning, design, construction and operational readiness. Retail is also explored in this part, an important part of T5's and indeed BAA's history, and with a slightly different approach to the main T5 Programme.

Part 3 starts to explore why T5 broadly has been a successful UK multibillion-pound project. The hypothesis is that the leadership involved were not always dealt the hand they would have chosen, but they pulled off the project, supported by an intelligent and involved client who put in place the right infrastructure and investment to set the integrated supply chain team up for success.

Heathrow's Terminal 5: History in the Making   S. Doherty
© 2008 John Wiley & Sons, Ltd

The front-line people story is also explored in this part, set up for success by the client and led well by those involved.

Part 4, the ending, explores what may still stop T5 from being a success, the predicted verdict.

Appendixes. For those wanting a takeaway from the book, these include some helpful questions that may be of use to those starting similar projects. There is also a list of designers, key suppliers and consultants involved in T5.

This is a genuine and candid account of the T5 project and so does not shy away from covering events that didn't work out the way they were planned. Many of those involved in T5 over the years have kindly agreed to be interviewed and it is with their help and insights that the story is told. The intention is certainly not to detract in any way from the undoubted success of the T5 Programme or the teams and organizations involved, but rather to encourage others to learn from T5's mistakes and build on its successes.

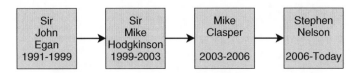

BAA CEOs

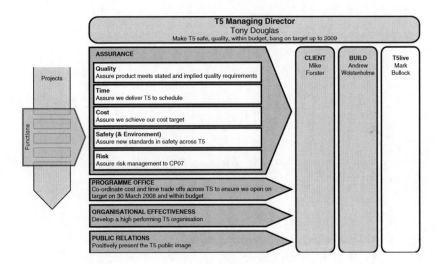

T5 organization structure

In addition there were 150 first tier suppliers,
2,000 third tier suppliers, 5,000 fourth tier
and 15,000 fifth tier

T5 principal contractors

CHAPTER 1

INTRODUCTION

Airports have come to symbolize progress, freedom, trade and the aspirations of their host nation on a global stage. At the same time they represent pollution, noise and fear to a world waking up to global warming. Airports are often loathed and opposed by the very people who demand cheap flights to their favourite holiday destinations.

Heathrow airport is a unique place, still holding its own as the busiest international airport in the world. Flying passengers to over 180 different destinations, Heathrow is a melting pot for all nationalities and backgrounds. The Queen and Prince Philip are regular users, and over the years such luminaries as the Beatles, Marilyn Monroe, Diana Ross, Nelson Mandela, Mikhail Gorbachev, Posh and Becks, George W. Bush senior and junior and the 2003 world cup-winning England rugby side have all passed through its gates; the Spice Girls' reunion in 2007, saw them opening the newly refurbished T3. Less welcome guests are also very interested in Heathrow – in 2004 Scotland Yard's flying squad swooped on

Heathrow's Terminal 5: History in the Making   S. Doherty
© 2008 John Wiley & Sons, Ltd

seven robbers trying to grab gold and cash valued at £80 million near the cargo area (BBC News, 2004). They are not the first and won't be the last to spot a financial opportunity at the world's busiest international airport.

And yet for so many the experience of today's Heathrow is not positive. The facilities strain under the pressure of running at over 99% capacity at all times, with no room for manoeuvre even in these troubled times of security alerts. Dealing with 68 million passengers in a facility designed to handle 45 million has been less than ideal for BAA, the airlines and sadly the passengers as well. As T5 opens in March 2008, over 22 years from the initial White Paper consent, there will be many who think that not getting the T5 facility open for the travelling public four or five years earlier was a real missed opportunity. If planning permission and regulatory settlements had played out differently, the UK could have built, and had open, both T5 and Heathrow East (tied to a third runway and first considered in response to a 2003 White Paper), which would have meant that by now 80% of the facilities at Heathrow would have been new and providing a world–class experience.

T5's opening date of 30 March 2008 was set in 2001 and a budget of £4.3 billion established in 2003. When the T5 Programme started, the predictions were that the terminal would open a year late and be a billion pounds overspent, an alarming prospect for the board of any plc. This is the tale of how leaders over time, from BAA, BA and some of the 20 000 suppliers who have been involved in T5, worked together in a different environment, with the tone set by a ground-breaking contract, the T5 Agreement, in which the client held most of the risk. This was a fundamentally different approach that in turn allowed 50 000 people working in integrated teams to deliver on time, on budget, safely and with care to the environment a good design and an even better passenger experience.

The planning, design, construction and opening of T5 have been a winding path that will be explored in some detail in this book.

The longest *planning inquiry* in UK history, which sat for 525 days, heard 734 witnesses, absorbed 20 million spoken words and carried out around 100 site inspections, ultimately gave the green light to build T5 with over 700 planning conditions.

Three different *design* schemes evolved over the years as planning hurdles were overcome and world events such as the King's Cross tube fire and the 9/11 terrorist attack meant that specifications needed to change. T5 is set in a mature landscape, including the 250 000 new trees and shrubs that have been planted, and is easy to get to with Piccadilly line and Heathrow Express extensions, a spur road built from the M25 and good bus and coach connections. Passengers will be greeted by dancing fountains in a boulevard-like interchange plaza that is home to 40 mature London plane trees. The 156-metre single-span 'wavy roof' and a glass façade afford passengers views of Windsor, London and of course the aircraft, while always feeling light and spacious. The iconic design will be challenged by some as being too costly, but has the potential ultimately to stand the test of time as a facility that looks good but works even better.

T5 was *constructed* on a site of 260 hectares, the size of Hyde Park, using the ground-breaking T5 Agreement commercial contract, in which BAA held most of the risk. It was made up of 147 subprojects, which clustered into 18 projects, and was led by four project heads, one for civil engineering, rail and tunnels, buildings and systems, and these collectively became the £4.3 billion T5 Programme. The main terminal building floor plates are the equivalent of 50 football pitches. There is 17 000 tonnes of steel in the roof of the main terminal building, which weighs the equivalent of 2800 bull elephants. To keep the workforce productive, 8000 people were being transported on 60 buses, fed in one of 18 canteens – and 18 000 000 metres of loo roll were used! As the terminal was being built it was the largest single construction site in Europe.

The *operational readiness* team has three opening events. The Queen will cut the ribbon prior to the opening date, there is an event on the actual day of opening and then the Saturday afterwards the Olympic torch will pass through T5 and the National Lottery will be hosted in the building. In preparation over three years, a joint BAA and BA team has worked to ensure that all of the people, processes and systems will be ready and working in the new facility on day one. Typically in airports such as Hong Kong or Denver it has been systems challenges that have delayed the opening date, so meticulous planning has gone into ensuring that this doesn't happen at T5. In the last six months of the T5 Programme, 72 proving trials each involving up to 2500 people will have tested how T5 works. By 26 March 2008 about 55 % of the first phase of the BA move will have taken place. Then on the evening of 26 March the first switch activity will move over most of BA's T1 and T4 short-haul services into T5, and its long-haul flights from T1 and T3. This move on the eve of the T5 opening will include 95 full lorries of equipment from inside the buildings, 2100 pieces of ground support equipment and 35 aircraft that are on the ground at night. The second switch takes place on 30 April 2008 and moves the remaining long-haul flights from T4 into T5.

HEATHROW, AN ECONOMIC POWERHOUSE

Heathrow's history

The roots of Heathrow airport (BAA, 1995) lie in the Second World War, when the Air Ministry determined that Northolt Aerodrome, which lies some four miles to the north of Heathrow, was too small to handle heavy bombers and large transport aircraft. In 1942 a survey of possible sites around London began for a second suitable military airfield.

A piece of land bought in 1929 between Bath Road and Staines Road, which had already been used for experimental flying and development, was deemed suitable for the site of the new military airfield. In 1944 work began on the construction of Heathrow, with initial plans outlining nine runways, three of which were to be to the north of Bath Road forming a triangle, and six to the south of the A4, which were designed to provide three parallel pairs of runways that would allow aircraft to take off and land into the wind irrespective of its direction.

By 1945 the first runway and some buildings on the north side of the airfield had been built and the first commercial flight took place in 1946, when British South American Airways carried 10 passengers to Buenos Aires. That year saw 63 000 passengers use Heathrow, in comparison with nearly 200 000 passengers a day now. By 1947 work had begun on a tunnel under runway one, leading to the central area, along with a control tower, office facilities, the Queen's Building and today's Terminal 2 (T2), which was opened in 1955.

In 1962 today's Terminal 3 (T3) was opened, providing a new terminal for long haul, and by 1968 Terminal 1 (T1) had opened for short haul. In the same year the cargo terminal on the south of Heathrow opened, along with a tunnel connecting it to the central terminal area (CTA). With more terminals and passengers the focus moved to surface access, with the M4 and spur road completed in 1965 and in 1971 work starting on the extensions to the Piccadilly line from Hounslow West to the central area or the airport, via Hatton Cross.

The first Boeing 747 arrived at Heathrow in 1970 and by 1977 some 13% of passengers were being carried on this kind of aircraft. The number grew and by 1979 this put such pressure on T1 to T3 that permission to build T4 was granted, along with the construction of a dual carriageway from the terminal to the link between the A3044, Stanwell Moor Road, and the A3113, Airport Way, which now provides direct access to junction 14 of the M25. In 1986 Prince Charles and Princess Diana opened T4.

The Heathrow we broadly know today has been developing since the mid-1980s. Other nations around the world continued to develop aviation infrastructure at a pace and Heathrow was to wait for over 22 years before the next significant step forward was able to be made – T5.

A new airport for London

When T5 comes on line in 2008, it will give Heathrow the capacity to provide a service to 90 million passengers a year within the existing runway capacity and also provide it with the breathing space to start to get back on the front foot with upgrading the other terminals. T5 has fundamentally changed the layout of Heathrow, which was originally built on a 'star of David design'. The opening of T5 signals a move to a 'toast rack'. This sets the shape that Heathrow East and future developments will start to follow.

Can Heathrow shake off its bad press and start delighting passengers again? Regulatory settlements allowing, there are plans for most of Heathrow to be refurbished or new by 2012 in time for the UK to host the Olympics. The new Virgin lounge opened in 2007; T5 comes on line in March 2008; additional refurbishment takes place in T1, T3 and T4; the closure and demolition of T2 and the Queen's building will make way for Heathrow East.

New facilities are only part of the answer when aiming to create a world-class passenger experience. Having an engaged and motivated workforce who want to protect and serve passengers productively is critical and is a difficult balance to achieve at times. To deliver this ambition for both airlines and airport operator requires significant work practice changes, which given that UK aviation is riddled with longstanding 'Spanish practices' is tough to deliver. By no means straightforward, this requires careful management of an influential group of trade unions, who understand the global impact of industrial action at Heathrow.

Why Heathrow is an economic powerhouse

Heathrow is the UK's only truly global hub, linking London to the rest of the world. It is the world's busiest international airport, with 90 scheduled airlines using it, flying 68 million passengers to 180 destinations around the world, resulting in over 473 000 flights a year.

Heathrow is used by 10 % of the world's airline traffic, the majority of this from three major worldwide airline alliances: Oneworld, Star Alliance and Skyteam, which now account for 80 % of Heathrow's

Heathrow Airline Alliances

Heathrow Airline Alliances	2004	% at Heathrow
Oneworld BA, Qantas, American Airlines, Cathay Pacific, Aer Lingus, Iberia (BA Share:)	34.5 mppa (27.9 mppa)	51 % (41.6 %)
Star British Midland, United Airlines, Singapore, Air Canada. Lufthansa, SAS	16.8 mppa	25 %
Skyteam Air France, KLM, Alitalia	3.3 mppa	5 %
Non-aligned Airlines (Virgin share:)	12.5 mppa (3.1 mppa)	19 % (4.6 %)

Figure 1.1   Heathrow airline alliances.

passengers (see Figure 1.1). There is significant local demand, with 83 % of the direct passengers in 2004 travelling from or to locations in the South East of England. There is a strong route network when compared to its mainland European competitors, with Heathrow offering the highest number of flight frequencies to the world's major destinations (see Figure 1.2).

Heathrow's European hub status is under threat, though, as Paris's Charles de Gaulle, Amsterdam's Schiphol and Frankfurt all have more runways and a greater land take (see Figure 1.3). While Heathrow is currently the most productive airport, the forecast is that it will be superseded by its European competitors by 2010 if it does not get permission for a third runway (see Figures 1.4 and 1.5).

Number Of Non-stop Departures Per Week - Summer 2004

	LHR	CDG	FRA	AMS
NewYork	135	60	35	18
Chicago	80	21	38	16
Washington	59	21	28	14
Los Angeles	59	23	17	7
Toronto	53	20	23	20
Singapore	49	17	28	18
Tokyo	42	33	21	14
Bangkok	32	14	30	17
Hong Kong	45	14	14	12
Dubai	55	14	21	7

Figure 1.2   Number of non-stop departures.

European Hub Airports Land Take 2004

	Landtake (ha)	Pax	000 pax/ha
Heathrow*	1.227	67.1 mppa	54.7
Paris (CDG)	3.309	51.0 mppa	15.4
Frankfurt	1.397	50.8 mppa	36.4
Amsterdam	2.147	42.4 mppa	19.7
* including T5			

Figure 1.3   European airports' land take, 2004.

European Airports Runway Capacities

	2004 R/ways	2004 ATMs	2006 R/ways	2010 ATMs (capacity)
Heathrow	2	67.1 mppa	2	54.7
Paris (CDG)	4	51.0 mppa	4	15.4
Frankfurt	3	50.8 mppa	4	36.4
Amsterdam	4	42.4 mppa	5	19.7

Figure 1.4   European airports' runway capacities.

European Hub Airports Capacity Comparison

	Current passenger numbers mpps	Runways	Destinations served	Current flights per year	2010 flight capacity	%Full (Current flights as a proportion of 2010 capacity)
Heathrow	67.7	2	180	473.000	480.000	98.5 %
Frankfurt	51.9	3	262	490.000	660.000	74.2 %
Paris CDG	53.5	4	223	522.000	710.000	73.5 %
Amsterdam	44.1	5	222	420.000	600.000	70.0 %

Figure 1.5   European hub airports' capacities.

The 2003 Future of Air Transport White Paper reinforced the view that Heathrow is much more than just an airport for London, recognizing that it delivers significant direct and indirect benefits to the local and national economy:

- *Employment generation.* Heathrow supports around 150 000 direct and indirect jobs in the local area and 68 000 employees actually work at the airport (BAA, 2005).
- *UK competitiveness.* Nearly 3.5 million foreign business trips are made to the UK through Heathrow each year. A total of £62.7 billion of UK exports are by air (Oxford Economic Forecasting, 2006) and 56% of all UK freight passes through Heathrow. International transport links are an important factor when companies decide where to locate. A survey of 500 of Europe's top companies found that 52% considered transport links a vital factor in deciding where to locate, while 60% identified access to markets, customers and clients as essential (Cushman & Wakefield Healey & Baker, 2005).
- *Tourism.* Of the 68 million passengers a year using Heathrow, over 9 million foreign visitors use the airport each year, with spending while in the UK estimated to be worth 1.5% of the country's gross domestic product (BAA, 2005).

Heathrow celebrated its 60th birthday in 2006. It has had an illustrious history as a key global landmark in aviation and a formidable economic force. As we look forward another 60 years, what will its fate be?

WHY SHOULD YOU READ THIS BOOK?

Written to appeal to those who enjoy both familiar and fascinating facts or an impossible challenge matched with human endeavour, and mostly for those who want to learn from a UK success story, *Heathrow's Terminal 5: History in the Making* is for those in the industry, those interested in modern history or simply those keen to explore details of how such a large-scale transformation was delivered.

We all know and have an opinion about Heathrow. The facts span all aspects of aviation and construction industry and are unashamedly used to try to share the scale of the task. It was a task that was at times predicted to be sure to fail, even after planning permission was finally granted. To design, build and open a £4.3 billion project on time and on budget was bucking the trend. Faced with failure companies and leaders can often take brave steps, and for BAA the T5 Agreement, the unique contract in which BAA held most of the risk, set a tone that permeated everything that was done on T5 and empowered key leaders from different companies to work together in integrated teams to deliver success.

Heathrow before T5

Heathrow after T5

CHAPTER 2

INDUSTRY TRENDS AND PERFORMANCE

**We had to navigate the multibillion-pound avia-
tion, construction and retail industries that were
changing rapidly, most of these changes were
not in our control and we couldn't always see
what was on the horizon.**

Mike Hodgkinson, CEO of BAA, 1999–2003

As BAA was moving from a public to private company
in 1987, Sir John Egan and his team were reviewing the changes
in the aviation and construction industry along with the emerging
opportunities in airport retailing. These were diverse industries, at
different stages of evolution, with quite different global opportunities, political challenges, environment implications and financial
risks that had to be navigated by a regulated company.

Over the 20 years of T5's lifespan, BAA boards continually
reviewed their operating context to make the best short- and

long-term decisions, and understand who they needed to influence and work with to ensure that T5 would 'make Heathrow not break it'.

AVIATION TRENDS

During T5's planning permission process, design, construction and operational readiness, the aviation industry has changed dramatically. It is useful to explore the changes in aviation and some of the external factors that have provided the backdrop to T5 and the context in which decisions were made and some subsequently changed.

The shape and size of the aviation industry

According to Oxford Economic Forecasting, in 2004 the UK aviation industry contributed £11.4 billion to the UK's gross domestic product and employed 186 000 people directly. By 2030 it is estimated that it will generate over £80 billion (Oxford Economic Forecasting, 2006). Today almost 70 000 of aviation jobs are at Heathrow Airport. Visitors arriving by air contribute £12 billion a year to UK tourism and generate a further 150 000 jobs. So aviation is a significant part of the UK economy and Heathrow is the horsepower that drives it.

Political landscape

Global deregulation of the aviation market

Markets have increasingly been deregulated, allowing new entrants into markets previously 'owned' by national carriers. The recent agreement on 'open skies' by European Union transport ministers allows European airlines to run transatlantic flights to any American city from any EU country, not just their 'home country'. Many of the outdated intergovernmental restrictions on how and where airlines can operate mask an inefficient industry, much of which is government subsidized, but over time the situation is slowly changing.

Over the years the changes have created mergers, new entrants and different pressures for space at Heathrow, all of which have needed to be managed.

UK planning and regulation

Although aviation is a critical contributor to the UK economy, the granting of planning permission to airports has always been a political hot potato, in the UK more so than nearly anywhere else. From White Paper to consent T5 took over 22 years. The impact of this for BAA was both financially and reputationally significant. If the time had been halved to 11 years, at 3.5% inflation the cost of T5 could have been half what it turned out to be. Equally, some of the many wrangles BAA found itself in with the press around Heathrow, summed up in the headline 'Our airports a national disgrace' (*Daily Mail*, 2007), would have been much less likely.

After granting of the final planning consent for T5, the debate has shifted to the general expansion of South East England. The 2003 White Paper, The Future of Air Transport, said that 'provision should be made for two new runways in the South East by 2030'; that 'the first new runway should be at Stansted, to be delivered as soon as possible'; and that 'the further development of Heathrow is supported, including a further new runway and additional terminal capacity to be delivered as soon as possible after the new runway at Stansted, but only if stringent environment limits can be met'. Since the White Paper was published BAA has been trying to deliver government policy for new runways at both Stansted and Heathrow airports as quickly as possible.

A significant amount of BAA's CEO's time is spent trying to get planning permission for additional expansion and gaining the correct regulatory settlement to be able to afford to build and operate the facilities. Sir Mike Hodgkinson was able to steer BAA to a regulatory settlement for Heathrow of 7.75% return on capital, which equated to 6.5 % above retail price inflation (RPI), for the quinquennium, the five-year period leading up to the opening of T5. He also gained a tacit understanding that all other things being equal, a similar settlement would be justified for the five years after opening, in order to reward BAA fully for the risks it took in undertaking a project that virtually doubled its market capitalization. Basically, that meant that BAA would be allowed to increase landing charges by the rate of inflation plus 6.5 %, hence by over 10 % p.a. in nominal terms, over the five years from 2002 to 2007 As things stand today, for the next five-year settlement the regulator is advocating that BAA should expect to receive a return on capital of only 6.25 %; the coming months will see the outcome determined.

Despite more than 10 % increases in landing charge in the five years to 2007, the offsetting effects of BAA's very large and successful commercial income streams, retail and property for example, meant that in 2007 as a passenger at Heathrow you still only paid £9.50 per flight, making Heathrow among the lowest cost of the world's big hub airports. Economically and competitively relevant though that might be in a global economic sense, for individual airlines operating at Heathrow that had grown used to settlements equal to or even lower than RPI, more than 10 % annual increases in one of their costs were a cause for much concern. They were vocal in expressing that concern, especially as the cause of this increase, T5, was ultimately going to benefit only one airline substantially, British Airways. Even for British Airways, such a large increase in its home base costs was cause for much scrutiny, rational and emotional, of BAA's strategies, plans and costs, even with T5 as the ultimate prize.

Managing competitive equivalence at Heathrow

While the T5 team focused on making the project 'on time, cost, quality, safe', trying to balance the current and future needs of all the airlines while appearing to be fair was the challenge of the Heathrow airport management team, led by Mick Temple, managing director 2001–06, and the board member responsible for Heathrow, Janis Kong. If all the airlines at Heathrow could see nothing beneficial to them from T5 to merit these increases, then the operational integration and cooperation that allow Heathrow to function way over its design capacity would be threatened. The other home-based airlines, bmi and Virgin, and the large airline alliances, OneWorld, Star and Skyteam, were looking for very substantial and tangible benefits that would allow them to continue to compete with BA and carry on providing the network of routes and schedules that makes Heathrow a compelling choice for air travel. Temple had always been very acutely aware of this need for 'competitive equivalence' and hence was often controversial in the positioning of T5. The real question was whether T5 would be the making, or the breaking, of Heathrow.

The big benefit that had to be sold to the other airlines was that the first move on the board, BA into T5, would allow the rest of the airlines to start to get what they wanted from a less constrained Heathrow. This was not a decision that was taken lightly, and Ian Badger from BAA spent several years in the 1990s reviewing the pros and cons before finally coming to this conclusion. Delivering competitive equivalence for the rest of the airlines at Heathrow – or at least managing a delicate path through that thorny subject – was Temple's challenge, supported by Hodgkinson and then Mike Clasper. Tony Douglas, T5 managing director at the time, and Andrew Wolstenholme, then T5 construction director, had to focus on making sure that they delivered on time and to budget. The idea of other airlines having to pay even more than had been anticipated for T5 on top of the more than 10% p.a. would be a hard pill to swallow.

Given the scarcity of space, slots and general capacity at Heathrow, every move on the board is scrutinized by the airlines to understand which of them are winners and which losers. Years lost in the public inquiry exaggerated this way of thinking, as the existing facilities were used at beyond their planned capacity for several more years than expected. Airlines fell into a number of groupings around how they approached 'competitive equivalence' and what they wanted by way of facility investment to achieve it. Virgin was resigned to BA getting T5, so it focused on trying to deliver a different, and in their view a potentially better, experience than T5. Temple worked with Virgin as he did with the other airlines to get their equivalent of T5. The T3 plans provided for a quick and exclusive Virgin experience, with upper-class passengers having the ability to drop their car off at an exclusive 'front door', walk through their own security experience and have as short as possible a route to their swish new commercially important passengers' (CIP) lounge, the 'clubhouse'. The experience for economy passengers, while not as private, would be exclusively Virgin and speedy. The other requirement was that the facilities should be ready to allow a launch around Christmas 2007, before T5. This was done in style with a certain amount of razzmatazz designed to upstage BA, involving Virgin boss Richard Branson and the Spice Girls.

For the Star Alliance, which includes key Heathrow airlines such as bmi, United Airlines, Singapore, SAS and Lufthansa, the problem was as much a question of timing as of appropriate facilities. Early on in discussions it was clear that if BA was to shift its operation from the eastern side of the airport, where T1 and T2 are, to the west, then the only logical solution for Star, as the second biggest grouping by far, was to congregate 'under one roof' in the east. This co-location would bring many opportunities for operational and customer service improvements among the alliance partners. However, since BA was not moving out completely until 2008, it would clearly be many years after before Star got facilities anything like those in T5. Even when Heathrow East, a new-build replacement for T1 and T2 on the site of the existing T2 and Queen's Building, was conceived and shared with Star, the thorny question of timing remained. BAA had to agree to spend considerable sums on the existing T1 to make it acceptable for Star's operational and service requirements until Heathrow East could be constructed. The plan is that Star will have a state-of-the-art facility comparable to T5 by 2012.

The promise for Skyteam was a refurbished T4, and with the advent of the open skies agreement this has proved even more important, as previously excluded transatlantic carriers Delta, Northwest and Continental airlines will want to move in too.

For both Skyteam and the Star Alliance, the main focus was being able to demonstrate numerically that they were getting a competitive equivalent to BA. This was often difficult to demonstrate in a timely manner, given the inherent limitations of a capacity-constrained environment. BAA also met with the non-aligned airlines, those not in any of the big alliances, and discussed their needs in bilateral talks, with a view to meeting as many of those needs as possible. In the main they moved to where there was remaining space, some more happily than others.

Many critical conversations took place from 2000 between Temple, Kong, Hodgkinson and Clasper and the CEOs of the world's major airlines, to develop the complex series of under-standings and agreements that sought to deliver a competitive and vibrant Heathrow for all its users. Mike Forster, at this stage the strategy director Heathrow, Mark Bullock, now managing director for Heathrow, and others have picked up these high-level agreements and developed them into signed contracts and move-implementation plans.

T5 is clearly a great opportunity for British Airways and BAA Heathrow, but only if the other airlines can find their equivalent home and be able to provide a passenger experience that meets their brand aspirations and of which they can also be proud.

Economic trends

UK passenger growth

While the Civil Aviation Authority (CAA) was unsure which South East airport could cope with additional passenger numbers, its statistics between 1991 and 2001 continued to indicate that in the early days the trend in relation to passenger numbers was up, and throughout the final planning permission process UK South East passenger growth had trended at 5.7% annually (CAA, 2002), with future projections following a similar pattern. Even the effects of the Gulf War in 1991 or the 9/11 terrorist attack in 2001 were seen as momentary blips before traffic levels returned. As passenger flying trends changed and aircraft turnaround times improved, it became clear that Heathrow's capacity, even with only two runways, could move to 90 million passengers, but that a new terminal (T5) would be required.

Low-cost carriers

Passenger number increases were being driven in part by increases in population. In 1999 there were six billion people on the planet, with a prediction of that growing to seven billion by 2012 (UN 2007 Revision Population Database). The ability of that population to afford to fly was fuelled by the explosion of low-cost operators. The first successful low-cost carrier was Pacific Southwest Airlines in the United States, which pioneered the concept in 1949.

In 1971 perhaps the most famous low-cost operator got out of the blocks, Southwest Airlines. It revolutionized air travel and notably has been profitable since 1973, a fairly novel achievement in American aviation. With the advent of aviation deregulation the low-cost model spread to Europe as well, the most prominent successes being Ireland's Ryanair, which began low-fares operations in 1991, and the UK's easyJet, formed in 1995. Low-cost carriers developed in Asia and Oceania from 2000 led by operators such as Malaysia's Air Asia and Australia's Virgin Blue.

Asian passenger boom and European hub competition

Heathrow is not a low-cost airport, but clearly the impact on the market of being able to get extremely cheap flights – for example Ryanair flies from London Stansted to Barcelona Reus from £5 – has been an increase in the number of flights. Full-price carriers such as Virgin or BA have had to review their offers and price points on short-haul flights. BAA has also had to review the impact that low-cost carriers have had on its other airports, such as Stansted and Gatwick, and hence on its ongoing planning strategy.

The growth of the Asian market in the twenty-first century has presented a very real and direct market opportunity for Heathrow. According to International Enterprise, Singapore, along with 10 leading airports in the Middle East, is pumping US$23.5 billion into new airports by 2012, providing capacity for 316 million passengers annually and expanding total airport capacity to nearly 400 million (*Business Times*, 2007).

The challenge for Heathrow of this huge market opportunity is that as the Asian economies boom, passengers want to fly to Europe, so Heathrow needs to maintain or increase its European hub status. That is a tough order given the growth of Paris Charles de Gaulle, Frankfurt, Amsterdam Schiphol and Madrid Barajas, all of which are vying to be the European hub of choice. T5 was a critical factor in Heathrow's positioning in Europe, and the world, for connecting flights.

Bigger planes with more people on them

The Boeing 747 had dominated the jumbo-jet market for more than three decades. Then the Airbus A380 was officially revealed in January 2005 and, after some teething problems, finally took to the sky on its first commercial flight in October 2007. This new plane has a standard capacity of 550 passengers, versus the 400 of the 747, and to accommodate the A380 at Heathrow runways have been widened and strengthened, while taxiways have been repositioned and enlarged to ensure that there is enough room for the aircraft's 80-metre wingspan. Baggage-carousel belts have also been lengthened. Fourteen of the 62 T5 stands will be able to be able to accommodate A380s from day one, even though the requirements were clearly not understood when the original design was agreed, with the capacity to convert others.

For Heathrow this development has enabled the growth of passengers. Without a third runway Heathrow is capacity constrained in a way that Charles de Gaulle, Barajas and other European hubs are not.

Retail creates a new airport revenue stream

Some economic opportunities were of BAA's own making. It has spent hundreds of millions of pounds developing its terminals to provide the right shops for airport visitors. Retailing now accounts for 40% of the group's annual turnover (BAA Annual Report, 2005–06). It was really under the leadership of Egan that the opportunities to change both the passenger experience and the revenue opportunity for BAA were understood. Both as a retail property landlord and the owner of World Duty Free, BAA has navigated this opportunity through its ups and downs, the most notable being in 1999 when duty and tax-free sales in the European Union ended.

Chapter 7 explores the debate about the pros and cons of airport retail and the passenger experience in T5. BAA understood the opportunities that retail presented, as investment in retail infrastructure and resources had taken place during the opening of Stansted and T4 in a more significant way than had been seen before. The conversations about building T5 included Nick Ziebland, retail strategy director BAA, and he remembered: 'Egan would look to me and ask are you happy with the new T5 scheme, and if the answer that came back from the retail team was yes, then the design could move forward.' T5 will represent one of the world's finest shopping experiences, one of which many high streets would be proud. It provides an opportunity for the airport operator to keep the landing fees down, as retail revenue is part of the regulatory pricing equation, while at the same time providing choice for the travelling public.

The advent of different airport technology

During the 1990s there were advances in technology in the airport environment, providing efficiency and passenger service opportunities.

Sensibly, the technology strategy for T5 has always been leading edge not pioneering. Since early 2000 significant changes have occurred in the use of online check-in, biometric technology for storing personal details, security machines right through to the baggage system, safety-critical technology around fire systems and flight information display system (FIDS) screens for passenger information. A significant opportunity was there to be exploited, bringing new efficiencies, improvements in the passenger experience and airport control. A careful path had to be navigated by Nick Gaines, T5's head of systems, to secure the right systems and then work within BAA and its third-party suppliers to integrate these systems and deliver these benefits.

Environment influences

More flights means more pollution

Aviation in volume terms accounts for less than 5% of carbon dioxide emissions, but of all modes of transport it has the highest growth potential as a source of emissions (*Times*, 2005). There are 15,000 commercial aircraft in the world. 'But in 20 years' time there are forecast to be 15,000 more,' says Professor Ian Poll, director of the Cranfield School of Aeronautics.

Aircraft are getting 'greener', but unfortunately, given that they are expensive, they will be in operation for 20–30 years, so even as technology creates more fuel-efficient aircraft, the replacement cost means that fuel-inefficient aircraft will be in operation for many years to come.

The challenge for airlines, and indeed airport operators, is to try to get planning permission for expansion given the strength of the green lobby. The market is a powerful agent of change. New engine technology, more fuel-efficient aircraft and new sustainable fuels will all help reduce CO_2 emissions from aviation. The existence of the Dreamliner owes much to Boeing's early realization that it had to answer environment questions. Rolls-Royce, the British engineer supplying engines to the Dreamliner, can also pat itself on the back. Its Trent 1000 turbine, which accounts for about a quarter of the cost of the £100 million plane, is integral to the concept of the aircraft and its environment friendliness. But financial considerations are at least as important as tackling green issues.

Oil price rises

The price of oil is important to BAA on a number of fronts. As a large consumer of oil, managing its use of energy in its facilities is important, but the increase in costs also puts airlines under more pressure and intensifies debates over landing fees.

The cost of crude oil has tripled in the last five years and by November 2007 oil had reached $100 a barrel. Airlines have traditionally used hedging via commodities futures to limit the impact of price rises, but the recent rises have caught them by surprise and most large carriers have only limited protection in place for 2008. Unless there is a dramatic fall in the price of oil, airlines will be stuck with the extra cost, which will either be passed on to passengers or erode profits.

Oil production in America and Britain's North Sea is already in decline. Demand from China and other emerging countries will mean, on present trends, a doubling of global consumption over the next quarter century. Reliance on energy very much sits in the hands of many states in the Middle East that have less than perfect human rights records and unstable political environments.

Terrorism on the increase

Terrorism has always been a consideration for those involved in aviation. Since Peruvian terrorists hijacked a Pan Am mail plane in 1930, there have been almost 1000 incidents of aviation-related terrorism. Hundreds of aircraft have been hijacked, while bombs in flight have destroyed dozens of others. Until 2001, the most lethal single act of terrorism had been the 1985 Air India bombing, which killed 329 people.

The use of four hijacked aircraft as piloted cruise missiles in the 9/11 terrorist attacks in 2001 raised the bar on terrorism and killed some 3200 people in less than two hours. In December 2006 an explosion took place in the car park building attached to Terminal 4 of Madrid Barajas international airport, and then closer to home in June 2007 one of BAA's own airports, Glasgow, was set on fire by a Cherokee Jeep loaded with propane canisters and driven into the airport, setting it ablaze.

For T5 the impact of terrorism has been a significant consideration. Since 9/11, and before that the bombing of Pan Am Flight 103 over Lockerbie in Scotland, the focus on passenger segregation and on security screening processes both for passengers and employees has required different design schemes, shared in Chapter 4, with increased investment in security machinery and more security staff. Equally, during the construction of T5 consideration was given to it being a trophy target, resulting in extra vigilance and security checks on security and sweeps for explosive devices.

Construction trends

Rethinking UK construction

In the early 1990s, when Egan was looking ahead at the multibillion-pound construction spend for BAA, the outlook was not good. Within BAA Egan quickly got to grips with the need to work with the supply chain differently and introduced framework agreements, creating long-term relationships. He could see opportunities to drive out waste in production and started to work with those partners to look at processes and equipment. Ultimately, this way of working led to the idea of BAA contractually holding the risk on complex projects. The case for this was cemented on the back of the Heathrow Express tunnel collapse in 1994, explored in Chapter 10. BAA had little choice but to try to get suppliers to work together to resolve the problem, and this was more important than arguing about who was responsible, given that there was a big hole in the middle of the central terminal area (CTA). The project was in fact delivered on time. This learning and significant research and internal debate led to the design of the T5 contract, the T5 Agreement.

Egan's thinking about significant opportunities to do construction differently was recognized in the UK. In 1998 he was asked to chair a construction taskforce on behalf of then Deputy Prime Minister John Prescott, working with Tesco Stores, Nissan, British Steel, Whitbread Hotels and Slough Estates, among others, to formulate a number of recommendations. The report concluded:

> the UK construction industry, was at its best, excellent. Its capability to deliver the most difficult and innovative projects was above the potential of any other construction industry in the world. Nonetheless, there was a deep concern that the industry as a whole was under achieving. It had low profitability and invested too little in capital, research, development and training. Too many of the industry clients were dissatisfied with its overall performance.

The report proposed a numbers of drivers for change in the construction industry, including committed leadership, a focus on customers, integration of the process and the team around the product, driving a quality agenda and a commitment to people. Key benchmark targets were also identified (Construction Industry Taskforce, 1998).

The Rethinking Construction report and debate formed an influential landmark in UK construction. Very publicly the industry had started to discuss poor performance and the need for cultural, process and contracting changes. In BAA, and for T5, some of this work was put to good use to start doing things differently.

As T5 has moved through the planning, design, construction and operational readiness phases, construction industry trends and innovations have continued to provide opportunities to learn, manage, mitigate risks and exploit opportunities.

The shape and size of the construction industry

The global construction industry is of economic significant in its own right, as well as being a key enabler to other industry evolutions. The

Department of Trade and Industry's (DTI) construction report in 2004 described the industry in three parts: residential, nonresidential and infrastructure. At this time the industry generated £74 billion, 10 % of national gross domestic product (DTI, 2004).

Construction is an industry with limited barriers to entry, so it is no surprise that it is skewed to small firms. In 2006 the DTI construction report showed there to be 168 000 construction firms in the UK. This number is growing, although the top 50 construction companies are consolidating. Directly employed and self-employed workers bring the employment pool to just fewer than 2 million employees working in construction, 1.2 million directly employed (DTI, 2006).

Contracts and relationships move to partnering

The different types of contracts and the approach to funding that spans the public and private sector are significant, with fixed-price lump-sum contracts at one end and open-book, actual-cost and trust-based agreements at the other. At the heart of contracting is the approach to risk management (see Figures 2.1 and 2.2).

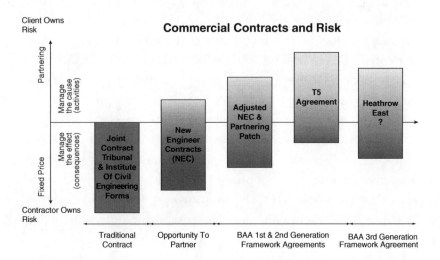

Figure 2.1 Commercial contracts and the approach to risk.

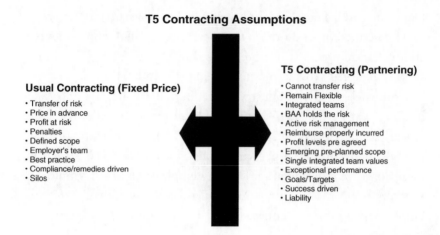

Figure 2.2 T5 contracting assumptions.

In a fixed-price contract, the contractor takes all the risk in the price. If there is no change in requirements, there is no increase in costs. If the client varies the requirement, the supplier may gain financially from the situation, with resultant losses being added to the contract price or blamed on the change. Fixed-price contracts often work for small or well-defined contracts and where the client does not want to hold the risk.

A cost-plus contract, in its simplest form, is where the client pays the contractor the actual cost plus a fixed fee, overheads and profit. The supplier charges what it costs him with some or no transparency over costs. The risk will be 100 % with the client, as the cost part is variable. On T5 BAA was very prescriptive about what is actual cost and what is meant by properly incurred cost. Although it is a form of cost-plus contract, it is being done in a much more partnering way, with an integrated team and in sophisticated manner, and in an environment where there is more trust but with the understanding that detailed cost verification may occur. This approach is good for projects where scope is not always known in detail, provided that the client is intelligent enough to understand and hold some or all of the risks.

Most of the T5 contractors who were interviewed for this book were very honest about the games that have been played with more traditional contracts. For example, 'Bid low to win the deal and then during the project your role was to safeguard your company's interest both financially and reputationally.'

Most of the contractors described the industry, particularly in the past but still in some quarters today, as 'aggressive, adversarial, with these types of relationships flowing from the type of contract the client puts in place'. These types of contracts don't get the best out of them, and more often don't deliver the most predictable outcome for the client, particularly in complicated jobs.

The T5 Agreement is quite an unusual contract in that the client decided to own most of the risk, insure the total T5 Programme and have a hands-on role. The advent of partnering that started in the oil and gas industry has slowly spread to other parts of the construction industry. The ideas of gain and pain share, using incentivization to try to bring about different behaviours, is gaining in popularity and certainly when contractors talk about these types of partnering contracts they are more positive. At an industry level it is difficult to tell statistically whether this more progressive way of contracting actually delivers more or fewer overruns, although we may find that the impact of poor initial cost estimations is now the most significant driver. This issue is explored further in Chapter 10.

Construction track record

Flybbjerg, Bruzelius and Rothengatter are academics, based in Denmark, Stockholm and Germany respectively, who for over 10 years have been tracking and reviewing £100 million-plus mega projects. Having reviewed 111 projects from 1920 to 2000, they conclude that the track record of cost and time overruns hasn't actually improved. 'If techniques and skills for estimating costs and avoiding cost overruns have improved, this does not show in the data,' they say. Reviewing 228 projects across rail, fixed links and roads in Sweden, the US, UK and Denmark, these academics were able to show cost overruns ranging from 40–80% (Flybbjerg et al., 2003).

Overoptimism in initial cost estimates, poor contingency costing and even a hypothesis that many projects would not get a green light for the realistic cost all drives the culture of 'price low and deal with the consequences later'.

The Rethinking Construction task force focused on what happened once projects started. Its members reviewed studies from the US and Scandinavia and suggested that up to 30% of construction was rework. Labour is used at only 40–60% of potential effectiveness, accidents can account for 3–6% of project costs and at least 10% of materials are wasted. The task force thought that these estimates were probably conservative, and that led it to suggest that there was at least 30% waste to be eliminated. While not commenting on initial cost estimations, the combination of Flybbjerg's work plus the inefficiency outlined by the Egan report do not bode well for cost and time predictability.

In recent years the track record of airport delivery has not been one to be proud of. Whether one considers Hong Kong, Denver or France's Charles De Gaulle, all have failed, regardless of the reviews and accolades some have received.

For BAA, these all held clues of where key risks to be managed were located and lessons that had to be learned. Visits by various teams to these locations and others helped T5 learn some painful and quite public lessons that will hopefully create a different legacy for BAA.

Hong Kong: Systems failure caused opening delays

Hong Kong's Chek Lap Kok airport opened in July 1998. The project was hampered by political uncertainty, as it straddled the handover of Hong Kong to China in 1997. Tough contract conditions (even when modified by the Hong Kong Contractors' Association), late design changes and challenges with contractor coordination were all par for the course. Today it stands as an award-winning airport and a benchmark that most others aspire to, and yet when it opened technical failings meant that it was dubbed by *The Economist* 'a fiasco', causing political embarrassment and said to cost the Hong Kong economy US$600 million (*The Economist*, 1999). A report from the time (BBC News, 1998) noted:

> Passengers faced long delays again on Tuesday as engineers tried to fix the computer problems, which have left flight information boards blank. Hong Kong's main cargo operator said on Tuesday it was temporarily moving most of its handling operation back to the old Kai Tak airport due to the issues. Hong Kong Air Cargo Terminals Ltd, HACTL, managing director, Anthony Charter, said: 'It appears we have got some sort of bug that is deleting records.'

Denver: Baggage system failures caused opening delays and cost overruns

Denver Airport in Colorado, USA, was originally scheduled to open in October 1993 with a single system for all three concourses. This became February 1995, opening with separate systems for each concourse, with varying degrees of automation. The baggage system's US$186 million original construction costs grew by US$1 million per day during months of modifications and repairs. The automated baggage system never worked well, and in August 2005 it became public knowledge (reported on Wikipedia) that United Airlines was going to abandon the system, a decision that would save them US$1 million in monthly maintenance costs.

Denver is perhaps one of the most famous and still publicly noted airport opening failures.

Charles de Gaulle: Delays in opening and roof collapse killing four passengers

Terminal 2E, with a daring design and wide-open spaces, was the newest addition at Charles de Gaulle. It opened in May 2003, after some delays due to construction issues, but in July 2004 a portion of its ceiling collapsed near gate E50, killing four people (CBC News, 2004).

In February 2005 the results from the administrative inquiry into the incident were published. The experts pointed out that there was no single fault, but rather a number of causes for the collapse in a design that had little margin for safety. The inquiry found that the concrete vaulted roof was not resilient enough, and had been pierced by metallic pillars and a number of openings that weakened the structure. Sources close to the inquiry also disclosed that the whole building chain had worked as close to the limits as possible, so as to reduce costs. Paul Andreu, lead architect, denounced the building companies for not having correctly prepared the reinforced concrete.

In March 2005, the airport operator ADP decided to tear down and rebuild that part of Terminal 2E, the jetty, where the section had collapsed, at a cost of approximately €100 million. The reconstruction replaced the innovative concrete tube style of the jetty with a more traditional steel and glass structure. Construction will be completed by summer 2008, and in the meantime two temporary departure lounges have been constructed in the vicinity of the terminal that replicate the capacity of 2E before the collapse.

After the collapse additional questions were asked of T5 engineering as to whether this sort of devastation could happen on T5. What was a more important lesson, however, was how multiple risks join up and create a calamity, and the T5 senior team spent time debating how this could be mitigated or managed differently. Given that there were so many variables, the conclusion was that each risk needed to be managed and then scenarios mapped, creating an extensive set of 'what ifs'.

Barajas

The winner of the 2006 Stirling prize, Barajas also ran into overruns and operational teething problems.

'Spanish Airports and Air Navigation (AENA) has decided to postpone one week the opening of the new terminal T4 airport Barajas, which eventually will take place on February 5 compared to the date of January 29 set so far, sources confirmed of the public body.' El Pais 11/01/2006

'The T-4, the new airport terminal in Madrid Barajas opened in February, continues to be a source of problems. In addition to the many difficulties involved (huge distances without communication still underground, etc.), the automated baggage system is not fully guaranteed. Last Saturday again fail, resulting in chaos for several hours and the loss of thousands of suitcases. Not enough apologies AENA and Siemens, the company in charge of the system.' [*sic*] El Pais 03/04/2006

UK construction track record

When the Suez Canal opened in 1869, its final cost was 20 times higher than the first estimate. The construction of New York's Brooklyn Bridge claimed 27 lives and cost twice what it was supposed to do. The Sydney Opera House cost 15 times the original budget. Work on St Paul's Cathedral was so extended and costly that Londoners had to pay a special coal tax to get it finished. It seems that time and location are not determining factors in project success.

Egan and Hodgkinson's thinking about the contracting strategy and approach to working with the supply chain was very much coloured by the catalogue of high-profile failures they had lived through. The Barbican Centre, opened by the Queen in 1982, started at £8 million and came in at £187 million. The Jubilee Line, ending at a doubled cost of £3.5 billion, opened late and was plagued with industrial challenges. The Dome did open on time and cost, but the UK taxpayer had to invest 'another £500 million' in its operation. The new British Library was almost £450 million over budget and 15 years behind schedule. The rail infrastructure from the north west of England to Glasgow after Railtrack went into administration in 2002 required the Strategic Rail Authority to intervene and steer a failing project to completion with £6 billion overspent (*Times*, 2003).

As T5 was being built, the other projects that failed or were of particular interest were Holyrood and Wembley Stadium. Stand-back reviews, looking at lessons learned about approach to design and construction, were commissioned by T5 managing director

Douglas, and at senior management meetings these lessons were shared as a 'cold shower of reality'.

Holyrood: Opened late and over budget

The £431 million cost, which started at £40 million, and three-year delay in the completion of the new Scottish Parliament building represent a management failure of 'gigantic proportions', the Fraser inquiry was told. John Campbell QC, counsel for the inquiry, made the claim in his closing submission that there had been a failure of direction and leadership at almost every level of official and professional involvement from the beginning (*Times*, 2004).

A Spanish designer, Enric Miralles from RMJM, was chosen, but died a few months after construction started. Miralles developed a grand design that he said was a building 'sitting in the land'. Seen in plan the Parliament is growing out of the site like a huge flower, with the leaves forming the different structures. Structures covered with grass run right up to the edge of the debating chamber. Garden paths and a series of ponds link all the buildings to the landscape around the four-acre site.

The outcome was a public embarrassment for the newly inde-pendent Scottish Parliament, but the initial cost plan was probably very unrealistic and provided a good example for the T5 team of a project with confused accountabilities, the grip on design being lost within insufficient programme controls and governance.

Wembley Stadium: Opened late and over budget

Wembley, a stunning 90 000 capacity stadium with a breathtaking 130-metre high arch, was scheduled to open for the May 2006 FA cup final. That game was actually played at Cardiff Stadium and Wembley didn't open until March 2007. It is probably the best recent example of how not to do construction, contract, design and management of industrial issues. Time and cost overruns meant that the Football Association and constructor Multiplex ended up in court (*Times*, 2006).

Wembley is an interesting comparison to T5, with less than 20% of the spend, much less complicated and a critical deadline that did end up being movable. *Construction News*, one of the industry journals, ran an inflammatory headline most weeks about strikes, cost overruns and high-profile fallouts between the client and contractor.

Green shoots of progress

Over the last 20 years there has been significant progress and innovation in how construction is designed, built and commissioned and in the controls that have been put in place.

Design

In design reputable architects want their designs to look good and work well, and hence they work closely with engineers and increasingly construction players. 3D modelling technology and single-model design environments allow faster, more joined-up design. The enemy of design continues to be change, and most good clients now realize this and either enforce disciplined processes or try to freeze design.

Construction

Prefabricating of as much as possible off site prior to construction has been a major development, reducing labour shortages and industrial risks, increasing the installation predictability of modules on site, and assisting with improved safety and quality. BAA understood these concepts and worked well with suppliers, listening to their ideas and encouraging this practice. This is explored further in Chapter 5.

There have been valuable cross-industry lessons for the construction industry from manufacturing the art of repeat-build processes. The Egan report suggested that up to 80% of buildings are repeated. Interestingly Tesco, which were one of the original contributors to the Rethinking Construction thinktank, at the time was embracing new approaches to technology and benefiting from it. The new Tesco Express store concept benefits from a standard module design that Tesco has worked up with Portakabin subsidiary Yorkon.

Standardization of products could give dividends, even though BAA has been a poorly disciplined client in execution of this idea despite strategically understanding the benefits. Schiphol airport is perhaps one of the best examples of a mid-sized facility that over the years has been added to in a consistent fashion. By contrast, if you look at BAA's airports, even individual airports like Heathrow, in different terminals and even within terminals there are different flooring, wall-covering and toilet schemes. A new standard has been created on the back of T5, and a good reason is then required to deviate from these agreed company standards.

The just-in-time logistics familiar in retail and manufacturing is a concept that is still in its infancy in construction. The theory works, but controlling multiple organizations with such a transient workforce is still difficult to implement.

Improved reporting systems enable more time and cost disciplines to be leveraged. 3D modelling is increasingly commonplace, not just for design but also in most complex builds. It was used by the team at Hong Kong Airport, with T5 building on that experience for the roof lift.

Benchmarking has been embraced along with quality- and value-management approaches. Safety process and behavioural techniques combine with a much greater focus on workforce welfare and skills training.

There have always been progressive projects where integrated teams have done good work. The T5 contractors, the likes of Laing O'Rourke, Mace, SPIE Matthew Hall (formerly AMEC) and Severfield-Rowen, had all had experiences in the early 1990s working on Stanhope office developments in the City. While these were projects in the range of £100 million and not open book, the spirit of the approach was partnering. Mark Reynolds from Mace talked of the 'beer and sandwich sessions' when there were problems, which normally helped the team find a solution.

Equally, as BAA introduced framework agreements with contractors it moved time and cost predictability on projects to over 95%. Critics would say that this predictability was bought with the cost-plus contracts that were put in place.

It's not all doom and gloom in the broader industry: there are good clients, working well with design and construction organizations that deliver on time and on budget. The Paris South East and Paris Atlantique high-speed rail lines and the Toronto Danforth rail extension are examples. Closer to home, the recent refurbishment of St Pancras station in London, using partnering techniques and lessons learned from the Channel Tunnel, delivered a splendid final passenger experience for £5.8 billion instead of the estimated £6.1 billion. Players such as Thames Water, some telecommunications companies and the large housing associations are also improving cost and time predictability through partnering-type contracts and increasingly their own involvement as intelligent clients (*Sunday Times*, 2007).

BAA is also keen to learn from other industries. Oil and gas has always been ahead of the building construction industry, and some of its early thinking on contracting, the approach to safety and the approach to project controls helped shaped the approach on T5.

SUMMARY

Faced with growth in aviation on the one hand, tempered by environment considerations and a failing construction industry on the other, there has been much to win or lose in the making of T5. Planning, regulatory and construction challenges against this backdrop have required big-picture thinking, drive, a different approach to trust, careful stakeholder management and an ability to get integrated teams to work effectively. These are qualities that the key leaders have demonstrated in sufficient quantum at critical times to deliver the T5 Programme successfully.

The opening of T5 will be a small step for the complex and changing aviation and construction landscape. Nevertheless, for successive BAA CEOs trying to understand the business context in which they have been trying to navigate, it has been a significant risk and opportunity to manage effectively. The T5 Agreement was the big idea that set a tone for the approach taken, which ultimately permeated that adopted by leaders, the client and the integrated teams.

Hong Kong Airport

Hong Kong Airport Interior

Denver Airport

Paris Charles De Gaulle Airport

Sydney Opera House

Madrid Barajas Airport

Holyrood

Wembley Arch

Projects that suffered overruns

PART 2

THE DIFFERENT PHASES OF T5

*O*ver 20 years there have been four different phases of T5: planning, design, construction and operational readiness. Although BAA understood these phases in theory, having opened other facilities and with a number of seasoned professionals in key leadership roles, practice is always more challenging. Over such a long period there was much to learn, many things that would not quite go to plan and need putting back on track, to turn T5 into a successful outcome. The phases were:

- *Planning*, getting appropriate consents.
- *Design*, deciding what passenger experience you want to create and facilities that will deliver what you can afford.
- Construction, when ideas and drawing become concrete, while delivering against the time, cost, quality, safety and environment agendas.

Heathrow's Terminal 5: History in the Making   S. Doherty
© 2008 John Wiley & Sons, Ltd

- *Operational readiness*, testing, proving and getting ready all of the people, processes, systems and facilities for opening day.
- Plus retail, which while not a phase will be covered separately in this section given its significance to BAA, T5 and the passenger experience.

These activities run concurrently in any project, but at different junctures the emphasis will be on a particular phase, type of leader and skill set. For something as big and complex as T5 the same process is followed, but the challenges, planning and numbers involved are all just a little bigger.

CHAPTER 3

PLANNING INQUIRY

In the time that it has taken to go through T5
inquiry, Hong Kong had developed, built and
put a new airport into action.

Rod Eddington, former CEO, BA
CSC Business Leaders' Forum, London 2004

*I*t's amazing that when T5 opens in March 2008 it will have
been over 22 years since the publication of the Airport Policy White
Paper that encouraged its development. The inquiry alone sat for
525 days, the longest in UK planning history, between 16 May 1995
and 17 March 1999. During this period, the inspector heard 734
witnesses and was presented with 5900 inquiry documents; over
20 million words were spoken and recorded on a daily transcript.
The inspector also carried out around 100 site inspections and sat
at 18 public meetings at locations around Heathrow at which over
300 members of the public gave evidence (BAA, 2007).

Heathrow's Terminal 5: History in the Making   S. Doherty
© 2008 John Wiley & Sons, Ltd

Roger Pellman, from the planning team at BAA, remembered some of the conversations:

> bat urine, fish, parrots, freshwater molluscs and the habits of tree sparrows were all subjects of debate. At one point there was an argument about whether the platforms at St Albans City railway station would need to be lengthened, and on another occasion a whole day was spent discussing whether dried sewage smells or not.

Such things apart, the impacts of any changes at Heathrow are considerable at a national and local level, so it is important that the right checks and balances are in place to ensure that all the arguments are understood and appropriately addressed, whether they are about CO_2 emissions, the effect on the local community during construction, employment opportunities in local boroughs or the impact on the City of London. With hindsight it is interesting that probably not enough time and energy was given to the need to upgrade the Heathrow facilities to allow passengers to experience a stress-free airport experience in what has become a new age with very different terrorist threats and customer expectations. Willie Walsh, CEO BA, described Terminal 1 and indeed the rest of Heathrow as 'organized chaos', as a facility for 45 million people strained to deal with 68 million passengers.

KEY PLAYERS

There are people who spend their time trying to pick their way through the machinery of national and local government to get planning approvals for big projects. Mike Toms and Alastair McDermid led the BAA Corporate team, and Michael Maine and Lynne Meredith led the planning inquiry team, supported by hundreds of planners, engineers, architects, lawyers, environment experts and airport managers. Ultimately, these teams took their steer from successive CEOs, who during this period were Sir John Egan and then

Sir Mike Hodgkinson. Both tried to ensure that government had in place a clear policy framework that would enable a way forward.

Making progress with planning included many twists and turns, both in government but also in BAA as it grappled with the financial and operational implications of this venture. The policy framework outlined in the government's 1985 White Paper identified key areas that BAA needed to investigate or take action on before it could proceed with T5 planning, notably the relocation of the Perry Oaks treatment plant and the solution to a number of surface access issues.

The business case for the new T5 was developed and approved by the BAA board in March 1992 and in April the company announced its intention to apply for consent. After the public presentation of its plans during 1992, BAA submitted the planning application in February 1993. It took a year for the government to appoint an inquiry inspector and he then held five pre-inquiry meetings before he finally opened the inquiry on 16 May 1995. The inquiry lasted until 17 March 1999. The inspector delivered his 618-page report on 21 November 2000, recommending that T5 should be permitted with strict conditions. Consent for T5 was granted, with almost 700 planning conditions, on 20 November 2001 and preliminary site work started in summer 2002.

The BAA and indeed the BA team involved in this long-drawn-out process talk about this as the 'the dark days'. Liz Southern, BAA head of development, explained 'whilst supportive of the public inquiry process we were all initially so excited to be involved in T5 but as time dragged on and on and on it became very difficult to keep people motivated'. It wasn't just the planning inquiry that the team had to deal with. In 2001, as the end seemed near for the inquiry, terrorist attacks hit the US on 9/11, followed not long after by the SARS virus. As the US aviation market fell away, BAA had to look at the viability of the new terminal. Over a few weeks the whole scheme was turned on its head, with options ranging from not building it at all to reducing the size or building it all but only using part of it. Common sense and long-term projections prevailed and T5 as we know it today got underway.

THE LOCAL COMMUNITY VOICE

The provision of additional capacity at Heathrow was opposed in principle on grounds of policy, need and sustainability. Behind that position, the principal concerns of the local community were air and ground noise, air quality, surface access, visual intrusion, the risk to public safety, loss and damage to the green belt and to the Colne Valley Regional Park, ecological harm and that the new terminal would inevitably lead to a third runway.

By far the greatest concern related to air noise. The inspector noted that aircraft using Heathrow caused substantial disturbance and annoyance over a very wide area, and that the vast increase in the number of aircraft using Heathrow had made the noise climate worse for many, particularly in the early morning. Night noise was also regarded as an unnecessary burden on the local communities. Many asserted that the method of producing the noise contours, which described exposure to different levels of noise, significantly underestimated the contribution that numbers of aircraft made to the overall impact. A limit on the number of aircraft movements and a noise cap were inevitable, and they have since become routine features of consents for major airport expansion.

There was evidence that T5 would increase concentrations of pollutants around Heathrow and cause a small increase in the risk to human health as a result of greater air pollution. Nevertheless, this would be a case of reducing the potential improvement in the area that would otherwise have occurred, as pollution was predicted to be less in 2016 even with T5 than it was in 1993.

Surface access to Heathrow and at Paddington was an issue for many. The road and rail infrastructure strategy that BAA proposed was thought to be capable of dealing with this, although the inspector did reinforce the strategy through the imposition of a cap on car-parking numbers.

T5 was regarded as visually intrusive. This concern were mitigated by the quality of the design of the principal buildings, but the inspector responded to objections by reducing the scale of the multistorey car parks in such a way as to emphasize the passenger terminal and permit more landscaping.

In terms of public safety, while there was no increase in the number exposed to an intolerable risk, more people were exposed to a material risk and T5 was thought to increase the risk of a major air crash involving many casualties on the ground.

Less was said about the loss or damage to the green belt, within which the Perry Oaks site was located, and the impact on the Colne Valley Regional Park, lying between Heathrow and the M25, which was judged in the context of its landscape character that was regarded as largely undistinguished.

The ecological harm was not substantial, but did result in costly mitigation. The most significant was a decision taken by BAA during the inquiry to address objections from the then National Rivers Authority, later the Environment Agency, by changing the design of the diversion of two rivers through the site. The rivers ran in inverted siphons beneath both runways and in open channel between them through the Perry Oaks site. It had been planned to link the siphons by placing the rivers in a culvert beneath the T5 development. In the face of intense objection by the Environment Agency, BAA changed the proposed solution to a diversion of both rivers in open channel around the ends of the runway and through the already intensively used landside terminal zone.

THE AIRLINE VOICE

While the inquiry was in progress, BAA was also trying to resolve which airline or airlines should occupy T5, and how it was going to work with any potential occupant to design world-class passenger facilities.

The basic proposition of T5 was to enable Heathrow to grow its traffic within the constraints of a two-runway airport. The proposition was to maximize the site available, and this was reckoned to be capable of taking 30 million passengers per annum (mppa).

When added to the estimate of a four-terminal Heathrow of 50 mppa, not 45 mppa as BAA and others now claim, this gave 80 mppa. No one believed that, and the inspector said he thought the capacity with T5 was 90–95 mppa. The task of the T5 planning team in the early 1990s was to determine how this additional capacity could be most efficiently and effectively used.

An extensive study and consultation exercise was undertaken with the Heathrow airline community during 1994–95 to determine the T5 occupancy issue. Four key selection criteria were used to establish suitable airline options: maximizing use of Heathrow's passenger-handling capacity, maximizing single-terminal transfer connections, minimizing the required number of airline moves, and meeting airline requirements.

The conclusion of this work was that British Airways was identified as the prime airline occupant of T5, on the basis that it would make full and efficient use of the infrastructure and, in doing so, would release large blocks of facilities in T1 and T4 that could be used efficiently by other airlines.

BA represents around 40 % of the traffic at Heathrow and its mix of domestic, short- and long-haul traffic generally offers a flat daily profile of traffic that allows the infrastructure to be used effectively throughout the day. BA also has high loads of connection traffic, so locating it in a single terminal provides a simpler journey for transferring passengers, reduces the risk of missed connections and avoids lengthy journeys across Heathrow to other terminals.

WHAT WAS ACTUALLY AGREED AND WHY?

The inspector delivered his report to the Secretary of State on 21 November 2000. The main report ran to 618 pages. It recommended that T5 should be permitted subject to strict conditions.

The inspector concluded that demand for air travel would continue to grow in the UK, and that most of the demand in the South East was concentrated on Heathrow. He thought that there was no realistic prospect of that demand being met at other airports in the UK, and that runway capacity was a fundamental limit on both Gatwick and Stansted. He believed that T5 would be consistent with the government's objective of fostering a strong and competitive British airline industry, and that the beneficiaries if T5 was not provided would be Charles de Gaulle, Frankfurt and Schiphol airports. He noted that Heathrow contributed some 1% to the national economy and played a significant part in attracting investment to the UK. Unless Heathrow was able to maintain its competitive position, there was a substantial risk that London's success as a world city and financial centre would be threatened.

The inspector recommended a limit on the number of air transport movements and a noise cap. He recommended that BAA should be required to extend both the Heathrow Express and the Piccadilly underground line to T5 and that car parking at Heathrow should be capped. He said that no further major development should take place at Heathrow after T5 and that a third runway would be totally unacceptable.

The discussion in the main report was confined to matters that the inspector viewed as relevant to the balance he had to strike; fuller statements of the cases presented to him appeared in the supporting topic reports that ran to many thousands of pages.

Planning consent

It was while the Secretary of State was considering the inspector's report that BAA discovered, in early 2001, that the scheme for the diversion of the twin rivers that ran through the site would not maintain their existing flows to their downstream destinations. The Secretary of State was informed of this in May 2001 and, following urgent discussions between BAA, the Environment Agency and the Royal Parks Agency as well as the local planning authorities, a new rivers-diversion scheme was submitted to the Secretary of State in August 2001.

Consent for T5 was granted, with almost 700 planning conditions, on 20 November 2001. Consents for the other 36 applications were granted at the same time.

None of the development permitted could start on any part of the site until planning permission had been granted by the local planning authority for the permanent diversion of the twin rivers. Otherwise, the principal conditions were:

- The Heathrow Express and the Piccadilly line should be extended to the site.
- A limit of 480 000 air transport movements should apply during any period of one year, allowing two runways and five terminals to manage 90–95 million passengers.
- A noise contour cap of 145 square kilometres, based on the 57dBA (decibels adjusted), 16-hour contour.
- Controls on the siting, by coordinates, maximum dimensions, by floor plate and height, and maximum floor space, by gross area of the principal buildings.
- Controls on the external appearance of the principal buildings.
- The provision of a public transport interchange at T5.
- Car parking at Heathrow was capped at 42 000 spaces; 46 000 had been asked for.

Following consent, a local kennels operator launched a legal challenge that was dismissed in the High Court in May 2002. In July 2002, the land at Perry Oaks was finally and formally transferred into BAA's ownership. In the same month, BAA was granted consent by London Borough of Hillingdon for the revised scheme for the diversion of the two rivers, and this allowed preliminary site works to start in August. The construction of T5 began finally in September 2002.

Design changes following planning consent

The T5 planning decision endorsed almost all of the proposals that BAA had presented to the public inquiry, and in particular the scale, design and architectural quality of the main terminal building; the principle of confining the development to the east of the A3044 despite the higher densities that this entailed for the principal T5 site; and the stepped profile of the main buildings in the landside areas up to the main terminal building.

Nevertheless, the Secretary of State's decision had a number of impacts on the proposals that BAA had put before the public inquiry that needed further careful consideration. In particular, reductions in the maximum height limits for the principal buildings within the landside area were imposed by the Secretary of State in order to reduce the scale of the landside development and to reveal more of the main terminal building; and the diversion of the rivers to a location adjacent to the principal site in turn reduced the area available for the supporting landside infrastructure. It soon became clear that this gave rise to a number of consequences that could best be resolved by revising parts of the proposals, particularly those for the landside area.

In August 2002, BAA submitted a planning application to vary a number of the conditions imposed by the main T5 outline consent. An application to the London Borough of Hillingdon sought permission to change the form of the main terminal building roof from an undulating waveform to a simple single waveform and the relocation of the forecourt to above the car park; to remove some of the buildings in the landside area, including an office block and a multistorey car park, reduce the scale and the dimensions of the other principal buildings and thus increase the amount of landscaping within the landside area; and to change the external appearance of the principal buildings within the landside area.

The main effects of these led to the following scheme changes from the plan approved by the Secretary of State.

The creation of a pedestrianized interchange plaza between the main terminal building and the multistorey car park (MSCP5), linking the various modes of public transport and providing an open-air space in front of the main terminal building.

In the landside area, the plan approved by the Secretary of State had the first row of buildings comprising a car park, a hotel and an office building. Instead, the first row of buildings closest to the main terminal building, but separated from it by the interchange plaza, would now comprise a 4000-space multistorey car park (MSCP5), with an integrated departures forecourt at its top level and a combined bus and coach station and arrivals forecourt at its ground-floor level. The height of MSCP5 slightly exceeded the height limits imposed by the Secretary of State for the row 1 buildings, but the design of MSCP5 and the introduction of the interchange plaza still allowed more open views of the main terminal building itself.

The second and third rows of buildings approved by the Secretary of State for car parks were now instead safeguarded for the development of a hotel, together with a second multistorey car park (MSCP2). The idea of a landside office building was dropped due to the size constraints of the site.

The ramps to the departures forecourt were realigned to achieve access and egress to the relocated departures forecourt at the top level of MSCP5 as well as to provide high-level access to car parking.

The overall number of car-parking spaces was reduced from some 8660 spaces in the approved landside proposals to some 4600, 4000 in MSCP5 and 600 in MSCP2.

The road layout, although remaining a broadly one-way circulatory system, was also realigned to reflect the changes set out above, as well as enhanced planting and landscaping provision.

These revised proposals maintained the key principles of the inspector's recommendations, such as the elegant and distinctive floating roof and the retention of the stepped approach to the principal landside buildings, and also addressed other concerns.

The creation of the interchange plaza not only led to improvements for the passenger experience, way finding and interchange, but also opened up views to reveal virtually the entire façade of the main terminal building and increase natural light and space adjoining the main terminal building, in order to improve the experience for arriving passengers.

The overall bulk of the buildings and scale of development was reduced, and the reduction in the scale of development created more space for landscaping, which enhanced the landside area and improved the setting of the T5 proposals.

The planning application was granted consent by the London Borough of Hillingdon on 27 January 2003. Thereafter, the many conditions attached to both the main T5 application and the supporting applications were discharged on a regular basis in order to meet the construction programme for opening day.

Key learning

Egan never believed that planning permission would have taken quite so long. The T5 planning permission timescale was sufficiently shocking to motivate the government into not one but a number of overhauls and improvements to the way it deals with major infrastructure projects, in order to make the system quicker, simpler and more inclusive.

Planning changes by government since T5

At the time the planning application for T5 was submitted, the Town and Country Planning Act 1990 was in force. The aviation policy context was set by the 1985 Aviation White Paper, but by the time the T5 planning inquiry opened this was 10 years old and was challenged as being out of date. So T5 was put forward for planning permission against a nonspecific and dated UK aviation policy, which meant that a significant proportion of time at the inquiry was spent debating the nature of government policy in respect to aviation and specifically Heathrow's contribution to meeting demand for air travel 10 years on from the publication of the White Paper. The Labour government did put this right and since 2003 there has been a 30-year national and regional aviation policy, which will be kept up to date. As part of the 2003 White Paper, the future direction of all the South East airports was out-lined, including support for the further expansion of Heathrow, but only if it could be demonstrated that strict environment criteria in respect of air noise and air quality could be met.

With government policy as a backdrop, airports are now required to produce master plans, a process BAA had previously done as a matter of course. The paperwork to be completed now for a planning submission has actually increased, given the additional focus on environment matters, but with a clear understanding of government policy and direction this can be dealt with efficiently.

Government still understands that there is more to be done to manage the tough decisions that need to be taken on controversial infrastructure decisions while balancing national, local and environment interests. A planning bill is currently passing through Parliament that will introduce a new process for dealing with major new infrastructure projects in sectors such as aviation, rail and nuclear energy. The commission of inquiry will be made up of high-profile independent experts, who will sit and listen to submissions such as those regarding Heathrow's third runway and once a decision has been given, neither the proposer nor the contenders can appeal the decision.

HEATHROW EAST: A DIFFERENT EXPERIENCE

What a contrast between T5, over 22 years in the making, and Heathrow East. Andy Wadham, Heathrow head of planning since the mid-1990s, has seen the planning landscape change in his time. 'East was set up in February 2006, submitted for consent in October 2006 and granted in July 2007,' he explains. 'The pain of going through T5 had set a blueprint of constraints for Heathrow East to work within, and indeed the CO_2 impact of a new, greener terminal will be positive. There was more paperwork to complete, but with the right environment advisers this could be achieved.' The very big learning from T5 for BAA was the approach to stakeholder management. Prior to submission the national, regional and local stakeholders were engaged, and their views were listened to and taken into account when making the submission. Heathrow East received a total of four minor objections that were dealt with fairly quickly before consent was given.

SUMMARY

Heathrow and the passengers using its facilities have suffered more than they might have due to the length of the public inquiry. The strain the travelling public has felt has intensified since 2000 as a 45-million capacity airport has dealt with the steady climb to 68 million passengers in 2006, with additional security measures creating a pressurized environment. With a more prompt inquiry Heathrow could now be on track not only to have opened T5 in early 2000, but also to be near completing Heathrow East and upgrading the rest of the airport. The judgements made have had significant consequences for the public, the airlines, BAA and potentially the reputation of the UK.

The landscape in planning has significantly changed over the last 20 years. The 30-year government aviation policy is helpful in setting the direction based on demand and supply issues, set in the context of economic and environment factors. T5 did establish a helpful framework for Heathrow based on surface access, air transport movements, noise and car parking. This clarity proved helpful when reviewing the Heathrow East proposals and in part was the reason for the quick turnaround.

The real test of the new planning process lies ahead. The government issued a consultation at the end of November 2007 that demonstrated how the environment tests for a third runway could be met by 2020; in 2008 it will publish its response to this consultation and finalize the national policy context in relation to the future growth of Heathrow. If the decision is to go ahead, then a planning application is likely to follow from BAA in 2010 and will be one of the first tests for the new planning commission process.

Other European hubs, however, like France's Charles de Gaulle, Frankfurt and Amsterdam, will by 2010 have significantly more passenger capacity than Heathrow, all with more land take and runway capacity in place. The Department of Transport has estimated that a third runway would allow Heathrow to handle around 116 million passengers a year by 2030 (The Future of Air Transport in the United Kingdom: South East – Feb 2003). Heathrow's request for a third runway brings into question the demand and economic benefits versus the local impacts and environment impacts. The future growth of Heathrow will be subject to similar debates to those made in the past, and the balance will need to be struck between the national, regional and local economic benefits. Decisions will need to be made about what expansion will bring, to maintain London's, and to some degree the UK's, competitiveness in an increasingly global market, deciding if the price to pay for this in the environment is worth it, having allowed for as much mitigation of those impacts as is reasonably possible.

Slurry farm before T5 development

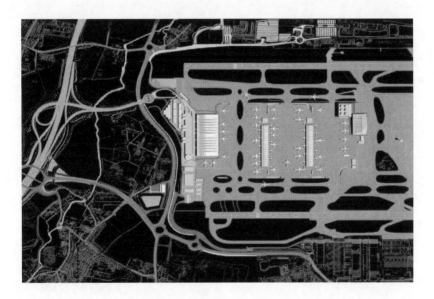

Graphic of aerial T5 view

CHAPTER 4

DESIGN

Looking good and working even better, that's the legacy we want to leave with T5.

Mike Forster, strategy director, BAA

In 1989 the Richard Rogers Partnership, now known as Rogers Stirk Harbour + Partners (RSH+P), won the national competition to design the new T5 for Heathrow, and then spent over 10 years developing its design accommodating the requirements of its client, the conditions of the public inquiry and the impact of world events. Mike Davies from RSH+P – or 'Red' as everyone knows him, as he wears red everything all of the time – has had 34 remarkable years designing extraordinary buildings and it's clear that T5 has been a project he and his team are very proud to have been part of. They have been helping to create a glimpse into the future for UK aviation and a passenger experience that will stand the test of time globally.

Heathrow's Terminal 5: History in the Making S. Doherty
© 2008 John Wiley & Sons, Ltd

BIG-PICTURE DESIGN

Lead architects achieve their acclaim in the bold architectural statement their buildings make to the modern age, and it is likely that T5 will achieve the award-winning status that the RSH+P have regularly come to enjoy.

As passengers approach by road they can glimpse the mature landscape within which an iconic building with its wavy roof nestles, and driving up the rounded car-park slope passengers will definitely know they have arrived for a different experience. After parking, they can wander across one of the four link bridges looking over at the plaza below, home to 40 mature London plane trees on either side, fountains dancing to the left, and move ahead into the main T5 building. The roof, along with exposed steelwork and glazed façades, which lean out at an angle of 6.5 degrees, give the building its distinctive shape.

The building is 40 metres high, 400 metres long and 160 metres wide, and the façades or sides are made up of 5500 panels equalling 30,000 square metres of glass that create a light and airy interior. Eleven pairs of huge steel leg and arm structures run the length of the building and not only hold up the dramatic roof, but turn its engineering into an architectural feature. Red is pleased with the combination of calm and buzz that the design of the building creates. What is perhaps even more spectacular and unique to T5 is that the totally glass building affords all passengers spectacular views, including Windsor Castle, the Wembley Arch, the London Eye and the Gherkin, all of which can be seen on the horizon. For those who just love watching aircraft arrive and depart, there are grandstand views of two of busiest runways in the world.

T5 concept design: Three different schemes

It was an interesting history lesson sitting with Red, having him reminisce on the three different designs that over the years he and

RSH+P had created with BAA. As he described critical meetings between all parties, you could almost smell the countless cups of coffee that were consumed as another planning permission hurdle or world event got thrown at them to resolve in design. Over the years there have been three T5 designs.

Flying carpet

The 'flying carpet', developed between 1989 to 1992, was the first concept and proposed a single level with three curves on the transparent roofing, creating a ripple effect that stretched T5 out to the west, through the green belt and stopping just before the M25. This divided the main terminal into three parts, each separated by a channel of light, between landside, check-in and passenger security and waiting areas on airside. Bridges connected these floor plates. As the public inquiry progressed, legal advice made it clear that building in the green belt was too contentious and would not be winnable.

Canyon

From 1992 to 2000 a series of other designs were developed, including a 'canyon' design. With less space the building now needed to become a multistorey stack. Canyon included three landside floor plates, for example for check-in and security, with a large canyon separating them from the airside floor plate that led down into the international departure lounge. This is a similar scheme to that at Barajas in Madrid, built later but following similar principles. Work was being done on the passenger experience and a focus was put on trying to balance the arriving and departing passengers' experiences, with both having the benefit of daylight. The concept was rejected on the basis that in the face of an ever-changing world, it offered less flexibility to be able to deal with changes. Maintaining flexibility in design for a building that would be built for the twenty-first century was considered an absolute priority.

Loose-fit flexible envelope

By 2000 the canyon concept had been replaced by a 'loose-fit, flexible envelope' concept, with large floor plates and the vertical circulation 'clipped' to the sides of the building rather than in the canyon. This final design boasts a building within a building: the roof structure is independent of the floor plates and no internal columns are required. This provides a flexible interior that can be readily adapted according to the changing demands of the aviation industry. The multistorey seven-level stacked building was developed, but now with only one giant floor plate at each level that allowed for maximum flexibility. The most important of these levels was check-in and security, which was now on the same floor plate, ensuring that future changes to processes or technology could be accommodated.

The main drawback of this design was the loss of natural light to the baggage hall, which was remedied by the use of clever lighting and by making it a double-height space, delivering one of the best spaces in T5.

Later on in design, the T5 team took the decision to change the master plan and remove the forecourt from the front of the building and place it on top of the car park, connected to the building by coloured bridges. This had the distinct advantage of allowing light to percolate down to the lower levels of arrivals, bringing back some of the advantages of the canyon thinking, and importantly it brought about the creation of the pedestrian interchange plaza.

FAVOURITE DESIGN FEATURES AND SOME AREAS FOR IMPROVEMENT

Now that the design is there for all to see, it is interesting to get feedback from those involved as to what has worked in the final design and what has not. Clearly these are the views of the designers, so the acid test will be what the passengers think when they pass through the terminal.

Favourite design features

Design area	Design description	Why this is a favorite
Enjoying the views as you approach the T5 main terminal building set in a mature landscape	250,000 new trees and shrubs have been planted, including 450 semi-mature trees, 100,000 evergreen shrubs. 2,000 metres of hedgerow, adjacent to the A3044, to help mitigate views towards the terminal. Along the western perimeter 18,000 ornamental grasses create an identifiable character along the road, with flower spikes in late July and bronze foliage in Autumn, while the welcome arch over this road is blanketed in green, having been planted with 35,000 evergreen groundcover shrubs.	Whilst a grand building, the time and attention given the landscaping mean the overall experience will be a green and mature one. The planting helps integrate this huge development into the context of its surrounding environment. This differentiates T5 from the central terminal area which is a concrete wasteland it enhances the passenger experience enormously.

Design area	Design description	Why this is a favorite
Fully integrated transport hub for easy access by rail, tube, car and coach	Six platforms, two for the Piccadilly Line, two for Heathrow Express and two for future rail opportunities, the station has some distinctive features. A unique transparent roof in the interchange plaza allows natural light to penetrate down to the platform and helps disembarking passengers to intuitively know which way to go to find the terminal, by following the source of this light. M25 and a spur road have been specially built linking the new complex to the motorway. Incorporated into T5 is a bus and coach station. Here travellers can catch coaches into central London or buses serving the local vicinity.	Whether passengers arrive at T5 by road or by rail the access into the departures level check-in hall is identical, i.e. via high level bridges above the interchange plaza, offering parity of service to all. It is anticipated that 40% of passengers will use public transport.

Design area	Design description	Why this is a favorite
Passenger interchange space before entering the main terminal building.	The landscaped plaza runs the total length of the main terminal building and is 30 metres wide. 40 mature London Plane trees, a dancing fountain, and the 'Moving World' Art installation by Langlands & Bell with seated areas all creating a boulevard experience. Digital screen by Nokia mounted at high level within the central courtyard of the interchange plaza will add another dimension to the space.	This social point, is a place for people to relax and unwind, while waiting to depart or meet relatives, friends and business colleagues.

Design area	Design description	Why this is a favorite
The main terminal building – 'loose fit flexible envelope'.	The fourth and final design that delivered a 156 metres single span roof in a seven-story building that is 68,000 square metres. Described as a building within a building the roof is a separate structure to the internal accommodation and as a result never touches the external envelope. There is one huge floor plate that houses check-in, security and airside processes.	Architecturally it is an iconic building with no supporting columns cluttering the floor plate at departures level, distracting the form, or encumbering its flexibility. The single span wavy roof for the operators offers a single floor plate. Over the years as the check-in, security and landside process change the building can be manipulated more easily.

Design area	Design description	Why this is a favorite
'The glass house' experience creating a light and open space.	The exterior of the building has a full height glazed façade on all of its four elevations. The internal walls are lined with 33,000 square metres of white back painted glass panels, the sizes vary so not worth mentioning. Max size is 1.1 x 3 metres panels.	Views into and out of and even from the aircrafts of T5 are quite spectacular. The glass house experience means amazing tones and interest is created as for example the aircrafts, trees or aircraft outside the building reflect on the glass walls inside the building. Glass is also just a great material. Environmentally friendly, durable, eas to clean and psychologically a material the travelling public are more likely to treat with care.

Design area	Design description	Why this is a favorite
Making it easy for passengers to use the facility.	The way-finding beacons, some of which stand at over 10 metres high and 4 metres long, in black and luminous yellow, BAA trade mark colours, at departures check-in and with the bag reclaim hall mean that although a vast space they enable the passenger to negotiate their way intuitively and with ease. The use of black tiles at processing point in check-in, security and immigration. The use of 'white saddles' at check-in, security and immigration to show this is where you interact or get processed.	The building has been modelled and has in-built obvious and more subtle design features to make using the facilities as easy as possible. The uncluttered floor plate allows the beacons to stand out clearly providing bold, clear way-finding elements. This aids the way-finding process but also break ups vast areas of a single coloured floor. They create tactile touch points throughout the passenger journey.

Design area	Design description	Why this is a favorite
Integration facilities into the building not adding them on as an after thought.	The five 18x9 metres towers that run up through the main terminal building act as an elegant feature to extract waste air from toilets, kitchens etc. mechanical and electrical, M&E, services run through the towers and house the stair cores that run through the building. The glazed wall linings again integrate many essential building functions such as some M&E services, signage, door access control, media, fire extinguishers, and temperature sensors to name but a few. The way-finding beacons house flight information screens, signage, displacement ventilation terminals DVT's, air-conditioning, Cameras, speakers, power sockets, fire extinguishers, emergency break glass units, media statutory signage, wireless LAN, cleaners power sockets, and general information screens For the first time within a BAA environment The retail & advertising experience is designed into the building's fabric.	Overall the well thought through integration creates cleaner lines and an overall better experience for the passenger. They are easier to clean and maintain and keep looking good for longer.

Design area	Design description	Why this is a favorite
Ceiling 'flying saucers' look good for a long time.	There are approximately 5,000 ceiling discs. In limited and specific locations some of the discs have lights in the centre of them.	The ceiling discs are fun and incredibly easy to work around for maintenance purposes. With relative ease they clip down allowing easy maintenance to take place without the ceiling being damaged.

Design area	Design description	Why this is a favorite
Use of lighting to create moods and a calm warm ambience.	During daylight hours natural light is able to penetrate into this deep seven storey building via the glazed walls and the roof lights which follow the main structural beams of the roof. These roof lights allow natural light to illuminate the side faces of these deep beams thereby creating the effect of a well lit, bright soffit. The beams themselves then act as effective "brise soleil" to minimise glare. During the hours of darkness the roof mounted artificial lighting has been arranged so as to provide down light to the Departures floor below and also to illuminate the sides of the main roof beams, much as the daylight does. This is so that the roof also appears as a light /bright surface in evening conditions.	For the passenger T5 will feel like a well lit and at night incredibly dramatic environment. To minimise energy consumption and maximise efficiently artificial light is used sparingly but for effect. Daniel Shipton, the electrical supervisor on T5, in chapter 9 tells his story of making sure the lights are perfect on day one of T5.

Areas for improvement

Design area	Design description
The immigration area.	In the heart of the building without natural light and a ceiling height of only 4 metres, this was less than ideal space for the team to work with. Clever use of lighting enhances the environment. The blue back lighting adds interest but also helps disguise the services sitting behind the ceiling discs. The use of lighting within the discs emphasises the disc form and focuses the eyes attention rather than beyond to the services behind which are in relative darkness.
The BA CIP, commercially important passengers lounge at T5 satellite building.	The exterior of the CIP, commercially important passengers lounge is closer to the structural trees than would ideally have been desired which results in compromising the spectacular views out. However passengers will be wowed by the interior experience that promises to regain the passenger's confidence and desire to travel through Heathrow.
Car park wall finish.	The team used a stainless steel mesh which at night may not be obscure enough to disguise the car park interior that sit behind it. The mesh, on the eastern face has an up lighting system that is intended to graze light over the surface of the mesh. This will limit the views into the car park during the hours of darkness. This system is not energised at present and therefore its effect cannot be judged. In addition, the internal lighting to the car park decks is completely controllable and therefore can be dimmed and switched to ameliorate this issue and to save energy. This system is also not fully commissioned at present. The up lighting system the western face of the car park was value engineered out to save money. This may have to be added back in.

BAA AS THE DESIGN CLIENT

Being an intelligent client in design is most critical when it comes to deciding what you want and can afford. BAA has not been perfect in this area, hampered by the length of time taken by the planning inquiry and changing world events, but on reflection it is clear that it has always known what it needed the T5 site to deliver and has been smart and agile enough as a client to manage significant changes along the design journey without compromising those objectives. This has been the case in both the big design picture and also in the detailed design.

Mike Forster, at the time development and design director for BAA on T5, was clear that 'if Heathrow wanted a world class passenger experience then having a world class architect was needed and found in Rogers Stirk Harbour + Partners'. Forster, a big picture thinker, was instrumental in building on some of the early ideas of his predecessor, looking at what T5 needed to be to 'delight the passenger' through looking good and working even better.

Key players

BAA's design client through the latter stages of the public inquiry was Raymond Turner, then group design director, but when the planning permission was granted and the project began to build up the leadership was handed over to Forster. In his team he had Liz Southern, head of development for BAA, whose team of development managers were responsible for writing the functional briefs, and Richard Napthine, head of development IT for BAA, whose job it was to write the system briefs that would enable the operational processes to work. In total over 300 functional briefs were scoped and signed off. In Forster's team there was also a head of design, initially James Berry and later David Bartlett, responsible for ensuring that the solutions proposed by the designers met BAA's aspirations and served the needs of future passengers, and a head of technical leadership, Chris Millard, responsible for setting the briefs and assuring that solutions were found for the engineering systems throughout the project. Together they drove the T5 product, balancing BAA's various and often conflicting requirements for the completed terminal and the constraints of programme and budget.

Stakeholders

Airports are stakeholder-rich environments. Red emphasized that on the T5 Programme 43 different stakeholders were involved. One of the key responsibilities of Forster's team, and within the development team, was to interface with all these stakeholders and ensure that their needs were captured in the briefs, as well as that the emerging design solutions met their expectations. Of these, the principal stakeholder was unquestionably BA, who as the future occupier of the building had an enormous interest in how it was designed. In fact the company had a team resident in the design offices working very closely with the BAA team, meeting weekly to review progress. The other two groups of key importance were the functions within BAA, such as security or safety, who had accountability across the whole BAA group for their areas of responsibility and therefore needed to make sure that T5 met their requirements, and the statutory authorities such as immigration, customs and the police, who were going to have to carry out their duties in the new terminal once it was finished.

T5 CAMPUS DESIGN GUIDELINES

In 2002 to 2003, as the planning process was drawing to its conclusion, it was important for both internal players and external stakeholders, Hillingdon Council in particular, to clarify how the design vision would actually look and work in detail. Starting from the initial drafts developed by RSH+P, Raymond Turner, now working as a consultant, and James Berry, the head of design at the time, spent a number of months creating guidelines that set out the principles for the design. These documents were intended to drive the design within the project, but in reality their most valuable contribution was to set out the design logic of the T5 campus, allowing those on Hillingdon Council to assure themselves that each of the many individual detailed planning applications they would receive over a number of years fitted together into an overall design approach. The design guidelines were very successful in achieving this. They were structured in a number of levels, each with increased detail.

Level 1: Design vision and values

The T5 vision was to be 'the world's most refreshing interchange', highlighting the idea of completely integrated surface access. This vision was important in the identification of the final option as described earlier, but as the project increased momentum the over-all vision became more focused on the delivery of the project and was changed to be 'to deliver the world's most successful airport development'.

For BAA and the design team that meant a multi-transport interchange; a positively refreshing experience for the passenger; a stimulus for change for those designing, building and operating the building; a world benchmark in terms of ease of use and ownership; enhancing value for BA and BAA; and improving the sustainability of the building in terms of its being future proof.

Level 2: Design strategies

There were then design strategies to direct the design of the campus, landside, the interchange, the terminal building and finally the airfield. In more detail the vision, objectives and the strategies to meet the headline objectives were outlined.

Level 3: Design concepts for each major locality

For the landside campus, Colne Valley, interchange plaza, main buildings and structures and the airfield, detailed drawings, materials, colours and finishes were packaged together.

THE DESIGN TEAM

At the centre of the project were a number of key design practices: Rogers Stirk Harbour + Partners, the concept architects led by Red; Arups, led by Tony Fitzpatrick until his untimely death in July 2003; John Thornton and Dervilla Mitchell, who provided the structural engineering; Mott Macdonald for civil engineering; DSSR for the services engineering design; Chapman Taylor, the retail consulting architect; and Hyland Edgar Driver for the landscape design. In addition to this were a number of specialist designers such as Spiers and Major, lighting designers, and Priestman Goode, product designers.

As the teams expanded they were joined by a significant number of design companies that took on elements of the design within the established framework of integrated teams on which the project was founded. The most notable of these were Pascall & Watson, architects and SPIE Matthew Hall, services engineers. In addition there were production designers who worked with most companies.

BA had also employed an architectural practice, YRM, initially to give it assurance around the emerging design, but such was the nature of working on the project that YRM too made a significant contribution to the end product. These companies were complemented at the end of the project by designers for the fit-out, CIP lounge and offices.

As the project moved through concept design to scheme design and then finally into production design, the client was supported by RSH+P, who had created the vision and guarded the concept. BAA would be big enough to say that partway through the T5 Programme it trimmed back on the RSH+P team's services too early and had to bring them back in to provide extra focus on the design detail. A full list of the design team is in Appendix B.

Giving designers the environment and tools to do their job

At its peak T5 had more than 2000 designers working on the design. To make this sort of environment work, careful consideration was given to the facilities required to do the job. Not all designers could be co-located, but the principle of a single-model environment (SME) was created, a real-time, off-the-shelf, 3D computer-aided design (CAD) system that allowed the team to share all the drawings, backed up by Documentum, software that was used to manage all the written design information.

The systems allowed the designers to take the most up-to-date drawings or Word documents out, work on them and then put them back for others to use. Clear protocols for data structures were critical to ensure that everyone followed the same rules. Bartlett, head of design, and John Milford, project head from buildings with multibillion-pound project experience, were critical to providing some leadership in this space, since the design community were relatively immature in their understanding of how to operate in this type of shared environment.

At one point in the T5 Programme there were more connected machines, more computer-aided design, more people and probably more data being produced on a single project than anywhere else in the UK.

What was different?

Integrated teamworking

In the spirit of the T5 Agreement, while the lead architect was absolutely critical to success, some of the most satisfying moments in the journey have come when that lead architect works as a team member. For example, in the case of the roof lift or the control tower redesign, architects, engineers and construction specialists all worked very closely together with mutual respect as peers.

In addition to working with one of the best lead architects in the world, RSH+P, BAA also brought around the table niche players such as Din Associates as concept interior designers to bring a fresh look to the design. From whichever angle you look at T5, designers from among the best in the world have been involved, creating a joined-up experience, because a strong client with willing consultants was able to deliver what was necessary for a world-class project.

The client team, who were also focused on the criticality of budget and programme, had driven the functionality of the building and the focus on the passenger experience. This did rely on the client working closely and effectively in collaboration with the concept designers. Some compromises to the purity of the overall design were knowingly made in the challenge of balancing time, cost and quality.

It was essential that during the project the client's team played their part in ensuring that the T5 Programme stayed on the right cost track. Value engineering, as it is known, looked at what designs could be simplified, specification lowered or scope reduced without having a detrimental impact on the passenger experience. For example, air bridges were redesigned, lifts and escalators were taken out and floor space was reduced. A good balance was kept, however, with Forster's 'pixie dust budget' that allowed the design team to speak up and say when there needed to be some more magic or focus on what the passenger will see or touch. When you see the dancing fountains, see if you agree that they got it right.

Progressive design fixity and LRMs

On a project as big and complex as T5, you can't design it all at the beginning – by the time the facility came into being much of it would be out of date. The design approach used was progressive design fixity or the 'Russian doll' technique as coined by Forster. Start at the outside, big picture and design in, getting closer and closer to the design that touches the passenger last. So for example on flooring, early on the team need to take a decision on the depth allowed for the floor finish, but the selection of the actual finish could wait until later. Progressive fixity is supported by a 'last responsible moment' approach (LRM), which mapped out the latest date that each design decision could be taken. However, speed of decision is also vital to keeping a project on time, and therefore after some initial teething problems Forster held a weekly surgery meeting, D^3 (development and design decisions), with his team to act as a clearing house before a design went through the project board process where stakeholders would sign it off.

Once the design was signed off, any changes requested would go back to the D^3 meeting for approval, or if they were very significant, they would need to be once again cleared by the project boards.

Client focus on detailed design

What has been very refreshing about T5 is that as much, if not more, effort has gone into the design that the travelling public sees and touches. Bartlett brims with excitement about how he believes the 'arriving and departing passenger experience is one if not the best in the world'. He's been nicknamed 'Mr Joined Up,' he laughs, 'since joining T5 in August 2004 I've been devoted to the passenger micro experience.' He describes a workshop he managed in November 2004 bringing together every designer involved in the arriving and departing journey in Heathrow's Academy. Everyone had been given pre-work to enable them to bring drawings and pictures of their effort, and over a two-day period they joined up all the different parts of the passenger journey. This way of working continued thereafter, and willingness to work like this was complemented by an assurance tool that was used to keep everyone on track – and this was visible to all.

To complement Bartlett's creativity Millard was recruited at a similar time. He was one of the many senior leaders employed from the car industry to bring the engineering rigour and process thinking that the construction needed. In 'old speak' Millard might be known as the chief engineer. His and his team's focus was to ensure that the system had fully integrated briefs and to own the system to ensure that what BAA needed was delivered. There were three types of system where the team looked for consistency across all of the 18 projects: design systems, which included things like internal wall linings, toilets and floor finishes; engineering systems, including the energy centre, electrical distribution, active fire systems and others; and IT systems, including security systems, third-party systems and communication systems. Project design and construction teams remained accountable for the design, engineering and construction of the system elements to deliver the required performance.

Millard took previous work to a different level, creating slicker processes for setting and monitoring standards, educating the integrated teams in a different way of working and leading a team of system owners who, on the ground, worked to prevent problems and resolve them if they arrived. What was most interesting talking to both Bartlett and Millard separately was the mutual respect and trust they had for each other, and how they formed a key element of Forster's expert client team, working together to hold to the vision for T5. Millard said, 'There were two questions Bartlett and I would always ask when we hit a difficult call. Are we being joined up and what is best for the T5 Programme?' Those two statements seemed to carry them through most things and led them to great, visually appealing designs, such as the three-storey way-finding beacons that assist passengers while integrating all of the essential systems internally rather than as boxes added on with metal mesh covering, as you can see in so many other airports around the world.

Key learning

When thinking about design there are two distinct ideas to hold in your head: the 'what' of design, or the brief, and the 'how' of the actual design process. As the client, BAA was invariably sitting on top of both design and construction. The management of the 'what' of T5 was pretty clearly in the remit of the expert client team, but with BAA's philosophy of integrated teams, the 'how' designers were managed by the construction project managers; the accountabilities for design process management were not as clear at times as they should have been. The disciplines that were established in construction, around having 80 clear, high-level milestones that were visible, not easily moved, clearly measured with individuals and with teams held to account for their delivery, again took longer to establish and embed in design.

The discipline of designing to a cost is also something that BAA improved on during the project and the company is now set up to operate this way on Heathrow East. In the early days there was some tension between the design and commercial teams, one trying to get the best design possible, the other watching the pennies. This culture was late in coming, and meant that at times value engineering was required towards the back end of the project to keep on track financially. This culture is now part of business as usual, leveraging creative genius and tight budgets.

Finally, the legacy of T5 design to the rest of BAA is the set of design standards and standard products that are now available and that can be applied at a reduced cost, which can be moved across to Heathrow East, the wider Heathrow and other BAA airports. Glass-panel walls, floor tiles, loos, ceilings, desks, balustrades, display systems – the list goes on and on. The modern standard has now been set and, working with the supply chain, energy and effort can go into getting best value. While there continues to be evolution, the change is managed by business cases.

SUMMARY

T5 is an iconic building and setting, which has changed the skyline of Heathrow. The BAA design team is braced for some criticism from the external design community, as there are a number of areas in the building that the team knows could have been improved.

Equally, design decisions were taken around the passenger experience that the passenger will find clear, but of which designers may be critical. For example, some may suggest that the large way-finding beacons distract from the form of the building, but they increase the ease with which passengers will move through the terminal. If T5 is as good as the design team have suggested, it may not win the award for the best-looking airport in the world, but it could be the one passengers enjoy using most, an accolade that on balance the design team would prefer.

There are many examples of design success. The design team set a clear vision for T5 and guarded that concept under pressure. There are great examples of integrated teamworking, with design, construction and end user, and of developing safe and cost-effective design solutions. On the other hand, finishing and freezing design took longer than it should have, and a more disciplined regime of milestone management should have been put in place to manage production design earlier.

Lessons have been learned about the design discipline required on mega projects and are already being put to good use on Heathrow East. The proof will be in the pudding when it comes to design. The prediction is that the travelling public will enjoy using T5, because it looks good but works even better.

T5 set in mature landscaping

T5 twin rivers

Fully integrated transport hub including Heathrow Express

4,200 space car park

View in to the main terminal building

A view from the satellite terminal building to the runways

Interchange plaza – A social space

Check in and fast bag drop in
main terminal building showing signage

Departure lounge

Baggage hall

Heathrow air traffic control tower
manages 473,000 passengers per year

Sunrise on T5

Sunset on T5

CHAPTER 5

CONSTRUCTION

**On time, on budget, quality, safely with care to
the environment was the T5 mantra for all.**

Andrew Wolstenholme, director, capital
projects, BAA

Planning permission for T5 was finally granted in
November 2001. By autumn 2002 the construction team had
started work on clearing the site, completing the archaeology and
creating the huge excavations required for the construction of the
substructures and service tunnels. One of the big challenges in the
early stages was the diversion of the twin rivers that split the principal
site in two, a task completed on time in May 2004.

As a head of steam built up, the assembly of the terminal building
roof got underway in October 2003. This phase was so critical that a
roof section had been trial-assembled in Yorkshire, and this exposed
125 errors that would have otherwise seriously slowed progress on
site. The roof, with its 156-metre clear span, was jacked up on six

Heathrow's Terminal 5: History in the Making S. Doherty
© 2008 John Wiley & Sons, Ltd

lifts after being pre-assembled on top of the main terminal building substructure by some of the most accomplished engineers in the world, learning from each lift, the next being more productive. There were stories of BA pilots feeling disoriented as they left one day and returned the next to find a 40-metre-high roof emerging from the earth. Three storeys of superstructure plus mezzanine floors were then constructed under the roof. The glass façade was lifted into place to protect the building from the weather. And there was no time to gasp for breath before the baggage team got into the basement to start their installation. An early start to these 30 months of activity was key to mitigating one of the most significant risks that faced the T5 Programme, that of not finishing on time. At the same time, October 2004, the 5500 mechanical and electrical modules that had been pre-fabricated off site started to be assembled. These modules contained all primary mechanical and electrical and water systems and were installed along with 131 lifts and 66 elevators.

With the last of the big items lifted into the building, it was pronounced weather-tight in early 2006. The fit-out team had already got underway in the internal facilities. The large retail fit-out was planned to start in February 2007, with final commissioning of the building by September 2007. From this point thousands of BA and BAA workers, alongside UK volunteers, stress tested T5 as all concerned tried desperately to pick up any final 'unknown unknowns' that might prevent the big day from going to plan.

From 2002 a new rail station was to be constructed, under the north end of the new terminal building, 10 metres below the apron level. At this time the Heathrow Express and Piccadilly rail systems were extended from the centre of Heathrow out to the new station at T5, along with a track transit system between the terminal building and the new satellite building that was to be completed in early 2007. Early into the programme it was decided to extend the track transit system to the second satellite building, which was to be completed by 2010. This involved extending the scope by constructing the substructures and associated cut-and-cover tunnels. The first aircraft stands and airside road systems were handed over to Heathrow for use in phases starting early in 2004.

When designing the T5 organization structure the principles were creating manageable chunks of work and expertise, for example putting all of the buildings together and managing the diversity that ranged from civil engineering to rail and tunnels, and from buildings to systems. That amounted to 147 subprojects ranging from £2 million to £300 million in size, 18 projects, listed below, and one T5 Programme:

- Earthworks, including earthworks for archaeology and phase 1 of the M25 spur road
- Airfield, including stands and runway links
- Western perimeter corridor, including the twin rivers
- Landside campus, including the car park
- Main terminal building
- Energy centre
- Satellite building
- Heathrow air traffic control tower (HATCT)
- Heathrow Express extension
- Piccadilly line extension
- Track transit system
- Baggage
- Systems
- Special projects, including working with Thames Water and the Highway Agency on M25 extension phase 1
- Central function, including finance, commercial, organizational effectiveness and risk
- Third-party projects, including work with BA and Air Traffic Control
- Site & Logistics
- Second satellite building

The challenge was to maintain clear messages and focus across this scale of programme and focus. These simple and powerful messages focused on being on time (originally 30 March 2008, but brought forward in 2007 to 27 March), on budget (£4.3 billion), delivering safely while building a quality facility. This was a consistent message from the CEO through to the men and women on the tools. After the first year of this message, it was amended to make it clear that the environment was equally important and that everyone on site needed to play their part. As the T5 Programme progressed and construction challenges evolved, these core messages remained unchanged, as did the targets.

KEY PLAYERS IN CONSTRUCTION

Norman Haste handed over to Andrew Wolstenholme in 2001 as construction director T5, BAA. BAA project heads were as follows: Robert Stewart, infrastructure; Ian Fugeman, rail and tunnels; Russell Batchelor, who handed over to John Milford, buildings; Nick Gaines, systems. The principal contractors and their representatives were: Laing O'Rourke, Mike Robins; Mace, Mark Reynolds; SPIE Matthew Hall, Grahame Ludlow; Balfour Beatty, Mike Peasland; Morgan Vinci, Chris Hughes; BAA, Andrew Wolstenholme.
A list of all the large suppliers by spend is given in Appendix B.

During the years of peak construction and then handing over the T5 Programme to the operational readiness phase in September 2007, other functions worked with these construction leaders to ensure that they had the tools and accurate data to be able to manage the £4.3 billion T5 Programme. These people are highlighted in the discussion below. While many are to be commended for their unique contributions to T5, those who led the construction must be recognized for their staying power, resilience and determination to lead an integrated team to deliver. The continuity of construction leadership has contributed to the overall success of the T5 Programme.

PROGRAMME MANAGEMENT

With the right contract in place to allow the effective management of risk, programme management allowed the client to stay in overall control of performance data and progress, and provided the integrated teams with accurate data to do their jobs better. Wolstenholme understood that this approach would provide him with the means to join together the many projects at T5. Accurate management information, especially on cost and schedule, is critical when spending £3–4 million a day across 147 diverse subprojects.

BAA had never done a programme of works on this scale before, therefore it looked to other sectors such as automotive and oil and gas for best practice. Colin Reynell and Jeremy Bates were brought in from the automotive industry to set up a programme management process, together with Andrew Hill, the finance director, the senior BAA team and the supply chain. They built on the early T5 handbook and created a way of working that allowed BAA to control the £4.3 billion T5 Programme in a disciplined and integrated manner.

What makes programme management effective?

The approach used at T5 focused on:

- Empowering the project teams to deliver and make their own decisions.
- Enabling tradeoffs across projects and understanding the impact of one project on another.
- Accurately tracking the progress of each project within a consistent programme framework.

Programme management enables control of the big picture to be maintained, drive value and seeing problems coming early enough to be able to do something about them. Predictability and transparency for stakeholders builds trust and confidence, and that allowed Tony Douglas to get the BAA plc board's approval to switch from £30 million to a portfolio of projects worth on occasion up to

£500 million. This was in part due to the team being able to keep track of every pound that was being spent. In turn, it allows those leading big programmes to get on and deliver and not get caught up in justifying their actions.

Programme management: People, process, systems and governance

The heart of the programme management approach was to use the 'earned value' methodology and an integrated schedule. The tool used to deliver this was Artemis, an off-the-shelf, highly customized project control system.

This system allowed the management team to understand not only progress versus schedule and actual costs incurred, but also the value achieved, earned value and the status of the programme versus its original baseline. To this key information was added the other dimensions of project management:

- Change control
- Risks and opportunities management
- Input and output measures for quality, safety, design
- Key production metrics

The final requirement was the right mix of review and governance forums to provide the challenge. This information is useful but impotent unless management understands it and takes action based on it.

When spending time with Anthony Morgan, a partner at PricewaterhouseCoopers who works on major capital projects all around the world, he was clear that many projects fail because of poor programme management. Either the client tries to use existing tools that are not fit for purpose in the construction environment, or while there is lots of data it is not accurate or integrated. He was clear that there was an 'inbuilt desire to please or to be optimistic at the front end of projects, as suppliers or client team members want their involvement to be a success story, so bad news is hidden in the hope that risks will not eventuate'. Without accurate, integrated data and effective challenges these trends are never fully understood or are kept from key players until it is too late.

Key players

The project controls team were: Andrew Hill, finance director, BAA; Steve Elliot, head of project operations, BAA; Pete Lewis independent consultant; Andy Anderson, master planner for the T5 Programme; Laing O'Rourke; cost and commercial led by TECHT, a joint venture between EC Harris and Turner and Townsend; John Williams in EC Harris and Mike Collings in Turner and Townsend, who handed over to Rob Stacey and Mike Knox. Project controls migrated to programme management in 2003, consisting of Colin Reynell, Jeremy Bates and Sarah Wenn, all from BAA.

This team, in its final form, had a wide range of diverse skills that provided its real strength. Experience in the team came from the construction, aerospace, oil and gas, automotive, IT and manufacturing sectors and combined specialist skills in construction management, general programme management, project controls systems, cost management and accountancy.

On time and on budget

Keeping time and cost together was a basic principle of how T5 was managed. In the early stages of the T5 Programme there was a greater focus on cost, driving out opportunities for savings. As time progressed it became the critical focus, as the way to drive down cost was to deliver improved, safe productivity.

The tools and frameworks put in place by the T5 team are outlined below. Most will be used in one industry, but potentially the discipline of the implementation and the management commitment to this way of working may be different on T5.

Earned value management

The earned value approach measured the 'heartbeat' of the programme. Cost performance indicators (CPIs) and schedule performance indicators (SPIs) provided management with easy-to-understand and simple monthly measures regarding spend and schedule. The challenge was always to have a ratio greater than 1.0; that is, ahead of budget or ahead of plan. These two measures, together with a detailed set of key milestones, meant that T5's status versus plan was always clear and unambiguous. That is not to say that there weren't challenges with the schedule; indeed, with the difficult winter in 2003, the schedule was at times only just within the boundary of the 'late curve'. However, armed with the right information, the recovery plan – or glide path – to the desired outcome could be plotted and tracked against.

Integrated baseline review

Periodic standback reviews of the health of the T5 Programme were held, using a process called integrated baseline review (IBR). This process started in July 2004 and the first review was incredibly painful. It was the first time that all 25 000 activities from 147 subprojects had been rigorously joined together in the schedule and a true critical path through to the opening date had been created. It was hard getting all of the data in one format, and then persuading the teams to believe that this was the right way forward. This could only be achieved by the management team taking a tough and uncompromising approach.

IBRs were held about every six months and there were six in total. Most found scope gaps that were not budgeted or challenges that had a negative impact on the critical path. While always an anxious time, the upside was that the team came to be comfortable with the process, and whatever came out at the end was then a joint challenge that would have to be managed as one team.

IBR5 was the review held in December 2006 and for the first time it exposed BA to this level of programme management. The detailed sequence of events to complete construction, operational readiness and start-up became visible to BA's management. This forced a series of tough decisions regarding the timing of handover of areas to BA. Significant replanning of the detailed, room-by-room handovers was required, a painful process for BAA, but without this level of cooperation and understanding T5 would have been delayed. Willie Walsh, BA CEO, remembers how BA's confidence was shaken, both in terms of what it needed to do to be ready and what the T5 Programme needed to deliver to allow successful trials from September 2007. It became apparent that both parties were not exactly where they ideally wanted to be. A quick response was needed and IBR 51/2 was called in February 2007, by which time both teams had worked together to fix problems. One year from opening BA needed to be confident enough to start planning its 2008 schedule and selling tickets with T5 as the departure point. The meeting was a success and the team continued.

Mitigating a cost challenge

IBRs identified integrated problems and the team would work together to get on top of these challenges and wrestle them to completion. An example of this was the cost challenges thrown up by IBR1 in 2004. At this point T5 was projected to be £350 million over budget, but it was clear to the T5 team that this was a very fixable challenge. Bates, who since 2004 has led the programme management and has been in the middle of more time or cost challenge discussions than he cares to remember, recalls that the management culture was always very upbeat: 'Every challenge could be turned around with the right management focus and team commitment.' The cost and commercial leadership of Douglas, Mark Bullock, at the time programme assurance director, Wolstenholme, Matt Riley, commercial director, and Hill, along with key suppliers, meant that it was always achievable.

To meet this cost challenge, the 'total cost management' team was created to look at all opportunities and risks. Could the team value engineer the design? Mike Forster looked at what could not be built or designed and built differently. Riley looked at getting better deals with suppliers by buying differently, having fewer knowledge workers, using site and logistics facilities differently or driving up productivity on site. Bullock was instrumental in getting a different focus and discipline in cost management. A framework of opportunities was created, using simple 'ABCs'. As were opportunities with costed plans that suppliers bought into, Bs were good ideas with a plan being worked up and Cs were just good ideas. Month on month Bullock, with the team, worked and challenged these plans. His talent to see through numbers and his ability to sit and absorb the detail, for days if need be, was probably unmatched at T5 and soon created a culture of 'don't turn up to a meeting and not know your numbers'. This quickly spread throughout the management team of each project and encouraged a different culture of 'knowing the numbers' and, more importantly, having ideas to improve those numbers.

Bullock was intelligent enough to know when a team had reached the limits of a reasonable cost challenge or when they needed help from other teams to achieve their objectives. This was where a programme approach really paid dividends, as Bullock was able to martial support from any other project or team, so long as it was the right thing to do for the overall T5 Programme.

Focus on risk financial management

At the same time, Bullock and the team focused on risk. When the original budgets were agreed, risk money was held within each project and was difficult to reallocate at a T5 Programme level.

While this approach worked well during the design phase, as T5 moved into the construction phase there was the need to react to changing priorities and reassess this. In 2004, Bullock decided to set some more challenging cost targets for each team, based on their current position. As a result, £100 million was removed from individual project budgets and held centrally as a programme-level contingency. From this point onwards the remaining risk money was managed more closely and as the time-bound risks passed, more budget was returned to the central pot to be reallocated where it was needed.

Change-control process

The final part of the approach to cost was the change-control process. In theory, the T5 Agreement could have made it easy for suppliers to add costs, but a change-control process meant that this was not the case. All changes to scope required a signed project leader's instruction (PLI), which could be authorized up to £100 000 by a project leader. Anything above that figure was escalated to the project director, managing director or T5 executive. Early identification of changes was encouraged through a system where anyone could raise an early warning notification (EWN) to alert management to a potential issue before the decision was completed. While the majority of the proposed changes were agreed, they were all rigorously questioned, and the combination of good, robust processes and relentless management focus kept a grip on cost.

30 March 2008 declared as the opening date

Time was managed with the same rigour, but there was also a little more theatre. What is perhaps most amazing about T5 is that 30 March 2008 was a date set in 2001 and declared to all employees, suppliers and external stakeholders. Some thought went into the date, but in the early days there were so many unknowns at the front end of the programme (such as the impact of weather and unproven roof-assembly techniques) and at the back end (for example final fit-out and operational readiness) that no one really understood the detail until it got closer. The decision to declare a date had been inspired by events during the Heathrow Express tunnel collapse, when creating a very real target, with stakeholders and public knowing and expecting delivery, galvanized the team to deliver. For Wolstenholme that lesson was a powerful one that he would bring with him to T5. This bold decision was based on the principle of declaring your future even if you don't quite understand every twist and turn of the journey to get there, and it definitely changed the probability of success. That was how time was managed from start to finish.

The milestone plan and LRMs

Very early in the programme Anderson, Elliot and the planning team had turned the more than 25 000 activities stored in the Artemis project-management system into what were known in the early days as the 70 milestones delivered by 2007 or '70 by 07'. Each milestone represented a critical path point on the programme when one team needed to be ready to hand over to the next team. To mark the significance of completing a milestone there was a ceremonial handing over of the milestone, a piece of rock with a gold-plated plaque, from one team to the next. Elliot recounted the story of how he had gone out with his wife to buy the milestone from a local garden centre. He chose an elegant piece of marble costing over £100. His wife said, 'You can't spend that much money, there's a big piece of rock, that will do, and it costs a fiver.' Sure enough, that rock came home with them and with great pride was passed around the site from team to team for six years. This ceremony was a great motivator to each team as no one wanted to publicly miss deadlines.

Last responsible moments (LRMs) came from the critical chain method of planning. On T5 decisions would be taken as late as possible on subjects like design or systems, where waiting until last moment reduced the likelihood of building the wrong thing or the technology changing. T5 was on a late curve for many early milestones, so this approach had to be followed. The planning team moved to a more traditional approach to planning as time progressed. LRMs were also used to manage key decisions with stakeholders.

After IBR1 this baseline was approved by all the project teams and converted into the '80 by 08' plan, which included the detailed operational readiness milestones through to T5 opening. Douglas then brought together the managing directors and key players from the supply chain to ensure commitment to their part of delivering the plan. After a typically robust and motivational speech, Douglas led the way and signed the schedule. All 40 other people in the room then signed it one by one to demonstrate their commitment to delivering T5 on time. This document was copied and distributed throughout the T5 team and supply chain and provided a very visible sign of the intent. What was always amusing was that there were actually 83 milestones, but never let accuracy get in the way of a good message.

Within these significant milestones were five regulatory milestones relating to T5:

- Completion of twin rivers – 31 March 2005
- Completion of early release stands – 31 March 2005
- Heathrow air traffic control tower handover to NATS – 31 March 2006
- Main terminal building weathertight – 31 March 2007
- Satellite building weathertight – 31 March 2007

Missing these milestones would have had a significant effect on BAA's profits, as a portion of the annual landing charges increase was linked to their completion. All were hit, but the Heathrow air traffic control tower was only achieved a matter of weeks before the deadline, despite having one year of contingency built into the original date.

The integrated schedule approach worked well for the strategic programme and gave great visibility on a monthly basis. However, there were always many activities where progress was so critical that a monthly sample rate was not sufficient. Reynell insisted on weekly production key performance indicators to be reviewed for all critical areas so that quick, reactive controls could be applied. This allowed many potential problem areas to be spotted rapidly and for senior management to step in and correct them before weeks on the critical path had been lost.

Construction handing over to operational readiness on time

Prior to opening on 27 March 2008, perhaps the most critical milestone for construction was 17 September 2007. This was when Wolstenholme's accountability for construction of T5 passed to Bullock, by now the managing director, Heathrow, to make it an operational facility. It was fitting that after the speeches at the handover ceremony in the T5 satellite building, Bullock hugged Wolstenholme and said a heartfelt thankyou for the years of hard work leading up to that moment.

Finally, the lasting memory of time on T5 will be the daily countdown. Huge clocks in offices and around site kept everyone informed of how many days remained before opening. Again, this was a very powerful and symbolic way to keep time at the forefront of everyone's thinking every day, every hour and every second as it ticked by.

What was delivered?

As it stands, T5 is on target to hit a £4.3 billion cost target that was set in 2003 and all major milestones have been achieved. The final cost tally cannot be declared until all accounts are final, a target Riley has set for completion in summer 2008, with most completed in 2007. Clearly, the most significant deliverable is that the original opening date is still on target. As the construction team handed over accountability of the site to the operational readiness team and BA, all parties were confident, including Walsh and Stephen Nelson, now BAA CEO, that without terrorist attacks, a fire or a strike, T5 would open on 27 March 2008 at 4 a.m.

What is perhaps more telling is that people like Walsh and Bullock are just as concerned about the detailed operational issues as they are about the grand statement that a building like T5 makes. The temperature of the coffee consumed on day one, through to the queue times at security and the cleanliness of the toilets – all must be perfect, as this will contribute to the passengers' first impressions. For them the real success will be measured at the first-year anniversary, after passengers have had a real opportunity to use T5 and the business returns are understood.

What was different?

Use of an integrated time and cost system to produce accurate data

The importance of the integrated time and cost plan that created an accurate, robust and transparent view of all 147 subprojects, 18 projects and one T5 Programme cannot be underestimated. While this was incredibly difficult to set up, the power and confidence it created were remarkable.

Introduction of the cost-verification team

The T5 Agreement was at times seen as having no teeth. So some suppliers were asked to leave, rework was not paid for and cost assurance was put in place. Hill created a cost-verification team that employed accountants to check that all costs were properly incurred; on a £4.3 billion cost-reimbursable project this was a necessity. This approach has netted some £30 million of savings to date. It's all too easy when spending these huge amounts to lose sight of the little things. Whether it was the 'every penny counts' campaigns in logistics or 'Project Leon', which had the cost-verification team looking at timesheets and removing individuals who had been dishonest, that balance was managed.

The leadership culture

There were of course many challenges on time and cost, but the senior leadership never panicked. There was a great belief in the ability of the T5 team to solve any problem thrown at them, and this was continually reinforced by Douglas and Wolstenholme. Their belief spread into the teams, motivating them and encouraging every individual to believe that they could personally make a difference. Douglas and Wolstenholme together were masters at turning bad news into opportunities, but were absolutely insistent on teams sharing their issues once they had been discovered. Keeping bad news quiet was frowned upon. This leadership culture was meticulously implemented throughout the various management and governance forums. Whether it was monthly project reviews or supplier principal contractor meetings, clear agendas, objectives, very specific attendees and descriptions of the issues were in place.

BAA demonstrated vigilant trust in how it worked with its supply chain. The T5 Agreement put in place an open-book environment and the suppliers really entered into the spirit of delivering on time and on budget. The supplier teams had been involved every step of the way and tools like Artemis worked for them as much as for BAA, with clever technology extracting data from their home base systems so that transparency was made easy. Bates said:

> 99.9% of the time as we worked with suppliers you could feel they had entered into the spirit of T5 delivering on time and to budget. They wanted to succeed for the T5 Programme, overcome hurdles and work together to not let the side down.

That supply chain involvement brought with it real shared account-abilities. CEOs and MDs always knew about cost challenges, never inappropriately leaked anything and entered into the spirit of working as a team to do things differently to save money.

Key learning

By the end of T5 there is a real sense that the tools, the frameworks and the management forums that were created could manage a big project successfully. This learning has been taken to Heathrow East and set that project up from day one. T5 has been a success story on time and cost, and its track record of declaring its targets publicly and delivering on them is to be commended.

The core team of Bates, Anderson and Wenn, together with a few others, has now been in place since 2003–04. They have held a picture of the T5 plan in their head and for years have gone to bed thinking about intricate details, risks and opportunities and always worrying about problem solving. This team was respected by and gained the trust of the BAA project heads and directors. The directors also knew how and when to call on this team for information and advice. In key senior meetings relatively junior programme office team members would be asked to share what was on their mind. The project teams learned to use this central resource to help them manage their projects better, and the embedded cost and planning team members worked as one team across the 18 projects.

The importance of the single monthly report produced and narrated by Hill cannot be underestimated. This report allowed the senior team of BAA corporate, Mike Clasper and Margaret Ewing, group finance director, to steer the programme and to assure themselves that T5 was on track and provided a single set of accurate data that all could use as a reference point. This unambiguous 'bible' of the T5 Programme allowed data to be accessed, understood and reacted to with a minimum of argument.

QUALITY

In Chapter 2 the catalogue of time and cost overruns in many projects was explored, and yet these projects resulted in buildings or experiences that the public enjoy today. There is even an argument to say that grand buildings would potentially never get funding if the real costs were proposed at the beginning.

As visitors attend the Scottish Assembly at Holyrood, or go to see their favourite team play at Wembley, or even sit on the Jubilee line travelling to Canary Wharf, they forget that all of these projects were over budget, late and in the case of the latter two had unremarkable safety records. That's a lesson for us all: ultimately though delivering time, cost, safety are important at any particular moment, the design and quality of the finished facility are what stand the test of time.

What is quality in design and construction?

The challenge for those involved in quality was to move the psyche of the project from quality with a small q to quality with a capital Q. On big projects time and cost are often the sacred cows, and safety, quality and environment come someway down the list. On T5 safety was positioned as a value not a priority, so it always came first. Quality and the environment were areas of focus that required education and significant senior leadership focus to signal their criticality to the overall T5 Programme's success.

Quality is about defining a specification and meeting that specification, and getting it right first time every time. A specification can relate to technical performance, level of heat or cold output, flow of water through a pipe or the decibel level of a particular noise. It can relate to the cosmetic performance of finish; for example for the back-painted glass used all over T5 as a wall finish, the cosmetic specification will relate to the colour, thickness, surface finish and even the gap between the panels.

Systems, process, people and ultimately a culture needed to be put in place across the supply chain to ensure that the specifications for the thousands of individual products or systems that run across T5 were achieved in the finished airport. The cost of rework as a result of the quality process is notable, but when completed work fails to meet the specification, the cost to correct it is significant. Getting that mindset and understanding to deliver the specification right first time, every time has been the challenge. T5 leadership focused on quality, developing a common approach across the site, but most importantly engaging the workforce so that they understood what good quality looked like, and the role they played in delivering it.

Using methodology tested in the car industry, the team created a six-step process to manage quality working closely with the construction teams. The 'right first time six golden rules' were:

- *Step 1 – agree specification.* Agree the specification to the right detail and with the right parties. On T5 this equated to over 10 000 specifications.
- *Step 2 – method statement and inspection plan.* Develop an inspection and test plan that will make sure that the technical or cosmetic performance standard will be met every time, produced by the suppliers. Supported by a method statement, this covers special equipment required for construction, or access requirements, the process to be followed and the inspection or test regime to be deployed to ensure that the specification is being met.
- *Step 3 – getting ready to start on site.* Ensure that the workforce have the right skills, are appropriately trained and have the right tools to do the job. This includes making a benchmark example of what 'good' looks like being completed. These benchmarks were laminated and put up around the site, so the workforce could see the quality standard they needed to deliver, and then stored in Documentum, a document database.
- *Step 4 – benchmark check.* Check work completed against the 1400 benchmarks of agreed standards by suppliers. When discussing this with Wolstenholme, he was clear that 'the power

of benchmarks was getting the workers on site to create the standard. The pressure to meet the standard then became personal or peer led, not management led.'

- *Step 5 – quality audits.* The central quality team audited about 5 % of the finished work. The enabling quality processes were also audited. In total on T5 over 700 audits were carried out, and 2500 issues were raised in these audits and closed out. In addition, many informal reviews took place during weekly quality work reviews.
- *Step 6 – handover.* Handing over the finished work had two steps, the little h and the big H handover. The scale of T5 with over 5000 rooms in the main terminal building alone dictated that a different approach was required, as many systems or parts of large areas would be completed but until all systems were complete and the final client ready for acceptance, the final handover could not be made. The little h was the interim handover, where a major system was completed; the big H was the final handover where the ownership of the completed asset would transfer to the client. In the case of a room, the small h involved the floor or roof being complete, the big H, involved total room completion, with windows, doors, lighting and all other systems and services checked against the quality standards. Before the room was ready for final handover, the team involved would have done a final review, the quality team from the supplier team would also have done a review and finally the technical leadership team would accept the room on behalf of the client.

Key players

David Long and Chris Little were the central BAA team, formed by Colin Reynell and handed over to Chris Millard at the end of 2004. They were supported by Mike Couglan of Parsons Brinkerhoff. Long and Little were joined by Geoff Sykes in the main T5 buildings project team to coordinate the team of quality leaders from across the supply chain embedded in the projects, with notable examples being Gerry Prickett, TPS, design; Stephen Parsons, Laing O'Rourke; Roger Wood, BAA building control; Richard Gammon and Steve West, Pascall & Watson; Barry Works, Integrated Project Management; Brian Crisp, Mace; Derek Gray, Balfour Beatty Rail; and Paul Cooper, Mott McDonald Rail. Together they championed the culture change and managed the processes.

This was not the only group focused on driving quality across the programme. They combined with the technical leadership team and the team providing building control services across the programme to provide a total 'product assurance' picture. This focused on reporting to the project executive against the key monthly objectives of an airport that should stand the test of time, work and keep working, raising key product quality concerns. This senior focus was invaluable to ensure that the topdown passion for quality was maintained and that significant non–conformance issues were quickly addressed before their impact threatened the programme.

What was delivered?

Simple key performance indicators were established that measured the performance of the 18 major projects against the six–step quality process. Each project reported monthly, giving 96 key measures that were analysed by Millard and his team. These were aggregated to an overall percentage score of success, with 100 % meaning that all targets were achieved right first time, a very demanding target.

As the project progressed and the q to Q enabling activities took effect, performance quickly climbed from 79 % in October 2004 to consistently being over 90 % in 2006. Targets were adjusted annually both to reflect the changing nature of construction activities and to set more demanding performance standards. This drove a continuous improvement in standards, with the score quickly climbing back to over 90 % after each target tightening.

The total cost of non-conformance was tracked through non-conformance reports (NCRs). These were reviewed monthly, root causes analysed and corrective actions implemented. The result was that the total cost of NCRs across the programme was £25 million, only 0.6% of the project total. Together with the observed finished quality of the building, this has provided ample evidence of the benefits of this multifaceted approach to quality.

What was different?

Frameworks were embedded through culture change

Once again, the approach to embedding quality as a way of doing business was carried out using frameworks, benchmarks, measurement and all of the technical things you would expect to find. What actually proved much more important was the cultural journey people were taken on. To capture the hearts and minds and to get people talking about quality, a 'quality week' road show kicked off, in which each project created a part of their site to show what good quality looked like, and every worker on site spent time watching a quality DVD on what the finished airport should look like, along with the role they played, and visiting benchmark-quality parts of the site. This was supported by quality exhibitions, a special edition of the *Site* newspaper and competitions. After that a strong quality message was added to the T5 induction process, and stepped up in the toolbox talks alongside other communication channels. The 800 supervisors were trained on 'right first time' and on their leadership role in leaving behind a legacy we would be proud of.

Wolstenholme and Millard did quality walkabouts talking to the workers about quality and looking at the work. Millard remembers:

> There were lots of areas we picked up for improvement on these walkabouts, such as work progressing without signed-off benchmarks, glass and tiling quality, and requests we could take back to line management to enable them to do a better job, but my real memory is of the pride the

teams would present their work. These walkabouts gave us a valuable opportunity to reinforce our commitment to quality and support the 'if you can't do it with quality, don't do it' message.

In total over 10 000 site visits to walk around or review benchmarks took place.

Quality was slow to get going as a full integrated approach, with joined-up communities, all the systems, processes, people and culture work in place. Candidly the management focus early in the T5 Programme had been given to safety and then the learning from safety was leveraged in quality. That said, as T5 draws to an end the discipline created of looking end to end from design, to construction into operational readiness has started to stick.

Key learning

As the work on quality moves to Heathrow East, the next mega project at Heathrow, the big message on quality is 'earlier', explains Millard. 'Setting the benchmarks and samples is being moved forward into the design phase, so that before construction starts client and supplier are clear on what good looks like.' As BAA moves to a more hands-off role, working with fewer third-generation suppliers, being much clearer earlier in the brief is critical.

The cultural change work on safety and quality will be more connected and start from the beginning of design and construction. There is still a lot of work to be done on getting quality to be a way of working, however, as rework during or after the job is a huge waste of money.

SAFETY

There are not many jobs that you start with a statistic that says you are likely to kill two people and have 600 disabling injuries over your tenure. While there is a downward trend in fatalities in construction, the Health and Safety Executive statistics for 2006–07 showed that 77 men and women didn't go home from work due to a fatal accident at work in the UK (HSE statistics, 2007). This is a declining number, but still completely unacceptable.

Wolstenholme took his accountability to create a safe environment for his workforce to heart. A family man, for him safety was personal, and to his credit for his seven years leading the T5 construction project he woke up worrying about this, and then came into work and built an integrated team with his suppliers who did the same. For many of those suppliers T5 was a life-changing opportunity. 'To have a client who expected you to put safety first, and really meant it, gave me the time to grow as a leader of safety,' explained Steve Cork of Laing O'Rourke. Mark Reynolds of Mace explained:

> The client facilitated thinking on safety from all of the different angles, most importantly from the cultural and people standpoint, and expected us all to put our money where our leadership needed to be, in making sure everyone went home safely.

There were two broad reasons safety was taken so seriously, and without doubt T5 is viewed by the industry as an example of what good looks like. First, the prospect of killing and hurting people as they do their job is morally wrong. Equally, it was understood that demonstrating to the 50 000-strong workforce that their safety was genuinely taken seriously meant that a different relationship could be developed between T5 and its workers. Mike Knowles, SPIE Matthew Hall, explained, 'I knew it was a different site when I saw supervisors pulling other team workers for unsafe practices. That just doesn't happen on other sites. The culture of 'don't walk by' was really happening on T5.' In repeated employee surveys, over 75 % of the workforce felt that T5 was the safest site they had ever worked on, and at the same time over 60 % thought it was a great place to work. By getting safety right you could then talk to your workforce differently about productivity. 'Safe productivity' was the phrase coined, challenging the idea that safety, time and cost were either/ors. The T5 team said that the language was 'and' not 'or': because it's safe we think it can be on time and on cost.

T5's approach to safety changed even the most hardened construction views on how safety can be done differently. In conversations with all of the main contractors about safety, they said things like, 'We didn't intentionally hurt people but for so many years it had just been accepted as one of the hazards of construction.' During T5 there were occasions when grown men were nearly brought to tears about safety. It was the one of the few areas where directors, trade union members and the people on the tools were genuinely 100% united. Safety was a value for the team, not just a very high priority, from Wolstenholme down. Come what may, safety always came first.

Mike Evans, T5 safety manager, remembers the turning point: 'A huge banner went up in front of the T5 entrance saying, if you can't do it safely, don't do it at all. For the first time top management had given, even instructed the workforce to take charge of their own safety.' For those working on site, the permission to say 'no' to unsafe working was not a signal to down tools and walk off site, but rather it was recognized that workers, management and trade unions needed to work together.

Key players

Andrew Wolstenholme, supported by Mike Evans, was in a leadership role for BAA. Other key players were Richard Rook, Laing O'Rourke site leader; and principal contractors Laing O'Rourke, Mace, SPIE Matthew Hall, Morgan Vinci, Balfour Beatty and JMJ, which became training provider Alkoomi.

Creating an incident- and injury-free site

From 2001 the groundwork was being laid for changing the way safety was approached on T5. Over the years the team challenged the approach to design, off-site prefabrication, the construction safety standards on site and how leaders work with people to get a different and safe site.

Appointing planning supervisors

The construction design and management (CDM) regulations stipulate that projects must appoint a planning supervisor. T5 appointed Bovis Lend Lease and a principal contractor (PC) who has overall accountability for safety on site. Given the size, complexity and contractual arrangements that were in place on T5, BAA was able to convince the HSE that the PC role would need to be done differently; a unique approach, demonstrating the leadership BAA was prepared to show. Morgan Vinci was the PC for tunnels, Balfour Beatty for rail and for the rest of the site, BAA, Laing O'Rourke, Mace and SPIE Matthew Hall were the PCs. This was perhaps a clue that safety on T5 was going to be a little different.

In design Bovis, the planning supervision team, entered into the spirit of integrated teams and asked each design team to identify a CDM coordinator. Working with the coordinators a 'red list' of products, processes or materials that were dangerous to the workforce or environment were created, meaning that if the design team wanted to use anything on the list they had to build a justification. The team of coordinators were tasked day in and day out with the challenge to design safety into the projects, and were brought together as a community to share ideas and create a network.

Off-site prefabrication

BAA encouraged a strategy of off-site prefabrication, or building and testing as much as possible away from the site in less time-critical environments, which was an important ingredient in the site workface being as safe as possible. Whether it was the roof, air traffic control tower, mechanical and electrical services modules or even concrete pre-casting, all of these helped to reduce the risks that workers faced on site.

Single set of site rules established

A common set of site rules was established, pulled from about 20 site construction processes and bringing together the best ideas from PCs, setting out one set of rules of engagement and the basic infrastructure. Common approaches to smoking, personal protective equipment, permits to work stipulating the approach to site welfare and logistics, and even training facilities on site to test safety competence were just some of the dos and dont's needed to make a big site work.

Getting everyone to take safety personally

Getting all of the right design, engineering and site rules in place was important. However, the '1 in a million, 1 reportable accident in every million man hours worked' safety campaign gave glimpses of cultural change that, while a step in the right direction, weren't good enough. The leadership engagement that was seen in this didn't go far enough either. In safety issues BAA had again looked out of the construction industry, using connections that SPIE Matthew Hall had in offshoring and spending time with Shell and BP. The PCs who had committed to making T5 different started to have a number of consultants who were involved in culture change tender to accelerate the activity, and the team finally picked JMJ Associates.

Most culture change needs to take place at the top of organizations and in this case a series of one- and two-day 'commitment workshops' were held throughout the duration of the project. These brought together CEOs, MDs and other key players from suppliers with key players from BAA to confront how they really felt about safety and what was acceptable to them.

For the first time BAA had involved industry leaders and made everyone face up to the statistics, and to personally commit to do everything in their power to get their companies to approach safety differently. Evans remembers early sessions where senior players watched video footage of a basketball team playing in a circle while a man in a gorilla suit runs onto the set. Eight out of ten people invariably don't notice the man in the gorilla suit, and in the same way they don't notice unsafe working practices as the brain goes into automatic pilot, seeing what it expects to see. The senior players thought they had been cheated and wanted see the clip again. Equally, debates with the senior site people showed that they were really struggling to see how it was possible not to injure anyone on site, and thinking aloud, 'That couldn't be possible, how could we declare IIF?' Slowly but surely, the conversations helped prepare a community of leaders to think about and lead differently on the safety agenda. These senior players would sign up to creating T5 as an IIF culture, incident and injury free.

At the core of this approach was getting everyone concerned to declare a different future and to free their minds from the past. To get out of this cycle the key is to focus on the future as a possibility. No matter how hard people focus on the future, thinking and behaviour are still governed by the past, even with the addition of a 'stretch target' or asking for that little bit more than people hoped to achieve. Therefore, through this focus on the past, behaviour becomes self-limiting and only a small amount of movement is possible, rather than a radical and fundamental shift. The declared future state helped everyone to sign up to delivering T5 IIF. It meant that the belief now was that T5 could be built without hurting anyone, doing everything with that value at the front of everyone's mind (see Figure 5.1).

Training went right through the ranks, with 800 managers going through the two-day commitment workshop, 1200 supervisors having a one-day training programme and every member of the workforce hearing about IIF at induction. This was then followed by half-day training sessions and refresher briefings. In addition, 150 in-house trainers, from within the frontline workforce, were trained to deliver the workshops.

Significant time and money were put aside to share the message, but the real power came in the shift in leadership behaviour that became visible. In the winter of 2003, Wolstenholme stopped the

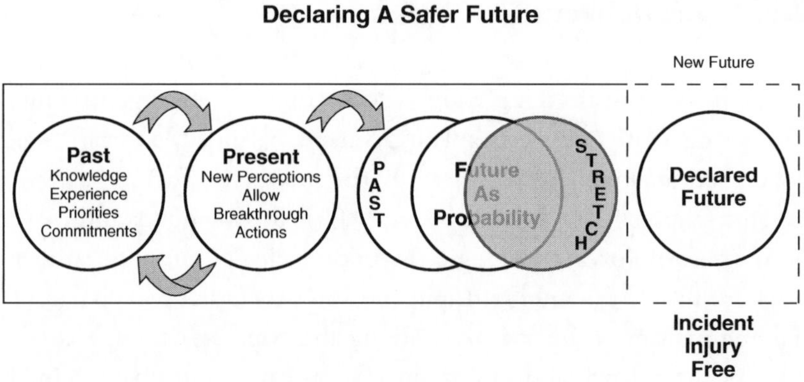

Declaring A Safer Future

Figure 5.1   Declaring a safer future.

site as he felt some unsafe night working was taking place, and he then gathered the key players in a room to ensure that safety was fixed. This was symbolic of safety coming before production.

There were a series of leadership forums at which key players would come together and talk primarily about safety. Monthly, 12–15 senior leaders met with Wolstenholme, and this cascaded to eight project leadership teams across the site. Matt Palmer, a BAA project leader, described these sessions:

> You never missed them, you made sure your holidays didn't coincide with them. It was like getting a monthly injection of good ideas or a boost to keep the energy alive.

In addition, there was a monthly health and safety forum, held on the second Tuesday of every month. This brought together 75 people in a room, with production leaders, construction managers and the key team leaders running the site. Attendance was always good, as the leaders on site knew this was critical. The team would look at photos from safety walkabouts, explore issues or new work-forces coming on site, identify what needed to be done, awarding a 'best-performing team' and always with an inspirational speech from Wolstenholme.

What was delivered?

To help shift the thinking about safety from 'preventing accidents to creating a safe culture,' explains Evans, a balanced scorecard was developed tracking every project, all the suppliers' measures as well as safety inputs. The balance was 70% focus on inputs and 30% on outputs, following the logic that inputs change outputs, so that is where to put the energy. Input measures included percentage of training managers, supervisors, training and competence, operatives meeting attendance and HSE course attendance, and finally bonus contribution. Outputs followed reportable injuries that must be reported to the HSE, including fatalities, major incidents like broken bones, or any injuries that required a worker to take three or more days off work. Minor accidents included anything put in the accident book, quite often trips and slips, and significant incidents or near misses were captured and reviewed for an opportunity to learn.

On T5 sadly two people lost their life, one on 13 August 2005, falling from 17-metre-high temporary works by the interchange plaza; the second on 27 October 2007, a man who was working in a lift shaft when the accident happened and was pronounced dead at the scene. So despite all the huge integrated team effort, T5 was industry average. More importantly, two sets of families are without their loved ones.

In terms of major injuries, statistically T5 should have seriously injured 600 people. This is the equivalent to the reportable incidents, and in fact T5 was three times better than the industry average. Over 6000 minor incidents were recorded, a number that cannot be compared to the rest of the industry as statistics on these are not captured and shared consistently.

What was different?

One of the darkest days on T5 was when two Laing O'Rourke workers were in the new multistorey car park at the western end of the site. The accident happened at around 3.30 p.m. on 3 August 2005, with both men falling 17 metres when the temporary works supporting a concrete slab they were standing on gave way. The men were quickly treated by onsite medical teams and emergency services, before being rushed to hospital by ambulance. Sadly, one young man died; the other, although seriously hurt, made an amazing recovery. Every person involved in T5 who has been interviewed said this was their low point on what otherwise has been for most the 'best job they have ever been on'.

Why was this different? Douglas had declared that if 'there was one fatality on T5 it wouldn't have been worth it'. The industry had come together and engaged with their workforce differently and genuinely all had believed that T5 would not have a fatality. So when over 2000 workers stood at the memorial service held on site on a hot August afternoon for the young man who had lost his life, Catholics, Protestants, Sikhs, Muslims and agnostics alike stood with their heads bowed. Genuinely there was huge sadness for the family who had lost a son and partner, but also the feeling that it 'shouldn't have happened on T5'. Counsellors who spent time with those most closely involved echoed these sentiments.

Great leadership was required by Douglas, Wolstenholme and Cork from Laing O'Rourke to go to the funeral, talk to the family who had paid too high a price, and to pick the site up again. The goal to have zero fatalities on T5 was not going to be achieved. Wolstenholme recalled an inspirational speech he had heard by Roger Black, an Olympic athlete who had only been able to win a silver medal. Despite the disappointment of not winning gold, he had run his best race ever to achieve silver. With a fatality, T5 now had to run its best race ever.

Paul Taylor from JMJ said he watched young managers after the fatality going into rooms with 20–30 men and trying to make sense of the accident while picking them up and trying to double their efforts.

T5 has shown that if you design, engineer and set up your site for safety, you will do a good job. What has been different is that in the most difficult times imaginable as well as in good times, the leadership commitment and qualities of the few who lead the many were unquestionable.

Key learning

The construction industry is a safer place as a result of T5. This is unquestionably the real learning that has truly transcended the T5 site. Why? Every individual and company spoken to in the writing of this book – Laing O'Rourke, SPIE Matthew Hall, Mace, Morgan Vinci, Balfour Beatty, Vanderlande, Sam Lloyd the stud welder, the project leaders, Sir Michael Latham and others – describe how IIF and T5 implementing it on such a scale have changed their lives or the industry. The extra training, the leadership commitment and the workforce engagement all come through in the examples and stories they tell of what they have done since leaving T5.

Rook talked about a job he was involved in Leeds:

> 50% of the civils workforce had come off T5 and the IIF culture was up and running within days. The men on the site refused to work in an unsafe environment, and felt empowered to take control of their own personal safety and look out for their mates.

The learning for the future is keep IIF fresh, keep talking and listening to the workforce, never become complacent, and just when you think you've got it, one moment of not thinking can lead to someone not going home safely.

ENVIRONMENT

The world has woken up to climate change, thanks to pressure groups such as Greenpeace or the Camp for Climate finally capturing the imagination of ordinary people and politicians alike. A recent radio programme claimed that Margaret Thatcher had been one of the first politicians on an international stage to raise the issue of global warming (Radio 4, 2007). Today leaders like Al Gore have helped the world set out an agenda for change involving countries, companies and individuals all working together differently to limit the damage we do to the environment. The UK aviation industry accounts for 5% of CO_2 emissions, industry accounts for 26%, households 25%, roads 24% and the rest is neatly known as 'other' (BAA, 2007). So it's a complicated story in a world where we all want to get somewhere fast, but we don't want to face up to the consequences of that convenience.

There are broadly three sources of impact on the environment: aviation in the air and while the aircraft are on the ground; the buildings and transport infrastructure that bring passengers to airports; and construction relating to the materials used in building and the impact on the local community during that construction.

Regardless of the facts, there are definitely two sides to the aviation and climate change arguments. On the one hand there is the environment lobby. On the other hand, airport operators and airlines are positioning themselves as treading a fine line between running businesses that have significant positive impacts on the economy and on quality of life for the traveller, and trying to mitigate the environment impacts.

BAA is on target to reduce its own CO_2 emissions from energy by 15% below 1990 levels by 2010. This is in excess of the UK's targets under the Kyoto protocol and despite a predicted growth in passenger numbers of 70% during this period. BAA has recently set a new target to further reduce CO_2 emissions from energy use in buildings by 30% by 2020.

Both in design and construction, and as an operational airport terminal, those involved in T5 have been very aware of the environment impact that had to be managed, and opportunities to improve today's performance were presented by the new building. When T5 started the ambition was to make everything 'best practice', but with so many years in design and construction many of the ideas that have been put into action will now be seen as the norm.

Key players

A team of seven at its peak was led by Eryl Smith, T5 managing director, and involved Liz Southern, head of development, and Beverly Lister, environment manager, supported by WSP environment consultants and the Environment Agency. All worked together to design, construct and operate T5 with the least possible impact on the environment.

The construction story

Archaeology

Archaeological excavations have been taking place in and around Heathrow airport for over 50 years. The construction of T5 provided a unique opportunity to learn even more about the history of the area. Archaeology started on site in 2002 once planning permission was granted, and that gave an over 80-strong team of archaeologists time to carry out excavations on over 100 hectares, digging 60 000 holes. Unearthing over 9000 years of history gave insights into how civilizations lived as long ago as 6000 BC, with artefacts such as 18 000 pieces of pottery, 40 000 pieces of worked flint and a hand axe dating back to 3000 BC all providing clues about the Heathrow of the past. The T5 main building was constructed north to south to allow the archaeological team maximum time to do their work, but this did create sequencing challenges, particularly around being ready for proving trials that the construction team had to and did work around.

Managing the impact on the local community

Working hours and noise limits were agreed with the local council. Deviation from these agreed working conditions was only allowed if permitted by the local council in advance. To avoid the impact of construction traffic on the local roads, contractors were not permitted to drive on designated 'no go' routes in local villages and residents' parking schemes were implemented to ease parking pressures. Deliveries of materials to the construction site were managed through the logistics centres to reduce congestion on the local roads.

Monitoring and mitigating air quality, dust and noise issues

A site-specific air-quality control plan was prepared and implemented at T5, detailing what measures would be adopted by the project team to ensure that impacts on air quality were minimized. Baselines for air quality started to be taken in April 2001, 18 months prior to construction starting. Monitoring taken at six locations around the site until the end of construction showed that T5's impact on local air quality had been negligible. Dust, though not a health hazard, is an inconvenience for the local community, so a great deal of effort was put into keeping it under control. Some 19 sites were monitored and data shared with the local community on a Web site.

The senior construction management understood the importance of being a good neighbour to the local community, and within their areas worked with the environment team to manage or limit the impact of their work. From day one even temporary roads were tarmaced and a rigorous damping-down and sweeping regime put in place. When planning required earthwork mounds to be left for over 13 weeks, they were seeded to reduce the dust blowing in the wind. Concrete crushing was strategically placed around the site and additional water sprayed on the concrete crusher conveyor belts.

Minimization of noise is a key consideration in the planning of works. Where possible quieter methods of working were selected, for example silent piling, or vibro piling, has been used at various sensitive locations across the project, rather than the noisier drop-hammer piling. Although the site working hours were 7 a.m. to 7 p.m., noisy works did not start until 8 a.m. and were finished by

6 p.m. Where works took place close to sensitive receptors, noise hoarding was installed, quiet plant selected for use, and all plant switched off when not in use. The T5 environment team used a portable noise monitor, and this data combined with the continuous static monitoring data allowed regular checks of activities to ensure that the agreed noise limits were not exceeded.

Materials used to build T5

At the outset it was recognized that materials specifications could have a significant effect on health and the environment due to the volume and scope of materials to be procured. Because of these issues, the project identified 'resource use' as a top environment priority and endorsed the following objectives: to consider lifecycle impacts in the choice of materials, minimize the use of nonsustainable materials, and minimize the use of toxic materials.

HCFCs and HFCs, which are powerful greenhouse gases, have virtually been eliminated from T5. Most of the timber was sourced from a sustainable supply, approved by the Forestry Stewardship Council. 300 000 tonnes of aggregates, such as sand, gravel or crushed stone used in construction, were recycled from site materials and 80 000 tonnes of recycled and secondary aggregate was brought onto the site. Crushed green glass from domestic household recycling banks was used as a base for roads and pulverized fuel ash, a waste product from power stations, made up 30 % of the concrete mixture that was used on site. 6.5 million cubic metres was moved during the project to avoid sending excavated materials to landfill; this earth was used to backfill excavations and landscape the terminal. In all, 97 % of the waste materials on site were recycled.

Twin rivers: An example of constructing responsibly

In Chapter 11 we deep dive on the twin rivers case study. However, while looking at T5's approach to environment issues during construction, it would be remiss not to draw attention to this area.

The Longford and Duke of Northumberland rivers ran through the middle of the T5 site, travelling in culverts under the north and south runways. To allow the construction of T5, the rivers were diverted. Two new river channels were constructed around the western perimeter of the T5 development.

To maximize their ecological value, 95 % of the diverted rivers have been placed in open channels, compared to only 50 % for the original sections of the rivers. Pre-planted coir rolls and hazel hurdles provide habitats for small mammals along the naturalized banks. In-channel enhancements maximize the ecological value of the vertical-sided channels, creating a meandering flow pattern that boosts river biodiversity. Recycled trees in the channels offer habitat for fish and macroinvertebrates (animals that live on the bottom of rivers), while gravel enhancements have been used to create a medium for over 84 000 native river plants. In addition to moving the population of water voles (see below), 40 000 fish were captured from the original river channels and moved to the river Colne. Over 1000 freshwater mussels and sediments from the old rivers, rich in macroinvertebrates, were collected and put into the new channels to kick-start the ecology.

The river diversion was completed in May 2004. Since then pike, chub, roach, tench, perch, gudgeon, bleak, minnow, three-spined sticklebacks and eels have been found in the new river channels. Ecological surveys have shown that the fish stocks have increased each year, and the size distribution of the species captured suggest that some of the fish are very likely to have been born there. Kingfishers have also been observed fishing on the rivers.

A small population of water voles was resident in the Duke of Northumberland river. When the river was moved as part of the construction works the voles also had to be moved. In 2001, six pairs of voles were captured and installed in a captive breeding programme at the Wildwood Centre in Kent. In early 2002, a further 18 voles were captured and translocated to a local receptor site identified by English Nature and the London Wildlife Trust. By June of the same year, surveys found feeding signs and droppings of juvenile voles, suggesting that the population was expanding up- and downstream of the immediate release areas. Following further habitat improvements, a further 25 captive-bred voles were released in April 2003.

The operational airport story

T5 will process 30 million passengers a year. With a new facility this has presented an opportunity to deploy new methods and thinking to make it a more environmentally friendly building than the rest of the current Heathrow portfolio.

Water, energy efficiency and waste management

Water was recognized as a precious resource from the outset, hence the team set out to reduce the amount of potable or drinking-quality water used by 70 %. At the rest of Heathrow about 40 litres of potable water is used per passenger; T5 will hit a target of 17.5 litres. To help meet the challenge a water taskforce from Black Veach looked at every opportunity to capture 'grey' water (nonindustrial waste water) from across all the T5 campus and use it appropriately. All toilets in the terminal buildings have the capability to be low-flush toilets with flush volumes as low as 4 litres. All taps and showers are fitted with water-saving devices such as automatic on and off sensors and aerated flow taps and showerheads, and the BA CIP lounge has vacuum-flush toilets that use just 1.2 litres per flush.

Energy-saving targets were built into the design principles. The main terminal building is glazed on all sides, reducing the need for artificial lighting. A digitally addressable lighting interface, or DALI system, controls the lights at T5. This will allow individual lights or sets of lights to be turned on, off or dimmed according to the requirements of the area at a particular time of day or for certain weather conditions. Energy-efficient fittings have been specified throughout the terminal buildings, and only centrally chilled water supplied by superefficient ammonia chillers in the T5 energy centre will be used cool the building. This negated the need for individually chilled air-conditioning units and refrigerators throughout the building.

BAA worked closely with the retailers and other concessionaires to ensure that energy and water efficiency was designed into their shops. Concessionaires were required to complete their own environment plan for each retail unit to demonstrate how they intended to meet energy and water targets developed with BAA.

BAA has a target of recycling or composting 40 % of its waste by 2010. By 2020 70 % of waste will be recycled, with zero waste being sent to landfill. From 2008, waste that currently goes to landfill will go to waste-incineration plants, with some of the energy produced being recovered. BA has been working closely with BAA to realize opportunities in waste minimization and has set its own targets for recycling and recovery of waste.

Noise control during operation

T5 presented the opportunity to look at the noise generated by the airport and include features in the campus design to minimize and contain this noise. The wavy wall constructed at the southwest corner of the airport provides a noise barrier. Fixed ground electrical power is provided at all stands, and pre-conditioned air is provided at all pier stands at T5. Aircrafts can 'plug' into these, negating the need to keep their engines running while on the stand to run their power supply and air-conditioning units. Without their engines running when on the stand, the aircraft are significantly quieter and less polluting.

Heathrow airport operates a noise and track-keeping system to monitor on a continuous basis that aircraft follow predetermined tracks. This enables BAA to investigate and analyse the noise and track data of every flight and to identify where aircraft don't keep to the required noise-preferential routes.

Landscaping

The T5 landscaping strategy encompasses four main areas: the M25 spur road, the Colne Valley, the western perimeter road and the landside campus. The landscaping scheme creates a gradual change from the agricultural land to the west of the airport to the urban character at the terminal. Over 1000 semi-mature trees, 2500 semi-mature shrubs, 50 000 native woodland plants and 2000 metres of native hedgerow will be planted as part of the landscaping scheme.

Areas of the Colne Valley had been used for the temporary stock-piling of material removed from the T5 site during construction. The Colne Valley landscaping scheme seeks not only to restore but also significantly to improve this valley. The scheme was developed in consultation with local stakeholders, and includes provision of access and footpaths, creating a valuable regional wildlife haven and recreational resource.

What was different?

Working with key stakeholders

One of the things that the T5 management team sought to do at an early stage was to engage a cross-section of industry experts to advise on environment priorities for the design, construction and operation of T5 who would provide an expert view on best-practice environment performance as well as what was likely to be coming down the pipeline in the form of future legislation. These experts came from companies such as CIRIA, Forum for the Future and BRE.

The group was called the Environment Assessment Advisory Group (EAAG). It quickly got to grips with advising on key issues for T5. Its terms of reference did not include debating all the issues that were being evaluated at the planning inquiry, but were more about where the team should be focusing its design efforts in improving environment performance. Priorities were established around:

- Climate change and energy
- Water, reducing the amount of potable water used

- Resource use and materials
- Waste, reducing and recycling
- Air quality

Various teams presented back to EAAG the progress made on these issues. Southern explained:

> There was good debate at these sessions and whilst they knew that the decision on whether T5 would proceed or not would be made elsewhere, this group influenced the environment targets and performance of T5.

Proactive monitoring

An extensive programme of monitoring encompassing dust, air quality, noise, surface-water quality, groundwater quality and ecology was implemented to detect any variation in the quality of the local environment features attributable to BAA's activities. Throughout construction, the monitoring showed that there was in fact no detrimental impact on the quality of the local environment. Open and regular dialogue with environment regulators and the local community enabled stakeholders to share their concerns with BAA and ensured that any issues were addressed. Frequent inspections and audits monitored environment performance against standards throughout construction. Objectives and targets were used to measure environment performance both during construction and in the operation of the new terminal.

Frameworks embedded through culture change

Rebecca Garner, from the BAA environment team, felt the understanding of the environment agenda change in her four years with the project. When T5 started it was all about hitting planning targets, but by the end of the time the BAA leadership had gone on a journey of understanding and even hardened construction attitudes started to change. The central BAA team had a policing, but probably more importantly an educating role, working with environment coordinators from each project team to make sure that the message about why the environment was important got through, and which things to look for. As part of the T5 induction, every employee received an insight into the environment challenges and opportunities and the role they needed to play. Rebecca remembered a story of a big, burly construction worker turning up at her desk one day with a box of baby rabbits, distressed that they would die if left alone. He exclaimed, 'You're part of the environment team, we need you to take care of these little rabbits!'

Key learning

Advances in technology and awareness of the environment agenda potentially mean that every new piece of infrastructure built presents an opportunity to step-change the environment performance of facilities. While strict planning permission consents create 'a stick' to ensure that airport operators take this seriously, actually engaging the architect, design team and builders on site is what really gets ideas and energy around seeing and taking advantage of every opportunity. The environment, like safety and quality, needs to benefit from a culture change.

LOGISTICS

Constraints are the order of the day in every area of T5, so why should logistics prove any different! The prospect of 50 000 people and over £1 billion of plant and materials being involved in the construction made those involved in the T5 planning inquiry quite anxious, and as a result they were clear about the sorts of hoops that BAA and its suppliers needed to jump through.

Heathrow is the world's busiest international airport and is bounded by Europe's busiest road network, the M25 and M4, but is also right next to Longford Village, a small community of 600 people who clearly wanted to make sure that they weren't overwhelmed by tradesmen and lorries. In accordance with the planning consent, the workers began arriving on site at 6 a.m. Vehicle access to site was Monday to Friday, 9 a.m. to 5 p.m. and 7 p.m. to 11 p.m., Saturday 7 a.m. to 4 p.m., and no deliveries were allowed on Sunday, with nine no-go routes in the local areas surrounding Heathrow.

To this kind of constraint add those of scale and complexity. The construction site may have been the size of Hyde Park, but actually the space to lay down materials was limited. At its peak nearly 250 deliveries were being made per hour, and the site had to deal with the production of 1.5 cubic metres of concrete and 120 000 tonnes of rebar metal. Also 24 tower cranes, more than anywhere else in the UK, were being used productively. To keep the workforce moving, 8000 people were being transported on 60 buses, then fed in one of the 18 canteens. BAA was also committed to arranging sufficient accommodation for workers who required it in the local areas. In addition to a helpline, BAA built a caravan park for 260 caravans and had a further 20 rented houses able to provide overnight accommodation, as well as booking 250 000 hotel rooms at various times. As T5 moved through the different phases and different trades were needed, each month 1000 people would join and 1000 people would leave.

Key players

'30 years in the army commanding joint force logistics in places such as Afghanistan and Iraq have helped prepare me for some, but not all, of the challenges of running logistics across Heathrow, including T5,' smiles Shaun Cowlam, logistics director. His skill set is not typical of those found on a building site, but it was clear from the outset that the size of the challenge was so great that if we didn't take this critical function seriously, T5 and Heathrow would suffer a logjam.

Over six years Cowlam and his predecessors David Hunt, a manufacturing and retail logistics expert, and John Hardman, a longstanding BAA employee, took early logistics thinking and brought it alive on the T5 site, which is the size of a small town such a Marlborough. Over 700 team members ranging from bus drivers, chefs and electricians to traffic marshals and engineers supported both. Key suppliers included Lang O'Rourke, SPIE Matthew Hall, Eurest in catering, Indigo in cleaning, Accord in facilities management, PSL in security, and Wilson James and Menzies Aviation in bussing.

Logistics directors always sat at the top construction table, as key and equal team members to those involved in the actual building. With a budget of over £350 million and providing a critical service to all the projects, the success of logistics played straight through to all projects' time, cost and quality deliverables.

What was delivered?

There is still significant waste in the construction process that BAA has worked hard to drive out in all aspects of design, assembly, manufacture and construction. The typical site-productivity figures that are quoted for construction sit at 55–60%, but increased reliability and efficiency in the use of materials helped get this figure to over 80% at T5 in some areas.

What was different?

Approach to delivering materials

To ensure efficient management and delivery of materials, and to reduce the construction traffic on the local roads, an innovative logistics strategy was adopted. BAA created two logistics centres, designed to manage the logistics of getting vast amount of materials to the right workface at the right time and used a third existing facility. These centres provided a local buffer of raw materials, and by precise matching of deliveries with demand, construction-related traffic was reduced significantly.

The Colnbrook logistics centre (CLC) used an existing rail line to allow over 30 trains a week at peak to deliver steel, aggregate, cement and pulverized fuel ash (an additive to concrete) for consolidation and onward delivery to the main construction site.

Steel rebar manufacturing and pre-assembly of materials took place both at CLC and at the Heathrow south logistics centre (HSLC). As the project moved from heavy civil engineering work to the buildings and fit-out phases, the rebar factory equipment was removed and these facilities were used as consolidation centres, where materials were assembled into work packages prior to delivery on site.

The CLC site and the Heathrow consolidation centre will continue to cut the number of vehicle deliveries to Heathrow airport, through consolidation of deliveries, contributing to improvements in local air quality and reducing congestion.

Both centres were used to manage the flow of goods into the site. A simple material flow or approach to demand fulfilment was put in place. Pre-booked delivery times were accessed by suppliers on 'air build', a straightforward booking system, and prioritized by the team if appropriate. Before going to site the goods and vehicles were brought to CLC either to be consolidated appropriately, or for paperwork to be checked with access to the site just in time to go through the nine-lane entry plaza, but not too far in advance to create a back-up. CLC was also used for rebar manufacturing, the cutting and bending of steel reinforcement for concrete, and pre-assembly of materials. In addition, BAA had four concrete plants around the site that in total poured $1\,520\,170$ m^3.

The management of plant

For plant there was the 'T5 marketplace', one shared facility on site were all personal protective equipment for the $50\,000$ people was managed centrally. This worked well, but the same was tried with plant management, for example sharing cranes, and although some inroads were made, there was a real sense that this could have been set up differently from day one and a culture created to take this a step further.

Leveraging off-site prefabrication to manage risk

The strategy followed by SPIE Matthew Hall in off-site prefabrication and modularization is to be commended. In discussion with Grahame Ludlow, the company's CEO of Building and Facilities Services, he explained, 'On a job the size of T5 we needed to manage the industrial relations risk and also the volume of work risk.' In practical terms, the way the team designed the T5 main terminal building meant that in total over 50% of the mechanical and electrical work was done off site.

There were two main dimensions to this type of prefabrication. There were the volume items such as corridors or items a gang of six men could lift, which represented around 5500 modules, and the balance made up of large items such as plant rooms or the 11 chimneys that run through the T5 main terminal building.

For the assembly of chimneys prior to site, the team reviewed who would be best placed to do this work, and with SPIE Matthew Hall's offshore experience, it became clear that an organization like Babcocks, based in Rosyth and more used to assembling offshore rigs or battleships, was actually best for the job.

Providing good-quality facilities for people

With a strategy of respect for people, the people logistics also needed to set new industry standards. To deliver safe productivity the infrastructure put in place for the people involved needed to be of a different standard. For example, good bus services get people to work quickly, accessible and well-presented canteens keep the workforce close to the workplace, on-site occupational health means that ailments are treated quickly and people can get back to work. Equally, this kind of infrastructure means that those on site feel respected, and their trade unions will work with you as they can see that there are gains for both management and the workforce. There were good stories of people leaving T5 and then desperately trying to return, as they had over their years of working got used to a different standard.

But as always, getting the correct balance was necessary. If logistics ratings were too high then BAA was spending too much money; if efficiencies were taken too far there was a risk of having a negative impact on productivity or creating an atmosphere of discontent with the workers. Early on there was a bussing review that took out redundant bus capacity. The team was a little too matter-of-fact and hadn't quite brought everyone along with the changes, resulting in a backlash. At that time Hunt was at the helm and what was exemplary was that he put his hand up and said he'd gone too far, he met the trade unions, went into the canteens and got his team out of the offices and into the buses to listen and apologize to the men. In 48 hours the right service was up and running, and his team were always a little more careful in matching desk-based analysis with a healthy dose of talking to the project leaders, trade unions and people involved.

IT support to enable knowledge worker productivity

An often overlooked element of a project like T5, IT support was key to enabling knowledge workers to do their jobs effectively. During the early days of T5 fewer than 200 people worked in a single office with desktop computers and computer-aided design tools, but at the peak of construction over 3500 people were using computers over 30 sites in Heathrow, and connected from locations all around the globe.

Providing IT support to this demanding community of designers, engineers and workers was an interesting challenge. Nick Gaines pointed out:

> When we started, new people were joining the project at the rate of hundreds per month. It was like being in an internet boom start-up company. Then at peak, we had all the problems of a major international corporate IT function.

Joan Buszewska led the IT support team for Gaines. She had to manage £40 million of IT support activity including tools for project control (Artemis), design (AutoCAD) and document management (Documentum), all of which had to be scaled up to support the site and then managed down to integrate into the business at the end of the project. Despite the challenges there was always a sense of fun, and the team won industry awards for their solutions and service.

Key learning

So much has been learned about doing logistics professionally in the construction of T5 and a great deal has been taken from other industries. But this is still an area that presents much opportunity. There is still a step-change opportunity that is worth 5–15 % in construction costs to be chased, but it does involve a much more planned and disciplined approach. Resource planning has always been almost impossible to predict accurately, often for good reason due to changes in the programme, but disciplines and systems to keep this transparent are needed. Materials resource planning (MRP) delivering more of a just-in-time approach is still to be improved.

As the logistics function moves forward at Heathrow, the silos of construction, retail and airport delivery have been eliminated and there is now one logistics strategy and team increasingly looking across the total airport. The opportunity to reduce costs of deliveries, reduce congestion and reduce emissions is significant. For example, when Heathrow opened a retail consolidation centre the number of retail deliveries reduced from 49 000 to 8300.

SUMMARY

The construction story of a new ground-breaking contract, the T5 Agreement, over 50 000 people who came together from 20 000 companies and worked in integrated teams to innovate, solve problems and most importantly deliver, on time and on budget, a quality product with care given to the environment, is the stuff of myths and legends.

As long as there are no final hitches, there can be no doubt that the time dimension was delivered. In 2001 the 30 March 2008 deadline was set and through hard-nosed milestone planning and delivery, the project will actually open ahead of time on 27 March 2008.

There will be more critics on cost. Scope changes and outturn costs do make it difficult for the outside world to see absolute transparency on costs on any mega project. That ambiguity will fuel speculation, but if closing of final accounts goes to plan, the £4.3 billion target set in 2003 will be delivered.

There will also be those who are critical that T5 just cost too much, even if it was on budget. Some of the design is too elaborate, the T5 Agreement paid over the odds for risk management, too much was spent on the people and logistics agenda and there were too many BAA people involved micro-managing what suppliers should have been left to do.

At one level these are all valid challenges, but at another it is important to remember what could have been and some of the reasons. On industry predictions a year late and a billion over budget was the risk that BAA faced as it started T5, and in Chapter 2 there are a few examples of multibillion-pound construction success stories in the UK. Going into T5 BAA only had a 5 % risk pot, significantly smaller than most projects and yet with an approach to managing and mitigating risk that got integrated teams to perform differently. Much of the design look and feel were stipulated by planning permission consent, though granted not all. I challenged Forster, the T5 development and design director, about the £250 million single-span roof and whether it could have been built for less. His position was that Heathrow should be a world-class airport, acting as the UK's front door to the world. There was an ambition for T5 to be iconic. Finally, most of the innovation and discipline that were established on T5 had a BAA person setting an objective, facilitating an outcome or doing a job that in other projects a supplier would be doing, but with a different set of skills or focus to come up with new ideas.

On big projects time and cost are often the sacred cows, with safety, quality and environment coming some way down the list. On

T5 safety was positioned as a value not a priority, so it always came first. Quality and environment were areas of focus that required education and significant senior leadership focus to signal their criticality to the overall T5 Programme's success.

The T5 Agreement was a courageous approach to contracting that not all in BAA or in the suppliers fully embraced. However, there was sufficient support for it to act as a philosophy that enabled integrated teams to deliver in good times and bad. BAA's third-generation framework supplier agreement demonstrates that development and Heathrow East will take advantage of the T5 learning and that both the construction industry and BAA have moved on.

History in the making.

80 x 08 SMART Milestones

Making T5 Safe. Quality. Within budget. Bang on target.

"80 by 08" milestones signed by contractors

Programme milestone marker passed between teams

T5A M&E Below Apron team led by David Mason.

From left to right;
Marlon Lewis, John Fleming, Alan Frost, Mark Alexander, David Mason, Lee Godwin.

This team has been recognised for the excellent planning and installation of a secondary grid for support services providing good access for maintenance.

Sidney Hallwass, Eduard Borsukiewicz
Supervisors

They have erected the ceiling in the benchmark areas in T5A&B to an excellent standard. Since joining us just 4 months ago from Germany and Poland they are mastering the English language and have both been promoted to supervisors.

T5A/B Escalator Team
Left to right
Phil Toplis,
Graham Coppard,
Neil Austin,
Neil Rayment,
Ian McDermid (Team Leader).

Working on T5A, T5B & Rail Station they have been involved in the building, commissioning and protection of over 50 escalators out of 105. The approach of the team to their work is second to none.

Creating T5 quality heroes

Making safety personal

Memorial for the first death on T5 – 2,000 attend

THE Site

The award-winning newspaper for the T5 site   June 2006

"NOT GOOD ENOUGH FOR T5!"

SAYS MILFORD

Buildings boss up in arms over safety lapses in T5A

John Milford: He won't be happy until everyone takes personal safety as seriously as him

The most senior boss in the buildings team, John Milford, has slammed the 'slack' approach to health and safety in the main terminal building.

He was so angry after a walkabout at the end of May that he instantly summoned all workers and supers in Compound K to express his concerns.

"I can't believe what I'm seeing! This is a great site with great people who have a great record in terms of safety!

"But there are still some people willing to let the whole team down."

"It's just not good enough – some people are not even getting the basic stuff right," said John.

"I saw guys not wearing full PPE on site and others working at height with out-of-date scaff-tags – this just isn't the way we do things."

"It might be acceptable on other sites, but it's simply not good enough for T5," the furious project boss added.

Following the eye-opening walkabout, John has stepped up his fight to prevent workers risking their own safety – and others' – at T5.

And he's so serious that he has got all the other projects on

board across the whole of T5.

John said: "Workers not wearing full PPE will now be reported and sent back to the classroom for training in site rules and safety.

Off the job!

"If caught a second time T5 will block their ID card and block access to site while their employer investigates whether to take disciplinary action."

The whole site will be included in this zero tolerance approach soon.

"I also want to see more of the supervisors and safety reps out on site with their eyes open – we

will not let up on this issue. People risk losing their jobs if they don't comply," John added.

Since T5 introduced the full PPE ruling – which includes gloves and glasses at all times – there has been a drop in accidents on site.

T5 is one of the safest sites in the UK according to Head of Health and Safety Mike Evans, who's supporting the campaign.

"Generally we're very, very good on safety, but we need to stay focused on keeping T5 Incident and Injury Free.

"We're recognised as being the best, but can't allow our standards to slip.

He added: "The building team faces a tough challenge, with many new workers. But we must stay on top of things and make sure everyone lives by the IIF principles, which we have all signed up to."

The safety clampdown also has workers' backing.

The Site spoke to many who supported the strict 'safety first' policy at T5.

One T5A worker said: "It's a necessary evil.

"It's easy to be a bit slack with your PPE but at the end of the day, your first priority has to be to keep safe." *See more workers' opinions on page 6.*

Safety leadership – taking a stand

THE Site

The award-winning newspaper for the T5 site   July 2006

WIN! THE MP3 PLAYER OF YOUR DREAMS
A STUNNING IPOD NANO

SAFETY STARS!

U-TURN AS BUILDINGS TEAM TRIUMPHS WITH SAFETY AWARD

The buildings team are being praised after going from safety zeroes to heroes in just one month.

Last month's *Site* reported how the buildings team had been rapped by bosses for its poor safety performance.

BUT – in a remarkable turnaround reminiscent of Rooney's miraculous recovery from injury – the team has this month landed the T5 health and safety award.

Buildings chief John Milford had slated the team for their 'slack' approach after workers were seen without full PPE and working at height with out-of-date scaff tags.

The clampdown clearly worked. A drop in minor injuries of 25 per cent showed the lads had taken the warning to heart.

And bosses are delighted at the result. "The guys have put in a lot of hard work, and it's all about commitment", said team safety leader Geoff Sykes.

"We weren't happy with the safety trends in buildings, and decided we had to improve, so we've put a new system in place and early indications are that it's working."

As well as toolbox talks and team briefings, there is also a poster campaign underway while safety patrols go round the buildings keeping an eye on things.

"Basically, we are trying to bring IIF out of the classroom and put it into practice on the site," Geoff added.

Well done

All the hard work has not gone unnoticed. It's still early days, but John is in no doubt that the changes made so far are having a clear effect on site.

"Well done to everyone. Before, if I spent two hours on the site I would see at least 10 people with incorrect PPE," he said, "but last week I didn't see a single one. That's the difference it's made."

So the lads may have stopped the rot, but there's still plenty more to do to ensure the team maintains a top safety record, John warned.

"We've drawn up a six-stage process to cover all aspects of health and safety here at T5," he revealed.

Stages include: PPE, housekeeping and fire loading, environment and waste management, working at height and permit to work, and occupational health.

John Milford . . . a happier man thanks to your safety boost

Safety leadership – focus pays off

9,000 Years of History Unearthed

100,000 Evergreen Shrubs
Planted

24 pairs of voles put into captive breeding programme

CHAPTER 6

OPERATIONAL READINESS

Bringing T5live has been our focus for the last three years. Year one was about the strategy, year two the plan and year three has been about delivery.

Mark Bullock, managing director, Heathrow, BAA

What is frightening about opening T5 is not that in its own right it is a top 10 airport, connecting into the world's busiest international airport, Heathrow; or that in one night 60 % of BA passenger load moves to T5; or even that this triggers another 54 airlines starting to move around the rest of Heathrow. What is frightening is that if T5 experienced a Denver baggage failure, or a Hong Kong systems problem, it would have a devastating impact on BAA, BA, the rest of the Heathrow and even the UK economy.

With the challenge of not distracting Heathrow operational airport too early, the team had to keep the current environment, although less than perfect, processing 68 million passengers a year in a facility built to process 45 million, and build a terminal that will plug into the rest of Heathrow while step-changing the passenger experience. Mick Temple former Heathrow managing director faced what he saw as an easy decision:

> In the early years the operational readiness team, or T5live, needed to be separate from the Heathrow operations team so as not to distract, and as opening got closer the T5live team needed to nestle back into the airport team. The difficult question was when was the right time? On balance the move in 2006 was probably about right.

Bullock picked up accountability for the opening of the terminal in 2004, before ultimately becoming the Heathrow managing director in 2006. He gave the T5live team a three-year high-level plan: a year to work out the strategies, a year to plan and a year to implement in the run-up to opening. What became clear during year one was that while opening T5 was going to be tough, the real challenge was to integrate it into the rest of Heathrow. Hence the T5live team started to become a subsection of a 5T (five Heathrow terminals) integration team from 2006.

The volume and complexity of change at Heathrow in the run-up to 2012 is very significant. The challenge is not to miss an operational heartbeat as all of these changes are taking place. To achieve this a fundamentally different way of thinking about change needed to emerge, more programmatic and quite similar to the type of approach used in T5 construction. A team embedded in Heathrow airport, and many coming from T5, was developed to coordinate any changes that are significant or more than three to six months away. Some of that change then gets delivered in new facilities, others in the existing facility, but always with a new way of working.

Both BAA and BA during the lifetime of T5 have become more planned, process-oriented and measured companies. There has been movement from things getting done because people have been here for a long time and do it that way, to processes being understood, standardized and then improved for the short, medium and long term. This shift has proved painful for management, employees and trade unions alike, but it is a journey that continues. Therefore, a key challenge for T5 was that as this new way of thinking emerged for both organizations, much of the early work done on the design of the T5 facilities and processes, in the absence of these ideas, had to be changed or a workaround created. This was less than ideal, but it was a consequence of company evolution.

KEY PLAYERS

BAA managing director Heathrow, Mick Temple, handing over to Mark Bullock; BAA, Heathrow and T5 HR and organizational effectiveness director Sharon Doherty, handing over Heathrow to Liz Neighbour at the end of 2007; BAA T5Live director Paul Fox, handing over to Debbie Younger; BA Projects Director T5 Colin Clarkson, handing over to Geoff Want, BA; Jonathan Council, handing over to Paul Burton as head of the T5 Programme; Representatives from the Border and Immigration Agency, Her Majesty's Revenue and Customs, the Metropolitan Police, the Port Health Authority and Munich Consulting spent two days a month with the team. The team involved in operational readiness started as a handful and grew to a team of 85 at its peak.

WORKING WITH THIRD PARTIES

Chapter 11 describes the integrated team relationship between BA and BAA, which has spanned all phases of T5. The team has moved through an informal meeting of minds, getting to grips with the functionality the building needed to deliver, and then through the inevitable changes required to get ready for the move.

All of the other third parties have had issues to resolve with their facilities, but the Border & Immigration Agency, a critical part of UK security, has presented some of the most interesting challenges. The security issues around its data have meant that key systems were not able to be tested until the appropriate data controls were in place. T5 also has a single departure lounge for domestic and international passengers, which meant that some form of biometric data needed to be taken from all domestic passengers at ticket presentation. At the gate fingerprints and photos are checked to validate the passenger's identity, a challenge for BA given that an average of 17 minutes is available to board domestic flights. This new approach involves significant security implications and all concerned need to ensure that it works effectively.

Kevin Bennett, who took over from John Bullen on third-party management, had to assure Younger that the third-party plans were on track and would deliver. As in construction the client, while not the master of every company, has an accountability to ensure that all players deliver and that they don't let the team down. Bennett describes how he 'speaks to the third parties, reviews their plans and gets confirmation of their progress'. This includes talking with operational staff in BA's existing terminals to see how BA is progressing with road testing its new T5 processes. 'Some of this is a science and some of it is gut feel. In many cases you have to take people's words at face value and trust them,' Bennett explains. Much like the way Willie Walsh likes to see the whites of the BAA construction teams' eyes to see if he believes they will actually deliver for him, there is a reciprocal 'whites of the eye gazing' going on for BAA.

The airport operator's role is to facilitate this type of working. For T5 the BAA team has really tried to encourage all parties involved to take deadlines as immovable and to view T5 as an opportunity to set new standards.

HAVING A PLAN AND MITIGATING RISK

The T5live plan has formed part of the integrated baseline review that spanned all of the T5 Programme since 2004, as the T5 milestone plan moved from the '70 by 07' plan to the '80 by 08'.

As the team get closer to opening, the detailed integrated plan for the last 90 days has taken shape, 'looking in absolute detail at the last responsible moment for every final point,' explains Bennett. This enables all key activities to be coordinated effectively, while allowing contingency plans to be mobilized if LRMs slip or the T5 Programme changes.

In addition, Bennett's team is developing detailed checklists for every area, with roles, and ultimately names, of those accountable to deliver the specifics. Kevin Bennett had the benefit of learning some hard lessons when he worked for Cathay Pacific in Hong Kong during the move from the old airport at Kai Tak to the new Chep Lap Kok airport. He says:

> It was little details like people going home with keys in their pockets and no one knowing where the spare keys were that caused problems. That's the sort of thing that won't happen on T5.

Planning for T5 doesn't finish at its opening. Nick Dent, the business leader for T5, will have a team from operational readiness working alongside his team for at least three months before opening, and for a month and a half afterwards. He says:

> In an existing terminal there is only the business lead and his team to run the operation and deal with anything else that happens. At T5 in the run-up to opening and immediately afterwards, the operational readiness support team will deal with all the opening plans and issues arising from proving trials before opening or teething problems.

Once T5 is a live terminal, Dent and his team are left to focus on building the new operational team and then the daily pressures of running a facility of this scale.

Using the same approach as was used in the construction phase of the T5 Programme, inherent risks have been understood, mitigating actions put in place and contingency plans developed. Reasons why T5 might not open on time are outlined in Chapter 12.

PEOPLE FAMILIARIZATION INDUCTION TRAINING

The people strategy for T5 has been worked on for over four years, focusing on the organization structure and roles in T5, the employee engagement and communication approach and the employee relations approach. In each of these areas, trying to balance the opportunity that T5 presented to start afresh in a state-of-the-art terminal, creating a new employee proposition with the employee relations risks of mishandling any changes.

The organizational structure, processes, management capability and culture were not in place in the rest of Heathrow in early 2002 to allow the T5 team to import the current way of operating. This presented a challenge as to reduce the employee relations risk at T5, in the main the strategy was to have most of the controversial structural or working practice changes in place prior to T5 opening, but in the case of new technology or specific rosters this wouldn't be possible. It wasn't in anyone's interests to get into disputes around the opening of T5.

A similar strategy was followed by BA, who also negotiated and broadly put in place all changes to working practices in T1 and T4 before the move to T5. For Heathrow in 2002 that meant that a significant journey of change was required at a time when BAA was finding it challenging to settle a national pay deal with the trade unions.

There were green shoots to be built on: some progressive work had been done in baggage and engineering at Heathrow, demonstrating that, even with a highly unionized legacy workforce, the company working with employees and trade unions could deliver positive change for both passengers and employees.

ORGANIZATION AND STRUCTURE

Brigitte Vanderwilk, head of organizational effectiveness T5live, working with Paul Fox in 2003 to 2004, did a lot of the early thinking on how eight layers of management in Heathrow could be streamlined to four, along with the philosophies and principles that needed to be in place to deliver a different employee experience. BAA built on this work and in 2004–06 implemented the Delivering Excellence Experience (DEE), a change programme with streamlined structures, new processes and some systems across its South East airports, again a scope of change that the trade unions engaged in professionally. It took nearly a year to work with the trade unions to get this new junior and middle management structure in place, with people assessed, exited from the business and new players brought in and trained; about 80 % of these managers were in trade unions. Again for many businesses this sort of change would happen every two years. For many of the employees at Heathrow, prior to these changes a new job title had been distressing, so this was a change of substance that required careful handling and strong leadership.

The work started on new systems and processes and structure, and selecting a new management cadre was underway across Heathrow and the rest of BAA when Ferrovial bought BAA and then the August 2006 terrorist alerts struck. Both acted as significant distractions for management and also put huge pressure on a new and relatively inexperienced management team.

EMPLOYEE ENGAGEMENT

Having spent my first few years in BAA working on T5 and then picking up accountability for Heathrow airport in 2005, I knew that the level of employee dissatisfaction was significant. Having spent three years on T5 with a third-party workforce who felt part of making history, by contrast the longstanding BAA employees didn't trust management and didn't feel part of delivering the business objectives. Heathrow wasn't untypical of the other South East airports, but many of the issues lay in too many layers of poor-quality management who had for years been promoted due to length of service, and unfortunately lacked the management capability to lead teams and work constructively with the local trade unions. Even those managers who were good quality found themselves hindered by layers of management and poor systems and processes.

This was the backdrop against which the T5 people team needed to start trying to engage the Heathrow BAA security officers, information assistants and other junior roles across the campus. The approach to T5 was subtle, being sensitive to talk about the Heathrow transformation, not just T5. As an aside, when T4 opened in 1986, those who didn't go to work there called it 'paradise island', among some other more derogatory names. T5 did not want to be divisive, but rather to signal the shape of things to come for Heathrow, with Heathrow East not too far away and in the interim significant upgrades of a number of the other terminals.

T5 is very much part of Heathrow and for some teams of staff – airside, trolleys and maintenance, for example – T5 will become part of their remit. In these areas teams are on a journey of change, working with employees and trade unions. Other roles will in the main be T5 specific, security being the largest, but others will include roles like information assistance or the new customer host as it will be known; that is, not behind a desk, but interacting with the customer. In the case of security, a self-selection system has been set up allowing employee choice, although for those in T2, the terminal closing after T5 opens, that wasn't the case, they will need to move. Again, from an employee relations standpoint this minimized the risk of disputes, although it also reduced the ability to select employees for T5. For hosts and junior management roles selection processes have been put in place and in the main these jobs have been significantly oversubscribed.

Veronica Kumar picked up where Vanderwilk left off, and with Younger has taken the ideas and completed the detailed work to bring the early thinking alive. In December 2006 she launched an expression of interest campaign. This encouraged interested employees to come and meet the team and find out more about T5. On trips around mess rooms, most people were excited about T5 and genuinely wanted to be part of this new opportunity. A total of 1100 employees expressed an interest in 900 roles and the T5 'shape of things to come' face-to-face sessions and tours started. Around 95 % of those attending these sessions signed up, understanding that there would be changes to how they worked, but wanting to have further conversations about roster changes.

Once an employee signs up, or for nonsecurity roles is selected, to join T5, there is a one- to three-week training programme that all go through. This includes an 'inside five' induction for all BAA, retailer, BA and NATS (National Air Traffic Service) employees, 30 000 people sharing the vision with Bullock and Walsh, and at the same time the importance of safety and security at the terminal is reinforced. Groups of 30 employees with facilitators then walk the passenger journey for three hours, doing pit stops to talk about what is different.

New approaches to teamworking and extra emphasis on service and communication are all plans to try to use the opportunity of a fresh start as a catalyst to step-change the service proposition.

TRADE UNION ENGAGEMENT

Any changes to working practices or conditions have been clearly defined and risk assessed in terms of actual or perceived employee and trade union impact. A task Kumar worked closely with Martin Beecroft on, the Heathrow head of employee relations. The team identified a number of must have employee changes, around the introduction of new technology, that needed to be consulted or negotiated with the trade unions, such as the track transit system or biometric data gathering at ticket presentation. Another essential item was rosters, moving the 400 rosters currently in operation to seven. Rosters are probably the most critical issue for the workforce. The opportunity to work around child care arrangements or other jobs has a significant value to the employees, and for many individuals, they have over the years, been able to create their own rosters.

At a national level the trade unions are often aligned with BAA strategic objectives, they are supportive of Heathrow expansion, against BAA break up, and like their construction counterparts want T5 to be a success story. The challenge faced by the national and local officials is that their ability to influence staff opinion is at times limited, and hence on individual issues, or if emotions are running high on unrelated subjects, they find it almost impossible to change opinion. That can make it difficult for BAA or indeed national and local trade unions to find a path through to agreement.

The trade union engagement on T5 matters was done in parallel with a significant employee engagement strategy for those interested in moving to T5. As trade unions were being taken through all the T5 changes between October 2006 and and right up until opening. concurrently a loud, simple and compelling communication campaign was taking place master minded by Tom Everett. So when the T5 team hit a disagreement with the unions they could go and test it with the workforce, or present data taken from hundreds of people to the contrary.

On rosters in particular the unions did start to take an opposing side, however ongoing dialogue means it looks like a settlement has been reached. The T5 team have relied on a strong employee engagement plan, going out and having one-to-one discussions with the workforce, which is showing a significant percentage who still want to sign up to the roster changes. There is likely to be a shortfall for the less popular rosters, a gap that will be made up with new recruits internally and externally. What has been very powerful has been that the newly appointed 60 'Grow our own' service team leader recruits, who were plucked from security roles, have had these conversations.

Kumar, Young and Heathrow ER manager, Neil Moore have fronted the conversations with trade unions and employees, with full support of key directors and the broader Heathrow HR and organisational effectiveness team. The journey to change the people proposition at Heathrow will start in a significant way as T5 opens, and if Heathrow East goes forward it will continue there. Whilst a professional and supportive relationship with the unions has been achieved for T5, replicating this back to the other terminals will be tough because, unlike T5, they don't have new facilities to provide a real opportunity to start again. With a new team, motivated to work differently, there is a different service provided to passengers.

In September 2007 BAA announced its intention to close the final salary pension scheme. The fight to reverse this decision has been the top priority for the trade unions since that time. Strike action was only narrowly avoided in January 2008 and discussions were continuing, with the scheme still open to new employees, as this book went to print.

PROCESSES

Both BA and BAA had historically operated their businesses based on the knowledge of key people who had been around for years, and who carried how things worked and what to do in a crisis in their heads. In the early days of the design of T5, both the BA and BAA development teams tried to get their hands on written processes. Finding that this was impossible they started the thinking for what the operation would need to be like in five years' time.

During the T5 journey both organizations took over 900 existing processes and worked to simplify their number and complexity into a system that could be used to build up the operation and train staff. For BAA this meant creating 10 key operating models based on the flows through and around the terminal. Examples include the departures flow and goods in/goods out. The approach included the key strategies, operating principles and processes for the passenger and staff experience. These models were then worked through with BA, and other third parties, to produce a joint operating model. Eventually all of this information was collated into the T5 operating manual, a resource available to all BAA staff working at T5.

SYSTEMS

Airports are extremely complex IT environments where every aspect of business depends on integrated systems. BAA knew that failure to deliver and integrate systems was one of the key reasons for mega-projects overrunning, Hong Kong and Denver airports being classic examples. Therefore, early on BAA engaged first-tier suppliers with extensive experience of airport integration, Ultra Electronics, NTL and Honeywell, supported by Ove Arup.

On appointment as head of systems and IT, Nick Gaines, a former nuclear engineer with extensive experience in major projects, was told: 'Your job is to manage the biggest risks to the project. Few people will really understand how complex they are, and we are all underestimating the challenges we will face.' It took several years for Gaines to educate the BAA team, but eventually systems thinking was embedded into most aspects of the programme.

The systems team led by Gaines has broadly stayed in place throughout the project. The key members of the team have been Tom Garside from BAA, who led systems integration, Graham Stacey MD of Ultra, Tim Vince from NTL and Grant Levy from BAA, who in addition to managing the installation and commissioning on site also led the work on the highest-risk safety systems. The stability of this top team and the project managers who worked for them has proved to be a significant advantage in this complex area. While each person played many roles during the course of the project, the team remained strongly aligned around its core strategies, and hence the logic of decisions stayed consistent over the duration of the project.

The team ultimately identified over £150 million of systems and telecoms to be managed; £50 million of that initially sat in Gaines' budget, and the other £100 million was dispersed in other projects. To ensure value and become more joined up, all the systems spend was consolidated into one budget, a wise move. The work was organized into work streams covering telecommunications, security, building systems and airport operating systems. The systems delivered covered every aspect of the airport environment from traffic management through check-in, retail, gate and stand operations. IT systems were everywhere, monitoring electrical plant, lifts and chillers, controlling baggage, providing biometric identification at ticket presentation and so on.

T5 is the most technologically advanced terminal in the UK, and while people think of IT at airports in terms of flight information and check-in, today electronic technology is ubiquitous. Increasingly everything is a computer and everything is connected. An operator in T5's terminal control centre can monitor every aspect of the terminal's operation, much like an officer on the bridge of a modern warship. Because of these trends, at T5 the most complex and challenging areas have been around telecommunications and integration.

Systems strategies

The systems team continuously monitored the lessons and learning from other major projects around the world, and as a result adopted a set of core strategies that have underpinned the success of the programme:

- *Strategy 1 – avoid innovation where possible.* The team viewed much of the ambitious innovation that the IT industry encourages as dangerous. The temptations to dabble were squashed, and for any new technology the business value had to be clearly articulated and risks mitigated.
- *Strategy 2 – approach to innovation.* If innovation is required, manage the maturity of the technology and take it off the critical path. The team identified areas where innovation was required and looked carefully at the maturity of the technologies involved. Where risks were high, it worked with suppliers and the airport teams to experiment and prove new systems in lower-risk environments. For example, the new CCTV system for T5 was initially tested at Stansted and rolled out across Heathrow before being installed in T5.
- *Strategy 3 – approach to integration.* Integration should be driven by risk and value, and in general smaller integration is better than large-scale integration. In the early days of T5 there were ideas of a 'digital terminal' in which everything would be automated and

integrated. Gaines and the team challenged these assumptions, and only integrated systems where safety, business performance or value drove the decisions. Where the business case was not clear, the team designed in a way that kept the option available for low-cost integration in future.

■ *Strategy 4 – use open standards.* In delivering a project over many years, for a terminal that will operate for decades, the team was automatically at odds with the world of IT where products rarely last more than a few years, standards come and go, and fads drive the market. To address this challenge the team looked for cross-industry open standards that suppliers could commit to for many years, and where the competitive forces would cause the standard to be supported. By designing against such standards and avoiding the temptation to use the unique features of products, the team hopes that many of the T5 systems will have a long life and not become locked into the escalating costs of dominant IT suppliers.

■ *Strategy 5 – future proof.* Have a safeguarding strategy: the need to future proof technology is important. The team used the last responsible moment (LRM) approach in systems decisions, but also service-oriented architecture, which basically meant that the interface with T5 and the rest of Heathrow could be managed more easily, even if the rest of Heathrow changed systems.

■ *Strategy 6 – testing regime.* Test systems early and keep testing. A state-of-the-art systems test facility was built at Colnbrook in early 2004, and Gaines made it a rule that no system could be installed on site unless its interfaces had been tested successful in the test facility.

Systems test centre

Systems have spanned all phases of the T5 Programme, but the most important element has been the integrated testing of the systems that took place during the operational readiness phase. As part of operational readiness, the approach to testing has been absolutely critical. Catherine Tann, the test facility manager, has gone on a huge journey of discovery:

> When I started I thought it was all about systems, but as we get to the end of the project, I've learned actually it's all been about discipline and trying to get different people from different suppliers, the T5 Programme, BA and other parts of BAA to work together to solve the inevitable problems.

The test facility provided a safe area for the different systems and end-user communities to do testing, finding defects and resolutions. The advantage of a neutral facility off site cannot be underestimated. Tann explains:

> Overall there were about 10% defects found across over 100 000 different system requirements; that is to be expected in this space. The really helpful thing was that the pressures of finding errors on site was managed, the test centre was a shared and neutral space, where people could work within a less pressured environment to resolve the issues.

Risk management and mitigation

Systems projects, like all the other parts of T5, took a thorough approach to risk management. Tom Garside in particular has played a large role in this activity. For every airport process to be used on T5, he and his team walked through normal and crisis operations, sat down with process owners, analysed risks and designed tests that prove not only system functionality, but how system, people and process perform together in the real world. The team looked at standard processes with systems input, such as passenger flow or baggage, but also infrequent processes, such as the person who misses the flight. The team also planned for disaster scenarios of things not working on the day and what was the workaround.

An important learning for T5 has been not just what was put in place, but when. Says Gaines:

> As I reviewed other major projects all had test environments, but none that I can remember where able to have it

operational so early in the project. The T5 test centre has been open since early 2004 and been used solidly since then. From early 2007 we have been testing a 'slice' through the airport, one check-in, one gate, one stand etc, and as construction progressed we have been able to scale up tests to measure the readiness of the terminal to operate at volume. In September 2007, we were able to start the operational trials with real operational staff and processes under increasingly realistic loads.

PROVING THAT THE PEOPLE, PROCESSES AND SYSTEMS PLUS THE FACILITY WORK

From spending time with Munich Consultancy and Toronto airport, both experienced in opening airports, as well as from countless trips around the world looking at large facilities, BAA learnt the pitfalls and good ideas that needed to be adopted when getting ready to open a large facility. To BAA's credit, even before spending time with these players it had worked out what the two critical issues were. Work with the end operator, in T5's case BA, as you progress, taking on board its ideas and needs; and protect the operational window, for T5 that was six months, where the facility can test how the people, processes, systems and facility work together. The conformation for the team was that what had intuitively felt like a common-sense thing to do to manage risk was also the advice of those with recent experience.

Approach to proving

Mark Mercieca, the proving manager, was keen to highlight that the team on T5 was 'proving a little differently from other airports'. There are two approaches to proving, one that takes a volume of trials but with only a few hundred people, the second is a smaller number of trials but with large numbers of people. 'BAA are one of the first to actually do both to make sure it all works to plan on day one. We can't afford the facility to not be ready on day one, or even worse open and have to close again,' explains Mercieca. In total there will be 72 trials across landside, terminal and airside processes, over the six-month period including BAA, BA and all other third parties. Basic trials will have the appropriate number of people doing the same process over and over again, and there will be 35 of these trials on processes such security or gate check-in. Five of the trials will be advanced, including up to 2500 volunteer passengers and ultimately 15 000 people in total. Finally, there will be 32 unit trials that test processes such as aircraft turnaround.

It's also a first for BAA not only to capture issues during trials, which is the norm, but to look at operational performance. Queues have been put in place in the trials to see what T5 at peak looks like, even if it is only taking a slice through one process. T5 will process 80 000 passengers a day, starting on 27 March 2008, so from day one the ability to deal with that volume of people and give them a great experience cannot be left to chance.

This detailed plan also leaves little to chance when it comes to proving. The BA and BAA stakeholders confirm what they want to test and the team prioritizes on a risk basis, with new functions such as the track transit system or critical processes like security getting priority.

The joint trial team made up of BA and BAA personnel has a system that ensures that the proving trials meet the objectives. There is a volunteer coordinating team whose members generate and manage volunteers, who have to be checked to adhere to the security requirements of Heathrow Airport. The team who design the trials and the team who evaluate the closeout of each trial both work together to deliver the proving trials and their benefits.

First large-scale trial, 3 November 2007

Along with more than 500 other people, on Saturday 3 November I, along with my husband, went to T5 for the first significant proving trial. Families, pensioners, couples and individuals from every continent had gathered, all excited to have been selected from the list of 10 000 volunteers. I chatted to a local Asian family of four, who explained that they had watched T5 being built. Members of the family worked at the airport and they wanted a sneak preview. I overheard a lady talking to her son, explaining that it was an honour to be seeing T5 before it opened and he needed to be well behaved. After an introductory video with Mark Bullock from BAA and Geoff Want from BA explaining what T5 meant to their companies, we were left secure in the knowledge that the day was about finding the wrinkles so that day one can be perfect, and 'please let us know your thoughts on anything missing or not good enough'.

During the morning it was a fully integrated team effort. We were welcomed to T5 by BA at the fast bag drop, fully operational for the first time, moved towards ticket presentation, having to stop off for a VAT return at customs, where we agreed with the three female VAT officers that the signs needed to be clearer. Ticket presentation took longer than expected: the new system again in its first live test under volume was taking double the anticipated time as staff and passengers got used to the new biometric facilities. Into security, where the new BAA security machines looked hugely impressive and much more automated, though a little scary, as it seemed that if you didn't get to your bag quickly enough at the pick-up point it would shoot off into the system; this was clearly not the case, as the system was too clever and doesn't allow that to happen. Then free to roam and explore, we went on our way to the designated gate, using the new track transit system to get transported across to the satellite building. At the gate we had the pleasure of the police and sniffer dogs having a chat with us, and there were scores of observers watching every task, looking for things that need to be improved.

The volunteers were clearly enjoying the experience, and the views in particular as they sat waiting for their journey to start in full view of aircraft, the new Heathrow air traffic control tower and Wembley arch in the distance, all very visible on that clear day. We over heard one man on his mobile phone really getting into his role play: 'I'm off to Hong Kong, I'll see you in a few days.'

These are learning opportunities for the team who will operate T5. Dent was excited about his amazing new role and keen to take feedback, 'so that he can iron out every detail to make the first passenger experience perfect'. Younger was also on hand not as an observer but as a passenger. She was keen to walk the Terminal in the 'footsteps of a passenger' with her daughter.

I asked my husband what he thought overall: 'It's not like Heathrow, take away the teething problems that the trials are designed to sort out and it's fantastic, has great views, is intuitive, spacious and logical.'

MIGRATING BA FROM T1 AND T4 TO T5

Over the years the team has reviewed the pros and cons of both the 'big bang' and the gradual approach to BA moving into T5. In its deliberations the T5live team has had to take into account not only the BA moves, but the 54 other airline moves that will take place at Heathrow after the first. Huw Phillips, the migration manager, had led the creation and implementation of a strategy that might be described as two slightly smaller big bangs. On the evening of 26 March 2007 switch one will move over most of BA's T1 and T4 short-haul operations into T5, and its long-haul flights from T1 and T3. Switch two takes place on 30 April 2007 and moves the remaining long haul from T4 into T5, except for 757 fleet and Australian Services, which will move to T3 in the coming months and operate out of there until the second satellite comes on line in 2010.

Managing and mitigating risk

As is so often the case, Phillips' role has been about mitigating risk as much as planning the actual moves. He comments:

> Our role is to ensure there is a seamless switch of operation from existing terminals into T5. What make this project a real challenge is we only have a very small window on the switch nights, between 11 p.m. and 4.30 a.m.,

when the flight traffic is closed at Heathrow. We have one shot at getting it right, and have to make sure we have robust contingency plans for all types of eventualities. The contingencies we have had to plan for include bad weather on the night of the move, high winds, driving rain or fog that would delay inbound flights and reduce the precious five hours; disruption in T1 or T4, impacting on the start time of the moves; health and safety accidents during the loading, unloading process; and a breakdown in communication, so the control centre can't control activities on the night. These are all the things that keep me awake.

The BA move

Switch one will include 95 full lorries of equipment from inside the buildings, 2100 pieces of ground support equipment and 35 aircraft that are on the ground at night. The key to mitigating risks has been to get as much done in advance as possible, so all nonoperational critical equipment will have moved before the big night. Switch two accounts for about 45 % of the total move, so a few weeks later with additional lessons having been learned, a similar exercise will take place again.

Premier Moves is the removal firm that will work with the team during this phase along with 260 BA and 120 BAA staff. It has been a significant task to get that number of additional drivers and volunteers, with the appropriate qualifications, to move the equipment and then to have a workforce ready and available for work the next day. Critical to success has been the joint teamworking. There can be no margin for error on either side, and both must trust that the other is ready to do their job. That trust comes with developing the plans jointly, knowing the people and working through problems together.

BRINGING THE OPENING DATE FORWARD

'One of the most significant decisions that the joint team reviewed, and created a way forward that worked for all, was on the actual date of switches and commencement of flight operations in T5,' comments Phillips. T5 was originally due to open on 30 March 2008, a date set in 2001 and used right the way through the T5 Programme as an immovable date. 'As we got closer it became apparent that this date really didn't work operationally for BA,' Phillips explains. For aviation and BA 30 March is exceptionally busy. The winter to summer schedule kicks in, the clocks change, it's in the middle of the Easter holiday period, and for BA the lightest day for traffic is Tuesday night to Wednesday. As Phillips said:

> Psychologically putting the date back didn't work for BAA even if BA were relaxed about this, so T5 has come forward. Officially it will be delivered ahead of time, on 27 March, which is probably a first.

What was different?

Learning from other facilities early

BAA has taken the key lessons learned from personal experience of opening Stansted and T4, along with learning from other airports and complex facilities from around the world. While nothing is really unique, what is perhaps different is the thoroughness with which the plan has been executed and the extra focus on detail for over three years. Volunteers are not army personnel or students, but rather volunteers who have been profiled to create trials that relate to summer peaks with families or business peaks in the morning. The trials look at the issues that need to be raised as part of the mitigation strategy, stress testing the performance of the operation and asking the questions of what the processing times will be and whether the processes can deal with the volume of traffic.

Risk management, mitigation and contingency

The approach to risk and contingency management has left no stone unturned to try to limit issues and the 'unknown unknowns'. As the first flight comes into T5 from Charles De Gaulle at 4.30 a.m. on 27 March 2008, nothing will be left to chance, and scenarios have been put in place for everything to go wrong and the response required.

End-user involvement from day one

The strategic and tactical relationship between BAA and BA has been unusual in its duration and its intensity. Most airport operators do not identify the end user until much nearer the opening date, with the notable exception of Munich Airport with Lufthansa. The excitement that BA expresses about T5 is not just that it has a 'new home', but as much about 'we have a new home that we designed'.

Approach to employee engagement

Overall the approach to employee engagement has been unparalleled, certainly at Heathrow, and so far it seems to have allowed the team to work with the trade unions and navigate tricky issues. Equally BA, despite a few close calls with the unions in 2006, seems to have negotiated a deal to open and operate differently at T5. For both organizations success cannot be declared until at least six to twelve months after opening, as there will be the question of whether what have been agreed as new working practices are what actually get implemented.

Key learning

The handover from construction to operational readiness on 17 September 2007 was pictured as the time when all construction, except retail fit-out, would be 100% complete and there would be no overlap time built in as T5 became an operational environment. The reality has been different, and will always be so as final snags are sorted out, changes made and final construction work completed. The expectation is that in the future management of the airline and planning will take into account a period of gradual handover, with both working in the same space for some time.

Gaines explains that the success of the IT interface test centre has been such that this will now become a permanent facility for BAA: 'It will be used for Heathrow East, but also for all other change programmes that have a systems dimension.'

Kumar and her team have set a new bar in how to engage with a unionized workforce about change, working with trade unions well and also going direct to the workforce with thorny issues such as rosters. Heathrow's people transformation journey probably has another five years before a significant step-change in attitudes and working practices and hence business efficiencies occur across terminals. T5 shows how things can be done differently.

SUMMARY

The approach to operational readiness has been textbook, BAA learning the lessons from others and starting early and working with the end user, BA. There may be critics who say that BAA has been too cautious and hence spent too much money on this activity, but the alternative of scrimping on testing in such a complex and integrated environment is easy for those without the accountability to suggest.

This approach to opening and integrating new facilities has created certainty and more transparency in the run-up to opening. Operational readiness has developed into Heathrow integration, and the tools and methodologies are now part of how any new project or process is deployed across Heathrow.

CHAPTER 7

RETAIL

Putting the glamour back into flying is our
ambition. The iconic building, the great views
and the extensive and exclusive range of retail
will be breathtaking.

Nick Ziebland, retail
strategy director, BAA

I n the 1980s and early 1990s, BAA began to identify the
opportunities that airport retail could present to its bottom line and
the passenger experience, becoming over the years probably the best
in the world at creating a compelling retail offer in its airports. Retail
for BAA is big business and in 2005–06 that meant £889 million
net profit from retail, including all of the shops, restaurants, car
park, car rental and media opportunities. 30 million passengers will
use T5, though after taking account of return and multiple flights
for business or holidays, Nick Ziebland indicates that a base of three
to five million very valuable ABC1 customers remains.

Heathrow's Terminal 5: History in the Making   S. Doherty
© 2008 John Wiley & Sons, Ltd

There is real and quite divided debate, however, about whether over the years BAA has allowed the pendulum to swing too far, and has focused on retail at the expense of security.

The comments by Sir Michael Bishop, chairman of BMI British Midland, in *The Times* (*Times*, 3 May 2007) are illustrative of many similar claims. 'Echoing the concern' of a number of airlines, Bishop believes that BAA's lack of investment in security scanners has forced passengers to arrive at airports earlier. BAA recommends that passengers arrive four hours before an international flight and three hours before a European flight to clear security. Longer check-in periods give passengers more time to shop in the terminals. Bishop said:

> BAA asks people to come to the airport early only for the shopping. But people want to pass through as quickly as possible and that dichotomy has got to be solved, because what people want is seamless travel. People don't want to go shopping.

The idea expressed by Bishop and others catches headlines and is indicative of the gaming that goes on during this stage of regulatory settlements. Stephen Nelson, BAA CEO, had previously commented:

> This idea that we are a greedy retailer is just wrong, and shows that some people do not understand how we are regulated. Our returns, that is how much money we make, are set by the regulator. So the money we make from retailing actually goes to keep airport charges down, not to us. BAA's prices are set every five years by the Civil Aviation Authority. (*Times*, 12 August 2007)

This is a complicated debate and is not quite as straightforward as either player makes out. For BAA there is an opportunity, once regulatory prices have been agreed, to exceed the retail contribution and pocket the difference. For some airlines it might be helpful if they also measured their own check-in queues and staff discipline in informing passengers of what is allowed through security and baggage performance.

The real opportunity on which both airlines and airport operators need to work together is how the end-to-end passenger experience in airports can be improved. Over 90 % of the time at Heathrow passengers will wait less than 10 minutes to get through security; for too long after the August 2006 security crisis, that lead to changes in processes by the authorities, that wasn't the case, but it is reality today, despite the capacity constraints. New facilities and the 1500 extra security guards recruited during 2007 will improve that further. For most passengers many of their frustrations in airports are around the combined experience: check-in, owned by airlines; security queuing, owned by BAA; delays in flight departures or arrivals, with a combination of accountabilities; and baggage waiting time, down to airlines. For radical changes in passenger experience a one-team approach, looking at end-to-end processes, is what will get a step-change in the passenger experience. This is the real conversation that needs to take place. Some of that work and thinking has made progress in T5, but there is a way to go in both T5 and the rest of Heathrow.

This is the backdrop for the T5 opening on 27 March 2008. Its retail offer is impressive by any major economy's capital city standards, but will only be celebrated as a real advantage for the passenger if the total experience that wraps around it feels balanced and respectful to the core function of an airport. Passengers need to be processed onto aircrafts efficiently, with courtesy and most importantly making sure that they are safe and secure. The T5 team believes that this balance has been struck.

KEY PLAYERS

There has been a small central team of retail experts led by Nick Ziebland, including Charles Byrne, Jerry Sparks and Anna Butterworth from BAA. This team has worked with the central BAA retail team, Heathrow retail operations, in particular Wendy Spinks, head of retail operations, and Simon Scott from Chapman Taylor Partnerships, the retail designers.

THE APPROACH TO RETAIL AT T5

Most people accept that airport facilities at Heathrow are desperately out of date and that T5 presents the first big opportunity in the last 20 years to set a new standard. Trying to 'de-stress flying' and 'put some glamour back into flying' were phrases that both Nelson and Ziebland were keen to point out.

The aim of retailing at T5 is to offer the passenger choice. If a passenger wants to shop or eat, the 112 different shops and restaurants provide something for everyone; for those who just want to do nothing before getting on a long flight, the open spaces with comfortable seats and fantastic views are on offer; and for those in a rush, the clear and easy-to-navigate spaces smooth the way to the departure gate.

Many architects would quietly say that they dislike the retail space in airports as it detracts from the building architecture. BAA, lead architect Rogers Stirk Harbour + Partners and the retail designers Chapman Taylor Partnership have worked hard to integrate the retail offer into the building, and Ziebland, who has been taking most of the press around previews of the retail offer, suggests 'even those who are paid to be more critical seem to agree this has been achieved'.

Giving passengers choice and integrating retail into the five passenger promises that were created has been the acid test for each decision made along the journey. Listening to the T5 retail walkthrough DVD that was sent out in the early days to prospective retailers, a very sensual voice shares the five promises with you: 'T5 aims to surprise, tempt, respect, simplify and satisfy'.

The team has taken these promises and stood by them during the four broad phases of retail on T5:

- Master planning
- Merchandise strategies
- Tendering and retailer section
- Fit-out and operational readiness

Master planning

As BAA, with RSH+P, developed the four different designs for T5, from the flying carpet to the final loose-fit flexible envelope, retail was considered at each stage. Consideration was given to the square footage allocated to retail, the type of retail experience T5 wanted to create and how retail could be integrated into the design of the building.

Merchandise strategies

To develop the merchandising strategy and plan, BAA, uniquely for an airport, uses data-modelling tools developed by supermarkets to allocate space. With years of retail experience and more importantly consumer spending data, the team was able to use this technology to model at a high level the allocation of space to different product categories, leading ultimately to specific types of shops or named retailers. This sort of approach is also critical in deciding where best to put different types of offers. Ziebland said, 'Nationality, frequency of flying and the purpose of your trip are all significant factors for the type of retail experience that our customers will value.'

Tendering and retail selection

Once BAA knows what in theory will make for the most profitable and enjoyable passenger experience, there is then the need to attract the most suitable retailers. In some instances there is no choice: either the retailer is one of a kind, as in the case of a Boots or WH Smith, or it is a player with which BAA has had a strategic long-term relationships. Even with those players out of the equation, T5 was three times oversubscribed, so it is fair to say that there are a few retailers a little disappointed not to be in T5.

Contracts were awarded to 62 different retailers, making up the 112 different retail outlets and catering units. This has been heavily programme managed to schedule them into a very busy pre-opening fit-out and operational readiness programme.

Fit-out and operational readiness

Retail fit-out is notoriously bad in time management terms. Ziebland explains:

> Arrive at any shopping mall a week before opening and you would put a fiver on it not opening on time. 24 hours before opening, somehow the rabbit gets pulled out of the hat, but we wanted T5 to be different and indeed given everything else going on at the same time we didn't have any option.

With most of the contracts awarded in 2006 and a final few complete by May 2007, retailers had signed up to explicit fit-out slots, shared drawings and ideas of how they planned to meet the five promises. By December 2007 95% are on schedule to be complete, with the last few stragglers being addressed in January as allowed for in contingency. The 4000 fit-out 'men in white vans', as commonly referred to by the T5 team, have had to go through the T5 induction process to ensure that they understand what they are involved in and, most importantly, the safety culture of which they are a part. Even during the relatively short six- to eight-week fit-out period, many different drawings at different stages will have been submitted and logistics approaches complied with. The facilities management resource then constantly checks the actual promise and quality standard that the retailer is delivering on site.

THE DELIGHTS IN STORE FOR THE TRAVELLER

Those who do choose to indulge will find 18 580 square metres of retail space. This means that passengers will be able to enjoy more than a third of the amount of retail at Bluewater in Kent. For critics these delights will be viewed as an unnecessary new shopping mall in west London.

The space has been divided into two areas. At the southern end are the luxury international retailers; at the northern end more contemporary and aspirational shops, along with more family-oriented ones. Passengers will find names like Coach, the classic American accessories brand, Harrods, Links of London, Mappin & Webb, Mulberry, Paul Smith, Smythson, Tiffany & Co., with its only European airport boutique, and concept stores from Ted Baker and Kurt Geiger. For those looking for that all-important reading matter, there are stalwarts like WH Smith.

Passengers looking for something to eat they could do no better than the award-winning, Michelin-starred chef Gordon Ramsay. Alternatively, they could select from a range of dining experiences, including the Italian upmarket pasticceria Carluccio's, the Caviar House & Prunier, Giraffe, offering a mix of European and African-inspired dishes, Japanese offerings from Itsu and Wagamama, the Mediterranean-style tapas restaurant V Bar, and a brand new British dining concept, The Huxleys Bar & Kitchen. Anyone looking for refreshments or a light snack will be spoilt for choice, with names like boulangerie-patisserie Apostrophe, Caffe Amato, Caffe Nero, Eat, Krispy Kreme, Lovejuice, with its blend of smoothies and juices, and Starbucks.

What has been delivered?

Although still to be finally tested, a very confident Ziebland is sure that 100% of the retail and restaurant outlets will not only be open for business on the opening day, but will be ready to delight the passenger. Mike Clasper's challenge to Ziebland of 'having the temperature of the coffee just right is something he believes will be achieved'.

Financially T5 is expected to deliver 10% uplift in income per passenger. Clearly, this is a deliverable that only time can tell about.

For the passenger verdict on whether the five promises to surprise, tempt, respect, simplify and satisfy are met, we will need to wait a while longer.

What has been different?

Retail has always had a seat at the T5 top table

In the spirit of an integrated team, retail has always had a place at the T5 top table. Ziebland, or 'the simple shopkeeper' as Tony Douglas often referred to him, was a valued member of the team for his dry sense of humour, the clarity and simplicity with which he would see things, and for the ferocity with which he protected the passenger retail experience during the T5 journey. All of the T5 team members were genuinely interested in the 'wow' effect the retail offer could give to T5, and one of T5 directors' trips was to Bluewater to understand how this centre had developed its offer and some of the logistical challenges it had faced in getting ready for opening.

All the retail outlets have been experimental and creative at T5

By creating a sense of excitement and expectation, the T5 retail team has engendered a real sense of imagination in the retailers. All were challenged to do something different in T5, to use it as an opportunity to show their brand of in a different way. All have entered into this spirit. Whether it is small things like WH Smith introducing self-scanning technology for buying papers, or Tiffany putting on vintage jewellery displays and having private consultation rooms, each has tried to entertain its customers with product or shop fit-out innovations, or offering new and exciting services that will change regularly, catering for frequent fliers.

Gordon Ramsay's restaurant

To set T5 apart, the retail team always wanted something that symbolically said that T5 is a different and glamorous experience. Over the years ideas such as having a casino were rejected, and ultimately getting Michelin-starred chef Gordon Ramsay to open a world-class restaurant was settled on. The restaurant will be the first of its kind: the Ramsay team have worked on one- to three-hour menu options, depending on the occasion and time you wish to spend, which will put an end to the plastic, microwave reputation that food in airports has had. The lasting memory of getting Ramsay on board was a mark of the man and the standards he expected. If BAA wanted him to open a restaurant in T5 he wanted toilets in his restaurant, not public toilets outside, one set for his guests and one set for his staff to a very exacting quality. This was not the norm but was done to land the big name.

Key learning

The members of the small T5 retail team have worked closely with the central BAA retail team, and it is an approach that has worked, adding real value not only to the individual project but also to sharing ideas with the rest of the BAA portfolio. It is likely that the same approach with be used on Heathrow East.

Advertising in T5 has also been taken to a different level. A new standard in airport advertising has been set by building advertising into the design of the building using technology and creating 'amazing spaces', such as the five towers that run across the span of the building that will provide Nokia with 16 large screens to entertain the passenger, while subtly reinforcing its brand.

Retail fit-out and operational readiness is probably one of the more structured processes that most of these retailers will have been involved in, and something that Chapman Taylor Partnerships has said could be a real lesson for the retail industry. The precision of retail planning, the transparency of communication with retailers about expected start dates for fit-out, and the dogged determination to make sure that all concerned did what they said they were going to have been second to none.

SUMMARY

The T5 retail offer is impressive by any major economy's capital city standards, and will be celebrated as a real advantage for passengers as well as providing valuable income for BAA.

Retail will continue to be a double-edged sword. On the one hand, it provides BAA with income that allows the airport operator to keep landing fees down. On the other hand, for airlines and critics the total experience that wraps around retail needs to feel balanced and respectful to the core function of an airport. That means processing passengers onto aircrafts efficiently, with courtesy and most importantly making sure that they are safe and secure.

PART 3

T5 CRITICAL SUCCESS FACTORS

Having gained an understanding of what happened in each of the phases of the T5 Programme – planning, design, construction and operational readiness – it's important to step back and try to understand why T5 has broadly been an unusual UK success story.

Three key themes will be explored:

- T5 leadership through the different phases and what was particular about the leaders in the environment.
- The role of the intelligent and hands-on client, the commercial contract and other frameworks that were put in place.
- Getting integrated teams to deliver. Work gets done on site and leaders' and the client's work was ultimately about creating a place to work that allowed these teams to deliver on time, to budget, safely, with a focus on quality and the environment.

Heathrow's Terminal 5: History in the Making   S. Doherty
© 2008 John Wiley & Sons, Ltd

■ This part also picks up the people story and how leaders got the best out of front-line workers.

The underlying hypothesis is that T5 has been a project like most others with lots of problems and issues. Fundamentally during delivery the leadership team stepped up to the challenge and performed, making up for lost time and not everything being in place from day one of construction on site.

Part of that leadership achievement, particularly as a hands-on client who owned most of the risk, was to create a working environment that allowed engineers, project managers and all the other skills and trades to focus on doing the job, not reaching for the lawyer.

CHAPTER 8

THE LEADERSHIP STORY

Leadership was the difference that made the difference on T5. The judgement, passion, determination with which we got the best out of the integrated teams and influenced the key stakeholders was second to none.

Tony Douglas, Heathrow CEO, BAA, until 2007

*T*he bridge between great strategy and the end result being delivered, I would suggest, is great leadership. We have all seen the difference some individuals can make: they bring clarity to ambiguity, take courageous decisions, inspire people to give more by making them feel valued, and have the capacity to turn situations around. Most companies never have enough of these types of people or are unable to access the required talent pool at key times. T5 has been no different, for BAA and its suppliers.

Heathrow's Terminal 5: History in the Making   S. Doherty
© 2008 John Wiley & Sons, Ltd

Even some good leaders found the size and complexity of T5 daunting and needed to work in integrated teams requiring skills beyond their abilities. At other times good players for one phase found it difficult to be successful in the next phase. A few good leaders really became great leaders during the T5 journey, as the situation tested their personal resolve. The only thing that separated them from reputational ruin was their ability to lead.

There have been times when the T5 Programme came dangerously close to heading down the same path as the other construction projects outlined in Chapter 2, more than history will record, as key players from across the industry stepped up to the challenges and at times bridged the gaps.

Examples of leadership are explored in nearly every chapter of this book. In particular here I will explore the different levels of leadership on T5, the BAA CEO story, and the five T5 leadership characteristics that I would propose emerged. The judgment of whether these transferable to other projects or organizations is left to others, but maybe an environment that requires something a little different should consider these characteristics.

THE SIZE, SHAPE AND CONTEXT OF THE LEADERSHIP CHALLENGE

Every large transformation project, whether in construction or in corporate life, has a unique environment in which it has to be successful. There have been some unique challenges that leaders have had to understand and navigate on T5: taking over 22 years to get planning consent; building T5 next to Heathrow airport, the world's busiest international airport; the M25, and Longford Village with 600 residents who understandably didn't want that potential level of disruption on their front door; and finally the new type of contracting, the T5 Agreement, which had those who doubted its ability to deliver both inside BAA and the supplier organizations. So it is no surprise that there was initially an undercurrent that everything was going to unravel.

After that the challenge was tough, but similar to that faced by many projects: a £4.3 billion project had to be delivered on time, to the quality and design required, with due attention given to safety and environment issues. Understand the risks, manage the stakeholders and motivate the team to deliver – that's all that was required. The statistics suggested that the terminal would open a year late, be over a billion overspent, kill two people and seriously injure 400 others.

The risks were financial, business related, reputational, technical and HSE related. Some were within the T5 team's control, others such as terrorist attacks or Department for Transport changes were to be anticipated, but unfortunately not controlled. Stakeholders were in national and local government, city analysts, insurers, the media, environment, HSE agencies, the local community, air traffic control authorities, BA and other airline operators – the list goes on. The team that had to be motivated came from over 20 000 different companies, comprising 50 000 workers over the years.

Level of leadership – 10, 100, 1000

During the phases of T5, from planning to design, construction and operational readiness, there will have been between 10 and 15 senior leaders who with personal presence, vision and good judgement put T5 on a course for success, often challenging existing industry norms. There were perhaps another 100 leaders who made the critical difference, taking brave stands, interpreting new ideas and frameworks, leading by example, and ultimately creating an operating environment that enabled others to be successful. There were maybe another 1000 leaders who given that context were able to swim with the tide and do their leadership role in a demanding workplace that had little space for error.

The numbers are illustrative rather than absolute, but the more important point is that these three levels of leaders played different roles, at different times, but were all aligned to delivering a successful T5 Programme. These leaders were able to work over time to take the strategy and deliver it on the ground. The simplicity at one level of delivering big projects makes the leadership imperative easier than in corporate organization, unless in a burning platform situation, but equally the track record of mega projects is that great ambitions end in cost and time overruns.

Some of the 10 to 15 senior leaders were in other roles and T5 was a part of their brief. Sir John Egan, BAA CEO, or Ray O'Rourke, CEO of Laing O'Rourke, or Peter Gerretse, CEO Vanderlande were in this category. Others were selected to work on T5, such as Fiona Hammond, BAA legal counsel, Tony Douglas, Heathrow CEO, Mike Forster, strategy director, Andrew Wolstenholme, director capital projects, and Mark Bullock, managing director, Heathrow, who devoted years of their life to grappling with the T5 challenges.

The list below is also illustrative and tries to give a view of some of the 100 leaders from about 30 different companies. It is not comprehensive; to list all of the truly inspirational leaders in this category would test the reader's patience.

- *From planning and design:* Liz Southern, head of development; Chris Millard, head of technical leadership; Dave Bartlett, head of design; Dervilla Mitchell, Arups; Mike Davies, Rogers Stirk Harbour + Partners.
- *From construction:* Ian Fugeman and Rob Stewart, BAA project heads; Bill Franklands, Phil Wilbraham and Jon Oliver, project leaders; Peter Emerson, Severfield-Rowen; Selby Thacker, Morgan Vinci JV; Steve Cork, Laing O'Rourke; Henk van Helmond, Vanderlande; Richard Rook and Mike Evans, safety.
- *From operational readiness:* Paul Fox, Debbie Younger and Huw Phillips, migration managers; Mark Mercieca, proving manager; Colin Clarkson and Trisha Corstan-James, BA.
- *From functions:* Jeremy Bates and Andy Anderson, programme management; Dave Ferroussat, commercial; John Williams, TECHT; Veronica Kumar and Megan Wiltshire, BAA organizational effectiveness.

Finally there were men and women, sometimes at quite junior levels in the organization, the likes of Sam Lloyd, Daniel Shipton, Ryan

Kameg and Angie Young, who were excited by the opportunity to be part of making history. They had a positive energy flowing through them that was infectious and personally they made a difference. These characters are profiled in chapter 9.

THE BAA CEO LEADERSHIP STORY

The BAA CEO's have been some of the key 10–15 leaders. Over the lifetime of T5 there will have been four CEOs: Sir John Egan, Sir Mike Hodgkinson, Mike Clasper and Stephen Nelson. Each was a very different character, and each will leave a different legacy on T5.

Sir John Egan, 1991–99

Everyone would see Egan as the first really to stimulate a different way of thinking about a number of important issues in BAA. How the company approached building new infrastructure was absolutely at the heart of that new thinking. As the chair of the John Prescott-initiated 'Rethinking Construction' thinktank, Egan had many new ideas, fostered in the car industry as a consequence of the Japanese influence of opportunities to drive out waste by up to 30% and build long-term relationships with suppliers. He saw the power of integrated teams, process improvements and treating people in construction differently. These were all ideas that he used to help shape not only the direction BAA was to move forward in, but also the industry as a whole.

The Heathrow Express tunnel collapse had been the moment when Egan had realized the power, in difficult and tense situations, of the client holding the risk. It was then, as a client, he started building a team of people who were able to manage that risk, and getting the company with the supply chain 'match fit for T5'.

One of the senior players at Balfour Beatty, the main contractor on Heathrow Express, was also Egan's next-door neighbour, so entering into a trusting relationship for both organizations somehow seemed easier. This is but one of a few critical points that proved to be fortuitous and old friendships helped senior leaders take a leap of faith that may have proved more difficult to orchestrate.

Not all the memories of T5 were positive for Egan. If he had his time again he would have approached getting planning permission for T5 differently: 'That it would take so long to get planning permission was just unbelievable.' He wasn't completely sure what he would have done differently, but somehow he would have influenced national and local government to get an alternative and quicker outcome.

Sir Mike Hodgkinson, 1999–2003

Hodgkinson is a very smart and extremely driven man, who was acutely aware of stakeholder-related issues. He had been part of Egan's team for many years along with other BAA executives. He had helped stimulate and develop many of the Egan ideas, so as the new CEO the baton was handed over easily and the long-term big-picture thinking continued.

There are two areas where Hodgkinson can take significant credit on the T5 journey. First, he landed the regulatory settlement of 7.75% return on capital, which equated to RPI + 6.5% for Heathrow for the quinquennium leading up to the opening of T5 (explained further in Chapter 2) and enabled BAA to afford the building of T5.

Secondly, he worked in a very hands-on way with the concept architect and the design team to finalize the 'loose-fit flexible envelope' design, with the subsequent detailed planning submission. In conversations with Mike Davies from Rogers Stirk Harbour + Partners, there were times when the final T5 planning permission submissions were running into tough twists and turns, and Hodgkinson's ability to see the T5 campus in 3D and make value-adding decisions on solutions was second to none.

Mike Clasper, 2003–06

Clasper was a more classically trained business leader, whose greatest strength was his ability to build a good-quality team, get them to work together to create an exciting vision for the future, and then put in place the frameworks to deliver. He was unable to follow this through to conclusion due to the Ferrovial buyout of BAA in July 2006, and his predictable decision to move on having ferociously defended the bid.

Credit for the build of T5 can really be attributed to Clasper. In the early days before there was a proven track record for the T5 Agreement and the T5 senior team, he held his nerve, consolidated the stakeholder support that Hodgkinson before him had initiated and worked with the team to deliver.

On T5 he was very much respected by the integrated team. He chaired the monthly T5 executive at which he could keep a very close overview on programme performance. He spent time with key CEOs from across the supply chain and attended quarterly T5 BAA standback off-site sessions, regularly walking the site with the project leaders.

The relationship between Clasper and Douglas was one of vigilant trust and this meant that big decisions were taken with relative ease, as Clasper had a good grasp of what was happening. Over the years Douglas was always open and transparent, even when there was bad news.

When the £350 million cost challenges were tabled in 2004 (more details in Chapter 5), Clasper and Margaret Ewing, group finance director, were helpful in getting the team to see some different opportunities or ways to manage risks. They managed the external stakeholders and during these tense times the team always felt supported and trusted. Clasper never needed to get upset or shout, as the T5 team always wanted to deliver for him and repay the confidence he placed in them.

Stephen Nelson, 2006 to March 2008

Nelson, having spent six months in BAA as retail director and with a background at Sainsbury and Diageo, took over in Autumn 2006. To a great extent the die had been cast on T5 and in conversations with Nelson he was very gracious in attributing credit for T5 to his predecessors.

As the project has completed the fit-out work and moved into operational readiness, the opportunity for Nelson, working with Douglas and Bullock, was to ensure that the focus on the passenger was at the forefront of everyone's mind in the final run-up to opening. The foundation set by Clasper, looking at how BAA could delight the passenger in T5, was carried on by Nelson, who is keen to showcase T5 as a glimpse into what Heathrow could be like, given the appropriate regulatory settlement.

Nelson's real legacy will be if BAA can take the learning from T5 and use this to transform the rest of Heathrow, living up to some of the competitive equivalence challenges, taking the very best ideas and people from T5 and using them to help him continue the transformation of Heathrow and indeed the rest of BAA.

So there have been four very different leaders of BAA, who built on the work of their predecessors with regard to T5. This meant that the project never philosophically lurched from one idea to another, but always had a steady course forward with a hands-on client who understood why risk management was critical. They all comprehended why BAA needed to take a lead role and own the risk, and put a team in to mitigate the risks and exploit opportunities.

As this book was going to print it was announced that Nelson would be moving on from BAA and that Colin Matthews would become CEO of BAA from 1st April 2008.

FIVE LEADERSHIP CHARACTERISTICS IN ACTION

With so many companies represented in the project there wasn't a single leadership framework that all were selected against, but I do believe that there are some underlying characteristics in the 10 and 100 key leaders who planned, design, built and opened T5 that are worth exploring.

There are many good books, frameworks and great ideas on leadership, so I will not pretend to create another. Rather, through personal experience of working on T5 with so many of these leaders, and through interviewing over 100 of them for this book, I will make some observations about the real differentiating characteristics of those leaders who made a difference on and around T5. These leaders could:

- Think big picture
- Engender and operate with vigilant trust
- Drive for success despite the odds
- Keep stakeholders onside and aligned with objectives
- Get the best out of the integrated team

These leaders were from around the world, with different technical and professional backgrounds; most were charismatic and engaging, but not all; some were reflective; and all had a belief that delivering T5 successfully was in the best interest of BAA or their company, the UK construction industry, and UK plc.

Thinking big picture

Understanding and influencing the aviation and construction industries

The political, economic and social context in which T5 operated over 20 years meant that leaders needed to understand and shape a new big picture while working with a complex and changing set of stakeholders. They had to understand and navigate successfully industry-changing events, risks and opportunities, such as regulatory cycles, growth of the environment agenda and 40–80% time and cost overruns in construction projects. A broader list is outlined in Chapter 2.

Competitive equivalence

In an environment with scarce resources like Heathrow, the conflicting business opportunities that existed between competing airlines had to be managed. The tensions created around the timing of all the airlines getting competitive equivalence on the Heathrow transformation journey had to be facilitated carefully. BAA leaders faced a never-ending intellectual challenge in managing their way through this situation by means of relationships and thinking outside the box to use the Heathrow footprint differently.

T5 Agreement

The big idea on T5 was the commercial contract, the T5 Agreement. In this BAA owned most of the risk, provided insurance for all suppliers involved in the T5 Programme and had a hands-on role as a client. In return, suppliers were given a guaranteed margin ranging from 5–15%, depending on trade, and worked in an open-book fashion. The quality of the work needed to be at least industry best practice and there was a shared incentive approach that rewarded exceptional performance.

Over the duration of T5 there were leaders who developed this idea, suppliers who saw the opportunity it presented to work with a client in a different way and innovate to grow their companies, and leaders who month in and month out could take the idea and use it to make business decisions. Matt Riley, commercial director, typifies the ability to see the big picture. He was able in commercial discussions to hold the conversation at the level of '95% of this contract is in good shape', pulling together work packages from many different parts of the T5 Programme, and then have a tough but reasonable conversation about the last 5% while keeping the supplier on side.

Engender and operate with vigilant trust

As the BAA management team was being strengthened in the early stages of construction and the reporting and governance processes were being put in place, there were times when blind faith was in operation. As the right systems, processes and most importantly people were put in place, that was no longer so necessary.

During T5, all sorts of people had to enter into different relationships around trust. This was tested particularly as the T5 Programme moved from an idea into a live construction site spending £3 — 4 million a day. Many stakeholders were asked to trust in a different way. The nonexecutive directors and plc board had to trust the CEO of the day, Clasper, who took the brunt of this challenge during the bulk of the construction phase. The BAA executive had to trust Douglas and his senior team and trust was tested among the T5 integrated supply chain teams. Added up this represents a significant amount of trust for communities who had been trained not to trust.

Perhaps one of the biggest tests of vigilant trust was the action by the plc board to allow Douglas's sign-off authority to move from £30 million to £500 million. In practical terms the amount of money being spent made the previous arrangement unworkable, but equally Douglas was entrusted with sufficient funds to do serious damage to BAA if he spent the money unwisely. Clasper and Douglas did have a special relationship that had been developed over the years. Clasper was confident that if Douglas was in trouble he would be the first to know and he could see the people, processes and systems that had been put in place to give sufficient visibility that this money was being spent according to the plan.

A different approach to trust was established on T5 as a result of the commercial contract, the T5 Agreement, and how the principles within it flowed through everything. Not all were believers in the T5 Agreement. Some in BAA and some of the suppliers liked the theory, but didn't really expect it to work initially. The Heathrow air traffic control tower was the moment when trust in the integrated team was tested. This is explored in Chapter 11. However, the critical point is that BAA used this instance to build trust by behaving in a supportive way, not resorting to blame and legal advisers. The leadership of Wolstenholme, Riley, Emerson and Mitchell, alongside others, was textbook. Reputations were at stake; the T5 Programme could have been knocked off course if a solution had not been found. It is at these crunch points that it is possible to see the real test of leadership. Douglas would say, 'It's when things go wrong you see who the real leaders are.'

Drive to succeed despite the odds

On the T5 journey there have been many challenging hurdles, which for some people at some times may have felt insurmountable, but for the best of the T5 leaders this toughened their resolve to succeed despite the odds. On the ground this was probably the most pronounced characteristic that came through.

Both inherent and left-field challenges have been part of the T5 story: for example the length of the planning inquiry, and three different concept designs taking into account planning permission requirements and changes in airport building regulations given lessons learned from Kings Cross and the 9/11 terrorist attacks outlined in Chapter 2. In construction as the team started there was the prospect of opening a year late, a billion over budget, killing two people and seriously inuring 400 more. In operational readiness, during the integrated baseline review with BA the team lost confidence in the terminal's readiness for opening.

Failure has never been an option, though. T5 leaders have been charming and very personable, but that masked a drive and determination that were combined with patience and good judgement to know when to push harder and when to give support.

This intriguing mix of being highly analytical and numerate, with an ability to inspire, particularly during the construction phase, was a differentiator. Very senior players rarely lost their composure in public, even when the stakes were high and errors had been made. There was a level of statesmanlike behaviour that always went on, even though everyone was very aware that heads would roll, and long-term contracts would be affected if companies and key players were not at the top of their game, demonstrating total commitment to delivering objectives.

The Laing O'Rourke organizational ethos of delivery, particularly in the early days of the T5 Programme, set the tone for the site. A number of the early milestones that had suffered setbacks from poor site conditions during that first bad winter in 2003 were resolved due to complete leadership determination. Steve Cork and Aran Verling, both from Laing O'Rourke, and Rob Stewart from BAA, supported by key players from Blackwells and Balfour Beatty, achieved unsurpassed productivity levels, whilst keeping a keen focus on safety. These players knew that if they missed what seemed like impossible milestones, the tone of failure would be set from the start. This was drive and determination at the sharp end of construction. Walking the site, gathering together gangs of workers getting a focus on productivity metrics – you name it they thought of it, as early milestones were not going to be allowed to slip.

Keeping stakeholders on side and aligned with objectives

Stakeholders are a bit like stray cats: you can't choose who you get, they are very independent, and just when you think it's safe to stroke them they sink their claws in.

In this kind of mutual relationship, with the balance of power changing over time, there are a number of lessons that can be shared. Know them personally, understand their drivers and have a strategy for the particular stakeholder; have credible leaders to interface with the different players and be aware that the situation will be quite different for the different groupings. Put effort into building obligation and trust, if at all possible, into the relationship. Know when to be very clear about things and when it is actually in the corporate interest to take a difficult meeting on the chin, rather than being transparent, going on to fight another day on the bigger agenda.

T5 was not unusual in the breadth of relationships that needed to be managed: national and local government with regard to planning permission and future permission to grow the agenda for Heathrow, the local communities, the breadth of the media, the investors, BA and other airlines, and then every local institute, aviation and engineering association or body imaginable.

National and local government and the local community

National government's influence on the success of T5 reduced after the initial 700 planning consent orders had been put in place. The issue with this stakeholder group then moved to demonstrating that T5 was an example of national importance, that upgrading or increasing capacity at Heathrow was equally in the national interest, and that BAA was a responsible partner. Alistair Darling, while at the Department for Transport, was very interested and attended critical milestones such as the roof topping-out ceremony and the M25 spur road completion. Publicly he sited T5 as an exemplar project.

Local government, in particular the London Borough of Hillingdon, and the local community were stakeholders who on a weekly basis needed to be engaged. Wolstenhome recounts:

> For three and a half years I spent time standing in front of the local community. Initially they hated and mistrusted the T5 team. We worked hard to listen to their issues, fix problems and pre-empt possible issues for the future. Success for me was that about two years into these meetings, a more trusting relationship developed and T5 stopped being on the agenda, other Heathrow concerns being raised.

Phil Wilbraham, twin rivers project manager, and Julie King, community liaison manager, personally put time into working with local residents' committees, at times going and spending personal time with individual residents. Another strategy was to give the local community access to T5 to demystify it. Thousands of those in the local community attended T5 every Friday to take the tour bus, with Mike Pearman regaling them with interesting facts about the site.

Both at a national and local level, key leaders in BAA managed these relationships with their teams, understanding the importance of the specific issue at hand, but more critically understanding the value created for the future Heathrow and BAA strategic focus.

Investors and insurers

T5 had both equity shareholders Barclays, Lloyds, Legal & General and Prudential, and debt investors such as Schroders and Scottish Widows. With investors the key was around maintaining confidence. Clasper and Ewing worked closely with Douglas to manage both formal and informal conversations with this community.

Those that provided professional indemnity and other insurances, the most notable being Swiss Re, did it seems take a leap of faith in insuring T5. Talking to Richard Williams from Swiss Re, construction had become a loss-making industry for the insurance market in the late 1990s. The consortium of insurers who finally agreed to work with BAA spent significant time and energy understanding what BAA planned to do on T5 to manage risk differently and get a different outcome. The insurers partly managed their risk by appointing Dr Terry Mellors as an independent consultant to assure the BAA work, and also took a personal interest in the T5 project. They were recognized all the way through as important stakeholders.

The huge advantage that the construction project had with these sorts of stakeholders was the 'T5 smile test'. Most people if they get taken around T5 can't fail to be impressed, partly by the size, scale, site tidiness, discipline and people who are hugely motivated about being involved in it. Before starting any investor or insurance briefing, a 90-minute T5 site visit disarmed people, as they could see that it was a well-run site, and the opportunity to get out of Canary Wharf worked on a personal level. Care was always taken to show them what the team said they would do in the previous quarter and what had actually been achieved. This continually stressed the underlying drumbeat 'we said we would deliver these milestones and we have' and built confidence.

For both groups, quarterly formal meetings on T5 were in the diary, and informal meetings were always happening. At short notice any of these key players could visit the site, getting one of the senior players to take them, and the visitors they wanted to impress, around.

Media

The media ranged from the nationals, trade and *Skyport*, the airport and local community paper, to special-interest publications. These were the opinion formers and the underlying strategy was to 'build obligation' when things were going well, so that if something went wrong or it was a quiet day, they looked to Wembley Stadium rather than T5 to get a headline.

Douglas, Wolstenholme, Forster, and Bullock, along with the media team, got to know the key players personally. Relationships were built in an attempt to humanize T5, and reporters were always given time and tipped off on stories so that they could do their job, always being given a comment from the leadership team, even for difficult questions.

It is difficult to tell how successful this approach was, since the amount of negative publicity that would have been written if this hadn't happened is difficult to quantify.

Generally during 2007 BAA often found itself on the wrong end of the headlines. Some of that has been key people leaving BAA with some key relationships in the media and in government being lost, much of it has been due to the timing of the regulatory cycle and the Competition Commission inquiry, and a lot of it has been down to operational pressures caused by changes in security requirements that BAA have found difficult to respond to quickly. Queues at Heathrow frustrate everyone and make for easy headlines. T5 in the main has been left out of this mud slinging, but some of the rifts run quite deep and it will be interesting to watch on the final run–up to T5 how the press plays out. It's probably the case that any room for error that would be brushed over by a supportive press, keen to applaud a

UK success story, has probably gone. To get a positive thumbs-up T5 will now have to be perfect. Will even that be good enough?

Airlines

The relationship with BA was an important one to manage. Building a campus the airline would ultimately move into meant close working through planning permission, design, construction and operational readiness. The relationships with BA have been managed formally and informally, and at all levels, CEO to CEO to key players in the T5 Programme. Interestingly, even when BA has been publicly very critical on airport operational issues, it has always been supportive of T5. There have been points of difference and tough talking, but always the teams have come back around the table and moved issues forward in a timely fashion. Other airlines have always been very keen to understand that BA is not getting a competitive advantage as a result of T5 on key performance indicators such as baggage or flight connection time. This is explored in Chapter 2.

BAA

As a plc, and then as a private company, it has been critical that key internal stakeholders within BAA were managed, as for this group the key to success was building and maintaining confidence. This in turn would give the T5 senior team the time and space to get on with the core job of delivering the T5 Programme, rather than getting caught in endless committees justifying decisions. The nonexecutives and plc board members visited the site for tours, spent time with the team, and had access to the monthly performance report to be able to see progress.

Chris Fay was a nonexecutive director who with Shell had experience in exploration and production; his background most closely matched the T5 experience and Douglas developed a close relationship with him. That relationship was critical to seeking advice on matters relating to the site, but more crucially to have an informed and supportive board member at crunch times.

Clasper, Ewing, Ian Hargreaves, corporate communications director, and plc board members all attended the monthly T5 executive board meeting, and ended up knowing the T5 Programme and team intimately.

Across all stakeholders, Douglas's ability to keep these relationships informed, supportive and maintaining confidence in him and his team, even when there were tough messages, was remarkable. He was always sensitive to issues and how they may land with key players, able to find innovative solutions, and continually tending relationships to build trust for the future. Focused on delivery, he was very aware that stakeholder red tape could stop him from delivering, so he was clear with key players, such as BA, on the last responsible moments (LRMs) for key decisions, such as whether BAA would be building the CIP lounge for BA, explored in Chapter 11. The use of LRMs, not just for design or construction decisions but also to manage stakeholders who needed to provide input on the critical path, was a clever way of managing a complex environment and keeping to plan.

Get the best out of the integrated team

Key leaders on T5, led by Douglas, put in place a strategy and plan to manage the key supplier relationships, involving a small subset of the 60 first-tier suppliers at CEO and MD levels, considered management levels within the 18 projects, and also looked closely at how to get the best out of the 50 000 people from the 20 000 companies.

At a very senior level the strategy was about building obligation, getting those companies at a plc or board level to engage with the T5 objectives so that it became personal, not just another project. Examples were dinners, hosting their company's board meetings at T5, supporting their company objectives at public events and straight-talking conversations about how reputations could be damaged if all stops weren't pulled out to deliver. At times the relationship was about getting critical teams from key suppliers to work a little harder to hit critical path milestones, with suppliers moving resource in from other parts of the organization, or clearing the way in some shape to allow them to deliver. At other times, particularly after the £350 million projected cost overruns in 2004, data was shared with the key suppliers to get them to start to manage risks or look for opportunities for understanding in a different way. Where the temptation might be to leak to the press or go back to their plcs and go public with information, the strong relationships that were tightly managed kept them on side and part of the solution. It is worth distinguishing between owning most of the risk, which BAA did, and doing work to mitigate risk or exploit opportunities, on which the later suppliers were very much held to account.

The integrated project team was ultimately where T5 succeeded. This was partially through those leaders striving to deliver and equally due to the senior leadership culture that wrapped around their teams, creating an environment that enabled them to deliver. Programme management and governance processes provided good and timely management data, and allowed leaders to know where there were problems and successes. Just as important was management by walking around, always being inquisitive with site leaders about how many people were working on jobs, progress made on very specific areas, visiting manufacturing plants and chatting to the men and women on the tools without their bosses being around.

With this group, leading by example was also important. The Heathrow air traffic control tower setback epitomized how to get the best out of teams even when things are going wrong.

Galvanizing the 50 000-strong organization was all about getting the basics right, and having the right leadership judgement around where to make investments to create a good working environment was critical. The 'history in the making' communications campaign, outlined in more detail in Chapter 9, really acted as a glue to tie the site together and along with the incident and injury-free safety approach, provided a chance to build pride in the broader team and demonstrate different values. Every opportunity was taken to gather large groups together and say well done. The

Site newspaper was full of hero stories. The personal touch was always noted, where senior leaders would take doughnuts down to the people on the tools, sit in the canteens and listen, or go and shake a worker's hand for reporting a fraud. Douglas, Wolstenholme, Peter Emerson, Ray O'Rourke, Mark Reynolds, Henk van Helmond and others in the supply chain were masters at knowing when to go and say thank-you, and they did that daily right across the site. Small gestures by senior leaders from across the supply chain set the tone and got the best out of teams.

DIFFERENT LEADERS FOR DIFFERENT PHASES

T5 is definitely a game of two halves. In the first half it was the big ideas of the T5 Agreement, concept design and getting funding that Egan and Hodgkinson delivered, along with their trusted advisers. The second half, involving Clasper and Nelson, was about putting their money where their mouth was. Could they build a BAA team good enough to work with an integrated supply chain, to deliver even when the going gets tough, while managing the key external stakeholders?

The underlying leadership qualities didn't change during the different phases of the T5 Programme. What really changed were the emphasis and the intensity as the work moved out of planning into design, on to the big push for construction and then the dash for the finishing line.

Big thinking on T5 was probably more necessary in the first half as the landscape was framed, although many of those in involved in T5, such as Douglas, Forster and Riley, were then starting to engage with the Heathrow East and third-generation supplier framework agreements, so the second half saw many of those ideas being tested. Engendering vigilant trust and being able to trust others was a concept in the first half, but was really tested in the second half by all parties. Drive and determination in the first half were much more around patience in the face of the long planning inquiry, whereas in the second half they was about a relentless focus on performance and delivery. Stakeholder management has been a key focus right the way through, always to be understood and managed. Finally, getting the best out of the integrated team was a concept initially but came to fruition in second half, with leaders like Douglas and Wolstenholme embedding the concept.

SUMMARY

The bridge between great strategy and the end result being delivered is great leadership. The big idea on T5 was about managing risk differently through the T5 Agreement. This context allowed leaders to drive for success and trust differently while working with stakeholders and integrated teams.

The strategic alignment of those leaders over the 20 years in the making of T5 has allowed the T5 Programme to head broadly in the same direction, towards an on-time and on-budget objective.

BAA CEOs

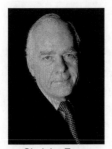

Sir John Egan
BAA CEO 1991–1999

Sir Mike Hodgkinson
BAA CEO 1999–2003

Mike Clasper
BAA CEO 2003–2006

Stephen Nelson
BAA CEO 2006 to March 2008

Key BAA Directots Who Delivered T5

Tony Douglas
T5 MD

Mike Forster
Development & Design Director

Andrew Wolstenholme T5
Construction Director

Mark Bullock
T5live Director

T5 BAA Director Team Away Day
Ben Morton, Andrew Hill, Matt Riley, Sharon Doherty, Paul Fox, Andrew
Wolstenholme, Mark Bullock, Nick Ziebland, Tony Douglas, Mike Forster

Principal Contractors

Mike Peasland
Balfour Beatty

Chris Hughes
Morgan Vinci

Mark Reynolds
MACE

Mike Robins
Laing O'Rourke

Grahame Ludlow
Spie Matthew Hall

Some Of The Development and Design Team

BAA Development and Design Team

Liz Southern
Head of Development

Mike Clasper BAA CEO, Mike
Davies RRP, Alistair Darling
Department of Transport

Dervilla Mitchell
Arup

Dave Bartlett
Head of Design

Chris Millard
Head of Technical Leadership

Some Of The Construction Team

Andrew Wolstenholme
Safety Briefing With T5 Workers

| Peter Emerson | John Milford | Rob Stewart | Jonathan Adams |
| Severfield-Rowen | Head Of Buildings | Head Of Civils | Head Of Baggage |

Colin Reynell
Head Of Operations

Steve Cork
Laing O'Rourke

Phil Wilbraham With Rob
McCarthy Of The Environment
Agency

Henk Van Helmond
Vanderlande

Ian Fugeman Head R&T and
Mike Clasper BAA CEO

Paul Fox
Operational Readiness

Debbie Younger
Operational Readiness

Nick Ziebland (Centre) And The
Retail Team

Shaun Cowlam
Logistics

Dave Ferroussat And Matt Riley
Commercial Team

Andrew Hill
Finance

Willie Walsh
BA CEO

CHAPTER 9

LEADERS MOTIVATING PEOPLE

History in the making, **one day you'll be proud to say 'I built Terminal 5'.**

50,000 T5 workers

T he employee engagement agenda was put together on the commercial premise that employees are more likely to be more productive and less militant if they are treated with respect, a message that had clearly come out of the Rethinking Construction report. Equally, some of the planning consents for T5 were based on BAA providing on-site facilities that reduced the pressure of a 50 000-strong workforce over the years using local facilities.

Having conversations with some senior suppliers in 2003 about the people agenda for T5, they told of 'some of the men on site being like animals'. It is true that racism, graffiti and destruction of lockers and showers are probably quite unusual behaviours for a workforce, but they are not uncommon on construction sites in the UK. The

Heathrow's Terminal 5: History in the Making   S. Doherty
© 2008 John Wiley & Sons, Ltd

senior players in BAA from the very early days of Norman Haste, the first construction director, saw things fundamentally differently. Haste commented:

> If you show the workforce respect most good-living people will respond to that, and treat their environment and colleagues with a similar respect, whilst working more productively and be less likely to walk out on strike.

At the peak of the project there were 300 BAA people working on T5, 2500 supplier knowledge workers and 5000 men and women on site working with their hands on the tools. Each month about 1000 people left the project and 1000 new people joined as it went through the different phases. During the life of the project the trades moved from civil engineering, rail and tunnels, to building mechanical and electrical, fit-out and to finally those who would be in T5 serving and protecting passengers. All races, ages and social backgrounds came together to deliver the terminal.

The overall strategy for T5 workers was one of 'respect for people'. In practical terms that materialized as a robust approach to employee relations, a common and good-quality approach to site facilities and an employee engagement plan. Careful not to try and do what the suppliers did best, there was always due consideration about what BAA should take a leading role on, whether it should be *hands on*, providing a *guiding hand* to facilitate the development of frameworks, implementation programmes and assuring delivery; or *hands off*, allowing the suppliers just to get on with the job.

EMPLOYEE RELATIONS: THE BIGGEST PEOPLE RISK TO MANAGE

Employee Relations (ER) was one of the top three risks in the early days on the T5 risk register. With a value impact of over £100 million if mismanaged, it was a significant number for the project. Memories of the Jubilee line being brought to its knees by militant action and similar problems with the building of Wembley

Stadium were always a reminder of what poor employee relations could do to damage your project. On ER matters BAA was definitely hands on, although it was always keen to stress with trade unions and the press that ER matters were for the suppliers to deal with, as all of the official work was done with and through the suppliers and never directly by BAA. The architects of the very early thinking in 2000 were Haste and Sylvia Cashman, the ER manager. Haste had bitter experiences of very militant trade unions in the 1970s and his experience of poor treatment of workers on construction sites motivated him to come up with some different people ideas, which required investment and a different approach from BAA and supplier leadership. The ideas on T5 – being a directly employed site, getting a single Major Project Agreement (MPA) for the mechanical and electrical workforce, and really looking at the site facilities differently to demonstrate a new commitment to people – all came from him.

The MPA brought together all the mechanical and electrical suppliers and over the years on T5 kept a united front with the workers and trade unions. Mike Knowles of SPIE Matthew Hall said of the MPA:

> It created harmony of the workforce and delivered some performance improvement through bell-to-bell working and critically and somewhat unusually, no industrial action, better than industry norm attendance and increased pay for workers.

Being critical, the obvious productivity benefits were hard to prove, but the single approach for all suppliers, the trade union goodwill and the common and transparent disputes process that it brought with it meant that the MPA was very much good value.

On T5 the trade unions were engaged from day one. Bob Blackman, National Officer from TGWU, was very clear: 'We felt part of T5 and wanted it to be a success.' During the T5 journey even when there was a dispute, the dialogue was managed either formally or informally through Joint Consultative Forum meetings with trade unions. The Joint Consultative Forum ran for six years, chaired for two years by Haste and for four by Andrew Wolsten-holme, construction director. This kept dialogue going even during tough times and effected some peer-group pressure. T5 definitely benefited from having a strategic relationship with the trade unions, who demonstrated real leadership when T5 was in tight corners, to keep what was one of the best-run sites with the highest standards of employee welfare in the UK working.

To build on the skills of Cashman, I brought in Martin Beecroft and Steve Smith to continue to develop the overarching ER framework; educate smaller suppliers on the need to manage ER matters differently on such a big, interconnected site; deal with the weekly assurance required on pay parity and transparency for all trades; and clearly help to manage the way out of disputes if that position was reached. Tony Douglas, T5 managing director, Wolstenholme and I, as organizational effectiveness director, added to the core ER team quarterly to review progress on strategic issues, and as needed in a dispute. That grouping of people with some help from our key suppliers steered T5 through what is almost a textbook example of how you would want ER to play out on a £4.3 billion construction site.

The formula was reasonably straightforward: the right team of people, key directors, ER experts, key line managers and suppliers, worked well together with the views of all the core team being taken into account. There was a clear strategy, the ER risks were mapped and significant action put in place to mitigate these risks (see Figure 9.1). When in a dispute situation a team was assembled with clearly understood roles to manage pre, for the period of and post the dispute. The BAA Executive was interested in this area and at critical points would sign off the ER mandate. Equally, the City analysts and insurers at the quarterly briefing wanted assurance that employee relations matters were in hand, and they always were.

The strategy and the approach to surface and mitigate ER risks were taken seriously, but also had their lighthearted moments. Each project team spent time with the ER team reviewing their ER risk profile against the workforce's and took this seriously. Equally, after a period of education the commercial team became really valuable eyes and ears and quite adept at assessing supplier ER competence in the tendering process. Picking up any underhand pay-related

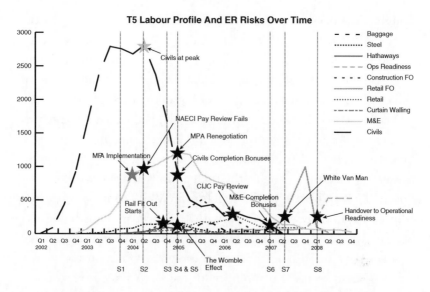

Figure 9.1   Labour profile and ER risks over time.

issues that created disparity in pay arrangements is often what caused disputes; with 20 000 suppliers involved in T5, even if suppliers were willing they needed coordination to ensure that they worked within an agreed framework. On a lighter note, a message came in from Margaret Ewing, BAA group finance director, who was about to show the ER risks to some financiers: 'What is the womble effect that is listed on the ER risk chart?' (shown above). The answer went back: 'When we have trades under ground and over ground that need to be managed!'

At times working with the suppliers was tough. Prior to T5 they had worked individually within construction sites and not across trades. The idea of working within frameworks and not being able to pay just a little more to get out of trouble and keep your workforce going was at odds with 20 years of custom and practice. The ER team was trying to strike a balance that maintained the natural order of pay in or between trades, so that pay terms didn't get out of hand. Following pay audit reviews carried out by Smith, or helpful tipoffs by the commercial team, Cashman would politely get the suppliers in for a chat and engage with them on why they thought they needed to pay their workforce more than was in the National Pay Agreement, and to explain that unfortunately on T5 that couldn't be the case. With the support of senior management very evident, suppliers understood that disregarding these sorts of conversations was just as serious as doing poor work on site.

Disputes were always tense and curiously, part of the strategy was to have a strike at T5, at a time that was least inconvenient and risky for BAA. A strike demonstrated to the City that T5 wasn't buying its way out of trouble, and to the trade unions and site workers that if pushed T5 and BAA would stand firm. While coming very close to disputes on a few occasions, with the most militant being the mechanical and electrical workforce, there was ultimately a T5 strike for seven days among the civil engineering workforce. After intense and long-term scenario planning with the BAA Executive, a mandate was agreed and a successful course of action steered through.

MASLOW'S HIERARCHY OF NEEDS: GET THE BASICS RIGHT

What was very refreshing about BAA on T5 was it followed up the right words 'we want respect for people' with the right investment, and millions went into the basic infrastructure to make the T5 environment safe and user-friendly for the workforce. There were 16 canteens and two mobile catering units, serving up to 22 000 meals a week, starting at 6 a.m. with tea and toast. Bus services transported workers from Essex and Kent, and flight discounts were negotiated for workers flying in from other parts of the UK. Good-quality lockers and shower rooms were provided, as well as a chapel and prayer rooms for non-Christian faiths. While there were always great headlines in the site newspaper on the quality of the facilities, such as 'canteens get a roasting' or articles that were critical of the buses, the reality was that the trade unions were very open about T5 being the best site for staff facilities in the UK. The late George Brumwell, the General Secretary for the Union of Construction, Allied Trades and Technicians (UCAAT), a witty man of great substance and a very real supporter of the T5 Programme, said: 'If employees are moaning about the size of the chip portions then we have a good site, and we're struggling to find things to complain about!'

An occupational health scheme was established with a dedicated on-site health centre, the first of its kind in the UK construction industry. A doctor and seven nurses provided essential medical services such as health screening, pre-employment medicals, treatment and emergency response. Angie Young, who is profiled later in this chapter, was an amazingly warm and larger-than-life Irish woman who saw T5 as an opportunity to reach out to 'an unseen population that normally slips through the healthcare net'. A proactive approach to health was taken, providing regular health-awareness advice and undertaking promotional campaigns, working with organizations like the Health and Safety Executive, Hillingdon & Berkshire Primary Trust, Flora Proactive and safety-glass manufacturer Bolle. Each month for the duration of the construction project, over 1000 workers received a pre-screening medical to ensure that they were fit for work, over 1000 per month visited the walk-in centre with cuts and minor eye injuries, rather than be referred to Accident and Emergency clinics or a GP, and 700 received a version of a BUPA-like health medical. For workers this was symbolic of T5 being different.

When the T5 team got it wrong they admitted their mistake and resolved the issue, as illustrated by David Hunt, T5's head of logistics, who went into the canteens and talked to the workers when they were not happy about the food or buses. Or Jonathan Adams, BAA baggage leader, who for a period of time knew that the baggage workforce were working in less than ideal conditions, and every Friday he went down with doughnuts and had a cup of tea with guys as a thank-you. Ultimately Wolstenholme epitomized treating people with respect: he would always walk a fine line between doing what he could afford and doing the right thing, and took a leap of faith when making the decision that treating a workforce with respect meant that they would be more productive and less militant.

It is alarming to think that men and women earning £40 000 or more working on the tools in most construction sites find themselves being treated badly and accepting third-rate conditions. T5 set a new benchmark on the basic staff welfare required on a construction site, and delivered on its promises. Many of the ambitions outlined in the Rethinking Construction report were actually delivered on T5.

ENGAGE THE WORKFORCE TO IMPROVE PRODUCTIVITY AND ER STABILITY

Once you put the basics in place for your workforce, you earn the right to start trying to get a different level of commitment from them. Most corporate organizations look at how they get 'voluntary, discretionary effort' from their workforce or get them to give that little bit more. In the early days Becky Martin, performance consultant, led this work on T5 for me, and put in place a simple approach that allowed the good work on people issues to fit together. Employee engagement or *employ, equip, engage* was the approach taken (see Figure 9.2).

Employ

BAA wanted to be hands off on these matters, allowing suppliers to manage their own resourcing, but given the size of T5 and the opportunity for suppliers to overlap in the recruitment market, there was a level of coordination that BAA needed to manage. It instituted a T5 recruitment system covering registration of interest, recruitment process tracking, referencing, confirmation of skills and qualifications, signoff on health and fitness to work by the occupational health team and induction.

This system ensured that all those who joined T5 had face-to-face interviews, checks on their right to work in the UK, skills checks and an induction process. This not only gave BAA a better quality of workforce, but also allowed a different working relationship with key government departments. The Home Office and the Department for Work and Pensions are known for doing sweeps at workplaces for illegal immigrants or tax dodgers, but at T5 the

T5 Employee Engagement

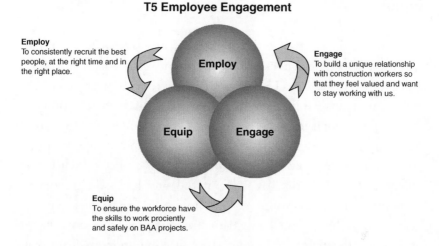

Employ
To consistently recruit the best people, at the right time and in the right place.

Engage
To build a unique relationship with construction workers so that they feel valued and want to stay working with us.

Equip
To ensure the workforce have the skills to work prociently and safely on BAA projects.

It's not just about getting good productivity, but getting that **voluntary, discretionary contribution** and maintaining a **stable ER environment**.

Figure 9.2   T5 employee engagement approach.

relationship was more collaborative. These departments were aware of the processes that were in place to keep the site staffed with legal and well-skilled employees, and in return they visited T5 at agreed times and worked in partnership with the team.

There was also a site-wide approach to managing poaching of employees between companies. The T5 resourcing manager would meet with the suppliers' resourcing managers monthly as a community to share experiences and work together if there were joint problems. The recruitment system did allow suppliers to transfer workers between companies, a functionality used, for example, when resource was being laid off.

Construction is still a very transient environment and indeed for many that is why it is attractive. There is still significant work to be done to change the relationship between the workers and the companies they work for. Laing O'Rourke employs most of their front-line workforce directly, and with that comes a certain degree of job security and benefits. They are the exception that reinforces the amount of change that is still to happen in the industry.

Equip

Once the right people in the right numbers have been recruited
and their references checked, getting them ready to do their job
quickly is critical. For T5 there was one front door that the T5
BAA team managed in a very hands-on way, the induction process
that was run for the 50 000 starters. This was held at Heathrow
Academy and everyone was welcomed to T5 and for a few hours
got to understand the size and shape of the T5 challenge; what was
different about T5; the basics about the site; high-level messages
on safety and the environment; and how they played their part in
helping make history on T5 by delivering the project on time, bang
on budget, to quality and safely. This was important as from day
one a different tone was set for the workers.

These basic messages were then reinforced as they moved to
their individual zone induction before finally being handed over to
the suppliers for company inductions. This approach was another
example of creating a framework, which suppliers engaged in, that
glued the site and its workers together.

Supervisor training was also very important to BAA, and while
at some points there were grand plans to send all site supervisors to
the military training facilities at Sandhurst, since they set the tone
and delivered productivity on site, in reality the release logistics
and costs didn't stack up. BAA did keep a keen overview, or gave
a guiding hand, on all site supervisor training activity, and in the
case of the mechanical and electrical community worked with them
and helped resource a site-wide training programme. Time was
spent by supervisors working on team building, five days on skills
training, plus training on employee relations and diversity. For most
of the supervisors this was their first exposure to such structured
nontechnical development.

Apprenticeship programmes have been encouraged and facilitated
at Heathrow in both construction and retail. Again, BAA has
worked as a guiding hand. In partnership with over 50 construction
companies, the Heathrow Construction training centre has been
open since 2003 and has encouraged over 100 16−19 year olds to

take up apprenticeships in bricklaying, carpentry, joinery, painting and decorating. The retail academy started in 2005 and, working with over 40 retailers, nearly 500 16−24 year olds have or are going through NVQs or apprenticeships

BAA looked ahead at resourcing requirements. For example to open T5 the retailers needed an additional 2500 staff in a sector that had found it difficult to attract staff and then retain and promote them. BAA also understood its commitment to the local communities. It has encouraged construction or retailers to get involved locally and has assisted with premises and helped gain government funding.

Engage

Perhaps the most innovative element of T5 employee engagement was the approach to employee communications, in which BAA was hands on. A team led by Megan Wiltshire from the organizational effectiveness team transformed everyone's views on what was feasible to do on a site with 50 000 people who didn't work for you.

The overarching employee brand on T5 was the 'History in the Making' campaign. The challenge was to try to engender pride in the workforce to bring alive the T5 strategy to the frontline worker. To this end the call to action was to work to make T5:

- Within budget
- Bang on target
- Quality
- Safe

This formed a balanced scorecard that everyone could affect as they went about their work on site and in the offices.

With the lead headline 'History in the Making', comparisons were made to the Eiffel Tower or the Empire State Building and many other iconic buildings of past and present, showing the individuals and teams of workers playing their part. 'One day you'll be proud to say I built T 5' was the message to make it personal.

The award-winning communication and engagement approach that permeated everything on T5 brought together the spirit of the site. The suppliers liked it so much that they paid for use of the brand, and that made the multimillion-pound communication and engagement campaign over the years cost neutral for BAA. History in the making was on the walls in the offices and canteens, on the buses, with huge banners everywhere profiling teams who were within budget, bang on target, delivering quality and focused on safety. It was used in presentations, the '80 by 08' milestone plan was linked to it, and when you walked the site and talked to people they talked about 'being part of history'.

This was a clever communications approach that became more than a campaign, it was a way of linking the big ideas to everyday actions. Wiltshire and Nigel Clarke, the authors of the campaign, really brought some magic to the T5 Programme.

This campaign was complemented by quarterly DVDs that showed the site growing and changing shape, highlighting the key focus for the months ahead, and by the infamous T5 *Site* newspaper, a tabloid newspaper format. This was the paper of choice for many of the workers, and Wiltshire remembers one worker offering to pay for it as she handed them out. The *Site* was a hard-hitting noncorporate magazine that initially BAA corporate and suppliers felt a little uncomfortable about. The desire was for a monthly magazine that was trusted by a cynical workforce, a magazine that picked up real issues for them and at the same time allowed the management messages to get through.

Individual and team 'high 5 awards', supported by little touches like the annual 'extraordinary day', sprinkled goodwill throughout T5. The extraordinary day near Christmas got the senior players out at 6 a.m. with a special edition of the *Site* newspaper and a goody bag saying 'Happy Christmas and thank you for all your hard work this year'. Combined with a free Christmas lunch, tribute bands in the canteen and perfume stalls to allow the mainly male workforce to have a chance of getting a little something to take home to their loved ones, this set a very different tone.

Sports, social and charity work should not be overlooked. There were good deeds done and goodwill created in the local community, but also the employee surveys showed that those who were involved or who took part in charity activities were four times more likely to think T5 was a great place to work. In the quest to keep employees engaged and motivated, this was another example of small initiatives coming together to create a different type of environment.

During the life of T5, a small group of people, initially led by Jonathan Crone, who handed over to Adams, created a programme of social activities spanning sports events such as volleyball, football and 'it's a knockout' to talent competitions, bowling and quiz nights. Thousands of employees from different teams across the T5 Programme got involved.

Good team building and lots of fun were had by all, perhaps no more so than at the annual summer charity ball, organized by Steve Dodds, themed and event managed, involving 500 paying guests, food, entertainment and dancing girls who, normally by the end of the night, would be joined by red-faced directors who just had to go and dance with them. This was all managed by volunteers from the T5 team, and would normally raise over £25 000. It was always a tribute to the spirit of the team and the genuine support of the suppliers.

The charity work in total raised over £300 000 during the T5 project and the charity committee that Adams chaired, of which Wendy Brown and Conni Piper were directors, identified local charities such as the Harlington Hospice; the Bedfont Nursery, whose library was destroyed in a fire and replaced by T5 funding; and the London Air Ambulance, which in cases of safety emergencies had come to the T5 site to help.

TESTIMONIALS: T5'S GUISEPPES

One of the stories that T5 communications told was the true story of Giuseppe Demarco, a man in his 90s who in the 1930s had been a rivet catcher on the construction of the Empire State Building.

His story was how he and his workmates had defied all the odds and built the Empire State Building. There have been so many people on T5 who have made unique and amazing contributions that it seemed appropriate to take the time to share the stories of a few.

Sam Lloyd, stud welder

Sam Lloyd joined T5 working for Laing O'Rourke in August 2003. He led a team of 15 men who installed 232 000 metres of structural metal decking and safety nets, over one million shear connectors and studs, and finished his work in the BA CIP lounge in March 2006. In simple terms, he led the men who once the steel frame had been erected on T5 then installed a metal deck, a permanent shutter that would allow the concrete to be poured to create the floors.

He explained that he had started working as a subcontractor prior to T5 on contracts such as City Point, Moorgate and the Citigroup building over at Canary Wharf, each building 30 to 40 floors high. Each had required him and his team to install approximately 50 000 metres of metal decking, so T5 was a big job. Lloyd, bursting with enthusiasm, told me that he had three children, each with a nickname from his last three big jobs, his youngest George being called T5 as he was born while Lloyd worked on the project and on the same day George Bush touched down at Heathrow in Air Force One.

The difference he made

Lloyd was very clear that there was his life before 13 August 2003 and his life after and the focus on safety. The professionalism of his new company, Laing O'Rourke, and the respect with which he had been treated had changed his approach to work.

Metal decking is viewed by the HSE as a dangerous trade, but Lloyd was proud to tell me that he had just received an email from Ray O'Rourke, the CEO of Laing O'Rourke, congratulating him on five years of no reportable accidents for him and his men, and the clock had started ticking on day one of T5. He was clear that in the early days working in an incident and injury-free way (IIF) was frustrating. 'We all felt like we couldn't get on with the job,' the method statements that were written down had to be right and followed to the letter and this was a culture he and his team were learning to operate in. After about six months working in this way, the team turned a corner and the conversations changed. Men who would have climbed into dangerous places to work started to refuse to do tasks if the site wasn't safe. There was a great cartoon in *Construction News* profiling Douglas being told by one of the workers that he 'was downing tools as it wasn't safe to do the task'. Culturally this was great news for T5, as it signalled that the men and women working on the tools were starting to own their own safety, and to work with management to keep them and their colleagues safe.

The team started to typify what was known as 'safe productivity', as the gang of three men – one setting the stud, one pulling the trigger and deck welding the shear connector to the steel beam, the third testing the quality – increased their average daily productivity from 1000 studs per day to an average of 3500, but who had at a critical handover point managed to deliver 6200 shear connectors per day.

Quality corners were not cut. Every one of the million studs laid was ring tested and 15 % were bent tested. The quality of this work was then independently checked by an engineer at every concrete pour.

Why T5 was different for him

Everything was different. Lloyd was very clear that he and his team were set up for success and treated with respect: 'We were looked after but it actually allowed us to be more productive.' Canteens were good quality and close, and there were cashpoints on site so you didn't lose time doing the basics. Materials were always there on time and the machinery they needed to do their jobs was in place. He said that this had been the only job he done where there were two stud–welding rigs, the guns that weld the studs into the beams. In every other job these have a habit of breaking down and the operatives have to wait for them to be repaired, as other companies tend not to invest the £20 000 to have a spare. That equipment was there on T5 and he never had downtime.

His team did little things to improve productivity, such as taking sequenced breaks rather than all going off for 40 minutes together. So whoever was leading production, be it the operative who set out the shear connectors or the one who pulled the trigger, would set their breaks. Management had not instructed the operatives that they had to do this, they understood the deliverables and worked out how they could execute quite explicit daily productivity rates.

While Lloyd was on T5 I had the pleasure of seeing him and Neil Bolton, stud welding supervisor, in action. Described by Steve Cork, the projects director for Laing O'Rourke, as 'the fastest and safest stud welders in the west', it had been a pleasure to see and chat to a group of men who were extremely proud of their work and knew they were at the top of their trade.

Some of the iconic photographs produced for T5 were displayed in canteens and compounds to everyone visualize the size of the challenge. Lloyd said that he now had one of these large pictures framed and hanging in his dinning room: 'When I pass away from this world my family will be able to travel through T5 and know that their own flesh and blood delivered this terminal.'

Angie Young, occupational health manager

Young has been on T5 since the beginning and many call her the 'mother of the site'. Absolutely passionate about improving the health of the workers on site, she and her team of seven nurses have worked to make a real difference to the lives of men and women on T5 over the years. She said:

> When I first started on T5, managers were suspicious that we would be taking their workers off the job and having nice cups of team with them, and workers thought we were management spies to wheedle out those who were ill and get them off site.

By the time T5 came to its conclusion, this nurse-led team was unanimously viewed by workers, managers, trade unions and BAA as one of the different ways of doing things that had paid dividends for all, and a large part of that was down to the way in which Young and her team went about their job.

Getting involved in construction industry in the late 1980s on the Channel Tunnel, she had fallen in love with construction and saw the possibility to reach out to a group of people, construction workers, for whom healthcare was often forgotten. After leaving the Channel Tunnel Young and her colleague Dr Pugh had enjoyed working together so much they wanted to keep in touch. Young laughs:

Our first cunning plan was to buy a barrel of whisky and let it sit for five years and make sure we came back together to drink it, but neither of us trusted the other not to drink it in the meantime, so when T5 came up, the opportunity to keep working together in construction was too good to miss and more likely to guarantee ongoing friendship.

The difference she made

Young and her team provided a range of services to the T5 site: occupational health, a treatment and emergency response service, a drop-in centre and lifestyle medicals, advice to designers and constructors on how to minimize health risks and a visiting GP service for those who could not easily get to their own doctor. The service was paid for by BAA, but ended up being cost neutral given the amount of time saved by people not having to leave the site to go to get medical help. It was also the case that in the planning inquiry the local community had been partly consoled by the assurance that T5 would not use local facilities, but provide healthcare on site.

Over 1000 workers per month went through pre-screening, those whose jobs might injure others if they suddenly became ill, such as crane operators. Screening looked at cardiac function such as blood pressure, pulse body mass index and vision, and ruled out diseases such as diabetes. Amazingly, 30 % of those seen had health problems, of which 50 % of them were previously unaware. The checks were not about excluding people but rather to help them get their health issues fixed. During T5 fewer than 10 workers were refused access to site because they would not get their problems sorted.

The drop-in centre also saw over 1000 workers per month for everything from minor injuries to routine health problems. Only 3 % of these workers were referred for additional medical advice. The downtime that would have been lost by over 50 000 visits to the GP or visits to accident and emergency was significant and helping keep workers healthy but on the job meant increased productivity. Young remembers a man who for a week turned up at the drop-in centre with a headache:

> Finally he got to see one of the nurses who had been out on site doing a toolbox talk about testicular cancer. He had felt too embarrassed to mention to the other nurses he had a lump, but had felt he could trust the nurse he had met previously. She was able to advise him and get him to do the right tests. That probably saved his life. We don't think he would have done anything about it if we hadn't been doing our job.

With six slots a week to do BUPA-type lifestyle medicals, 700 workers were screened to look at the impact of lifestyle on their health during T5 construction. The workers saw this as a real perk, an indication that T5 was a different type of site. Results from these medicals got Young working with the T5 caterers, Eurest, and changing the menus on site. Cereals were added to the breakfast menu of bacon and eggs, salad bars were introduced in one canteen for lunch and rolled out in all, as the myth that site workers only want greasy, filling food was at least challenged.

Why T5 was different for her

Young's previous construction experience had been about dealing with health after accidents happen:

> On T5 we got the opportunity to be proactive and I believe that helped us save lives, both in terms of workers who were heading for heart attacks, liver cancer and countless other

poor lifestyle conditions that could have led to them being a risk to others.

The focus on safety on T5 was so different that leaders really looked for the root causes of accidents and poor health, getting full management attention and support due to the benefits. This way was so successful that companies like Laing O'Rourke and Morgan Vinci have taken it to other sites. Young explains:

> T5 has been the highlight of my career. I got to work in an industry I love, with people who are straightforward, with no hidden agendas, doing ground-breaking work and seeing it make a real difference to people's lives. My nurses, Dr Pugh who came to T5 once a week, and the part-time physician knew this was a once-in-a-lifetime opportunity.

Young was a 'superstar', a phrase used by Douglas. She had a unique ability to make everyone feel at ease and gain the confidence of people whom society often overlooks and genuinely help them. She was full of fun, but at a moment of great tragedy on T5 it was Young who was at the side of the young man who lost his life in 2005.

Daniel Shipton, electrical supervisor

Daniel Shipton started his working life as an electrician and was at SPIE Matthew Hall for eight years, mainly in the Manchester area, working his way up through warehouses, schools and prisons before arriving on T5. When T5 came along as an opportunity in early 2007, Shipton remarks:

> It was really something special. T5 was an important project in my company, and a big deal in the UK, so getting a chance to do a job that would run right up to the opening was really something.

Daniel was leading a gang of men involved in the pre-commissioning stage of all lighting for the main terminal building. This included the intelligent lighting system, an advanced system that knows when people come into a room and can work typical usage patterns that turn the lights on and off as needed.

In the project the architects worked with Andromeda Telematics (ATL), SPIE Matthew Hall and Crown House to design and produce the lighting control elements of T5. The Crown House team then installed all of the lighting. Shipton and his team went room by room checking the 100 000 lights, ranging from those in offices and roof lighting to the many emergency lights. He commented:

> There are many snags that need to be picked up when you're working at this scale, and that's the role we play, going from space to space and checking everything is recorded correctly, works, and does what it is suppose to do, fixing it if it doesn't. We then hand back to ATL for commissioning to be done. Lights need to work with all the other systems on T5 as well as the people and processes.

The difference he made

T5 has 127 different lighting worlds, each with up to five control panels, which in turn have five gateways, which in turn control 50 lights. Shipton said of this complexity:

> Everything on T5 is so big, 100 000 lights with 75 miles of cable connecting them to the control systems, where do you start? It's a bit like eating an elephant, it needs to be broken down, and that's how the job gets managed. For the team and me we have to deliver 4000 to 5000 light checks a week. I've got a great team, and I trust them, so even if they are at a different ends of the building, I've know what the clear deliverables are for them and they get on with the job.

The lights at T5 are expected to set the stage. Mike Davies, from Rogers Stirk Harbour + Partners, saw them as one of the magnificent features of the terminal. In pictures at the end of Chapter 4, the view into T5 at night shows an illuminated building, but get closer and the intelligent lighting system dims depending on the strength of the sun, saving energy and keeping the environment in T5 pleasant for passengers. Shipton and his team have painstakingly made sure that every light on T5 operates in this way from the start: 'That's our target.'

Why T5 was different for him

T5 is a huge project and getting the opportunity to prepare it for opening has been a once-in-a-lifetime opportunity. 'When I go back to Manchester working in prisons just wont feel quite the same,' said Shipton.

T5 has shown him some different approaches:

> I've never been involved in a project that when I've finished, and the job is commissioned, it all gets turned into three dimensions. Ultra Electronics have created a 3D model of all of the lights, so if there is an issue after opening, the maintenance team are alerted on the panel, and can see what is going on without visiting the site, a real efficiency gain for the terminal.

Finally, for Shipton it's all been about his team, keeping everyone safe and making sure that they deliver on our plan: 'We had the challenge of eating the elephant and each day we came in, we've worked together to take another bite!'

Ryan Kameg, civil engineer

Having graduated with a civil engineering degree from Washington University in 1995, Kameg has been working 'hands on' with track transit systems in Singapore, Malaysia's Kuala Lumpur, Madrid's Barajas, and Dallas Fort Worth airports, among others. He became involved in T5 in 1998, having spent time in the UK working on the track transit system (TTS) at London's Stansted Airport. It made sense to assume the additional workload and pop down the road to Heathrow, to assist the Pittsburgh-based company Bombardier. 'When you're already so far from home, it was just another exciting challenge and a chance to learn,' he said. Later, he came to discover that it was a much deeper learning experience than he would have imagined.

Kameg and his family live in Pittsburgh, PA. Both his father and brother work for Bombardier as well, and all of them have been at T5 more than once over the years. Kameg explains:

> Bombardier is a family-oriented company. My father is a vehicle technician and was involved with training the vehicle technicians at T5 and performing vehicle repairs at T5, and my brother works in sales and marketing and was at T5 during the initial negotiations.

Initially, Ryan worked with the original design teams at Heathrow to integrate the TTS into the overall conceptual design of T5. Bombardier, supplier of the Automated People Mover System, was one of the original first-tier suppliers on T5 along with Mott McDonald for structural design, Crown House for electrical, and Richard Rogers as the main architect. After working diligently with all of the design teams, designing several options and performing value engineering exercises, the TTS was designed and integrated into the complex infrastructure.

The TTS is a dual-track Automated People Mover System (automatic train) that transports passengers between the main terminal building, T5A, and its satellite T5B, and will eventually run through to a future satellite T5C. The initial phase 1 system, running between T5A and T5B, consists of two or three vehicle automatic trains. Each vehicle of the train is capable of carrying 75 passengers. The APM system is capable of carrying over 4000 passengers per hour in each direction. The TTS must operate 20 hours per day, 7 days per week, with a 4-hour shutdown period during the night for preventive maintenance, to keep T5 operating per design.

The unique architectural design of the TTS is a painted dot matrix, created by one of the BAA designers and implemented by Bombardier and its suppliers. This creative style is captured throughout the design of T5.

The difference he made

Like so many people involved in T5, Kameg has devoted a large part of his working career to making the terminal a success. Starting in 1999, Kameg took advantage of this unique opportunity to learn and grow as an engineer. After completing the concept design in 2001, he worked with the other design teams to ensure that all of the unique details of the APM were captured in the detailed design drawings. As the design was being implemented in 2003 into final construction of the TTS tunnels, once again Kameg was there on site working alongside the contractors and ensuring that the unique items required for the APM system were installed so that there would be no need for rework.

In 2005, the infrastructure was ready for the unique installation of the APM trackwork, and the architectural and mechanical fit-out. This installation was unique as it required the expertise of Bombardier personnel as well as the construction management of Balfour Beatty. Kameg, along with his Bombardier colleagues, worked with Balfour Beatty to ensure that the TTS tunnels were complete and ready to accept the APM vehicles, scheduled for delivery in September 2006. Soon after the delivery, the vehicles were ready to be powered, with the first vehicle moved automatically in January 2007, a significant and memorable milestone for the entire TTS team as well as T5. 'The entire design, installation, and subsequent testing of the TTS has been a very successful team effort, one of which I am proud to be involved,' says Kameg.

His background as a civil engineer, the main reason he had been on site, was to ensure that the trackwork (running surface and guidebeam) was installed in a quality manor. This is essential for an APM system, as the trackwork reflects the system's ride comfort and passenger experience. After installation, Ryan inspected and measured the trackwork to ensure that the specified tolerances were achieved so that the vehicles will meet the ride quality standards. However, ride quality cannot be truly measured until the vehicles actually ride on the track, usually a year after the installation. The ride quality of the vehicle is measured by use of an accelerometer placed on the vehicle, which measures the passenger-perceived g forces in vertical and horizontal directions. Generally, during testing one would expect to see recorded high peaks on the accelerometer where the very tight tolerances were not achieved and could not be quantified in actual inspections. These findings must be translated to those areas on the track that require rectification. Because of the attention to detail by the entire installation team, there were no areas that required rectification after running the ride quality tests. Therefore, the ride quality at T5 from day one has been second to none.

Once T5 is operational, the TTS's reliability is an essential key to the functionality of the entire terminal. Therefore it is critical to BAA and Bombardier that the TTS operates to specification 99.5% of the time during its 20-hour operational period. In order to ensure and confirm the standard of reliability and teach the new maintenance technicians how to maintain and troubleshoot the system, a system demonstration must be performed as part of the contract. The demonstration must prove that the system over an average of a 30-day period can meet 98.5% availability during its operational hours. Generally this demonstration lasts up to 60 days due to the inexperience of the new technicians and the breaking in of the new equipment. However, at T5 the system demonstration was completed in 30 days. Kameg commented:

> I don't think that BAA paid extra for the quality of the system, we hit our milestones and cost targets also, but the team wanted the track transit system to be a great passenger ride and experience, a lasting legacy, so the entire TTS Team put every effort into that from day one, and it worked.

Why T5 was different for him

Like many of the early suppliers working on T5, Bombardier was impressed with the idea of the T5 Agreement, but was unsure how it would work in practice. As Kameg explained:

> I've worked all around the world and have not seen the type of teamwork that I've been involved in on T5, and

it started with the customer, BAA and their philosophy. This contact was unique in that BAA assumed all the risks associated with the project, such as currency exchange, non-conformance, or consumer inflation, allowing us to deliver on the contract. We were also challenged by the customer to continuously improve the design and installation to create a world class passenger experience, way-finding, simplicity of the stations, vehicle interiors, ride quality, etc. all contribute to the passengers experience. T5 has been the highlight of my career. Working in an integrated team has allowed me to understand the needs of the other players and companies within such a large-scale project. The teamwork approach allowed everyone to be proactive and pave a clear way to ensure things were done right the first time from day one. It's not been all smooth sailing, there have been a few rough points, but every person involved worked together and wanted T5 to be a success. That is what made the difference.

He added:

Eight years ago after becoming involved with the concept of T5, I never imagined it would take me to where I am now in my career. The people, the teams, the striving for excellence, have all taught me valuable lessons along the way. Things can be done and done well when the drive is there to do it. Although I spent several years away from my family and friends in Pittsburgh, I made a great deal of new friends working on T5. These people were all like a family to me. Now that T5 is nearly complete and I must move on, I will miss but will always remember the people, the friendships and the invaluable experience gained as being part of T5.

SUMMARY

The T5 people agenda was ambitious and proactive, primarily in order to reduce the likelihood of creating a militant workforce that would hold the site to ransom, as in the case of the Jubilee line or Wembley Stadium. However, of equal importance was the desire to try to win the hearts and minds of the workers, get them to be more productive, take quality first time seriously and to work with management to keep themselves and their colleagues safe.

The basic needs of the workforce were understood, such as bussing, canteens, showers and lockers. There were calculated risks taken on significant expenditures where the leaders expected to create a step-change in performance. For example, occupational health could be seen as a overgenerous facility and yet the statistics show that it more than paid for itself, reducing workers' time off the job; over 50 000 health-related visits were made taking an hour, as opposed to losing that number of workers off the job for a day. The workforce felt like they were being respected and that their health and safety were being taken seriously.

An industry that often treats workers badly should not be too surprised if its workforce is not motivated and aligned with company objectives. T5 set a new standard for respecting its workforce and the management verdict would be that it paid dividends.

We're making **history too.**

Just like all those who saw Grand Central Station as the symbol of human and technical achievement it is today, we're making history too. So that in years to come, each of us will be proud to say "I built T5."

(T5) The world's most successful
airport development

Associating T5 with other historically significant buildings

We're making **history too.**

Just like all those who turned the Thames Barrier into the symbol of human and technical achievement it is today, we're making history too. So that in years to come, each of us will be proud to say "I built T5."

(T5) The world's most successful
airport development

Creating pride that T5 people are making history too

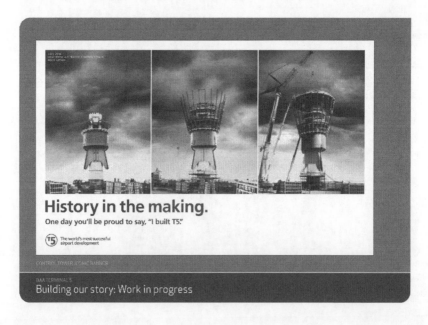

Making T5 Within budget.

Making T5 Safe.

Making T5 Bang on target.

T5 heroes making T5 within budget, bang on target,
safe and quality

Large scale communication programme on site

CHAPTER 10

THE ROLE OF THE CLIENT

A committed, highly involved intelligent client
who over the years has pioneered new thinking
and different ways of operating in partnership
with their supply chain.

Anthony Morgan, Partner,
PricewaterhouseCoopers

R eflecting on the catalogue of UK construction disaster
stories and the few success stories of big projects that have delivered
on time, to budget, safely and exceeding the quality metrics explored
in Chapter 2, it might be easy to vilify the UK construction industry
for not being up to the job. Some of that may be true, however
the proposal here is that at least equal blame for failure needs to be
laid at the door of the client. The client sets the contract, picks the
partner to represent it, or chooses to lead itself. The client decides
what is to be delivered and sets the tone when things don't go to
plan, alongside many other items.

Heathrow's Terminal 5: History in the Making   S. Doherty
© 2008 John Wiley & Sons, Ltd

There are intelligent clients who since the 1980s, like BAA, have been experimenting and learning what a client needs to do to set its project on the road to success. The big retailers have really started to perfect new store builds, some of the housing agencies and oil and gas companies have always led the way in projects of this nature, but there are still too many examples of the client who is a 'one-time buyer' or on complex jobs wants 'lowest-price contracting'.

There are a few interesting areas to explore when looking at the client focus on supplier partnering, such as the approach to contracting when managing risks and opportunities, as with the T5 Agreement and its next generation, and the other strategic frameworks and processes that BAA, as a hands-on client, uses to create an environment that allows leaders and integrated teams to deliver.

T5 AGREEMENT: A GROUND-BREAKING CONTRACT

BAA was very clear that it needed to play a different role to deliver T5 successfully. A number of steps were put in place to allow it to establish the right contract and then make that contract work commercially. Under the leadership of Sir John Egan and Sir Mike Hodgkinson, players like David Hall and Fiona Hammond, from BAA, masterminded the T5 Agreement and the philosophies that underpinned it. The implementation in the main was down to the team involved in construction from 2002 onwards.

Matt Riley was the perfect supply chain director to lead the implementation of the T5 Agreement and the six steps outlined below. He was smart, commercially focused, very pragmatic, absolutely understood the importance of behaviour and wasn't a quantity surveyor. The ability and style of the commercial director are probably critical in this area. However, competence alone would deliver failure. The person needs to embody the spirit of the agreement and work with the supply and project teams to deliver. Riley said that not being a surveyor:

actually lifted me out of the detail and helped me realize that the sum of the parts was greater than individual projects. The key conversations with suppliers in start-up, if challenges appeared or even at the final accounts stage needed to be about the big picture.m This always made it easier as 90–95% of the conversation was on common ground.

There were countless examples of this, but perhaps the most obvious was when the Heathrow air traffic control tower didn't go as expected. For a moment there was a small camp in BAA who started to think about blame and the suppliers were starting to get their legal teams lined up, but Riley was very clear and showed real leadership, along with Andrew Wolstenholme, T5 construction director, to commit to the integrated team approach and get the T5 Agreement working overtime, with the team having to fix the problem not blame each other. Chapter 11 has a case study of the Heathrow air traffic control tower construction.

For suppliers the T5 Agreement created a different way of working. Rather than always having most of their attention focused on managing their commercial position, that effort went into delivering the T5 Programme objectives. Noel Gaffney from Mace explains:

> The T5 Agreement helped suppliers make the right choice, deliver for the T5 Programme without always worrying about the commercial implications. Commercially it was open book, so we all knew where we stood, we were incentivized to perform at exceptional levels of performance, which normally meant having to work with other teams in a more collaborative way, solving problems together and worrying about getting the job finished.

Psychologically, the T5 Agreement seemed for many suppliers to free their minds of worry about financials. Many have said that they knew that as long as they were doing the right thing for the T5 Programme, even if they made a mistake they wouldn't end up in court. That liberated them to focus on what they had trained for, to be great engineers, project managers and the like.

There were six commercial steps that allowed the T5 Agreement to be delivered.

Step 1: Put in place the commercial contract

Even with a regulatory settlement of 7.75 % return on capital, which equated to RPI + 6.5 %, T5, or T5 going wrong, was a significant risk to BAA, financially and reputationally. On the one hand BAA had received a fixed price from the regulator and on the other it had gone into a flexible contract with its suppliers.

Fiona Hammond, BAA legal counsel and one if the founding thinkers of the T5 Agreement, stated that the traditional way of contracting, lump sum and fixed price, was so destined to fail in the UK on something as large and complex as T5 that a burning platform had to be created to 'do something different as it couldn't be any more likely to fail'.

Broadly, the construction industry track record of delivering on time and on budget was poor, particularly in the UK. Think of the Jubilee line, the West Coast Main Line, the Channel Tunnel, the Dome and the British Library. During the 1990s Egan, the directors and their advisers were involved in trying to come up with an approach to contracting that would deliver a different set of outcomes, and for years they explored and piloted many different ideas 'to get match fit for T5'.

Heathrow Express lightbulb moment

The lightbulb moment came after the Heathrow Express tunnel collapse in 1994, and this started to shape the T5 Agreement approach. This crisis got the powers that be to 'throw caution to the wind'; leadership, not legal thinking, came to the forefront. Hammond explains that the key directors at the time wanted to limit the reputational damage for BAA, and getting into a slanging match with key suppliers while there was a big hole in the middle of the airport didn't seem like a smart idea, regardless of where the blame lay. A single team of BAA led by Rod Hoare and key suppliers was formed, and Hammond advised that the ability in a single team to apportion cause and effect is so difficult that it's almost impossible to give away risk. Hence after the Heathrow Express tunnel collapse

BAA, under the leadership of Egan, confirmed to suppliers that BAA would hold the risk and that it wanted the team to focus on problem resolution. Heathrow Express opened on time.

Confidence that there might be another way of contracting started to win favour. In practical terms, key BAA players on T5, such as Wolstenholme, Ian Fugeman, rail and tunnels, Jonathan Adams, baggage, and others learnt about a different way of working on Heathrow Express and this meant that in the T5 leadership team there were people who had experienced a version of the T5 Agreement in operation. At times when implementing the T5 Agreement got tough, having this type of firsthand experience was valuable.

The Heathrow Express turnaround was a large project demonstration that the client holding the risk and working differently with the supply chain could deliver very tangible results as well as tangible added value.

Principles of the T5 Agreement

The T5 Agreement was a legally binding agreement that confirmed that BAA, on a £4.3 billion programme, held most of the risk, with the supplier exposure being loss of profit or insurance excess payments. To build something as complex as T5, the details of which were prone to change in 1998, a subcommittee of key players from the BAA executive needed to agree in principle to move forward with integrated teams and a contract that meant that BAA would hold most of the risk. In the same year the plc board officially ratified those proposals. Suppliers would receive a guaranteed margin that ranged from 5–15% depending on trade for delivering at least industry best practice, and a team incentive plan would be put in place, so that all the suppliers would have to succeed for additional bonuses to be paid if exceptional performance was achieved. The aim was to try to keep money in play rather than paying for risk, which meant that it became dead money once it was built into the suppliers' costings. The approach is outlined in Figure 10.1.

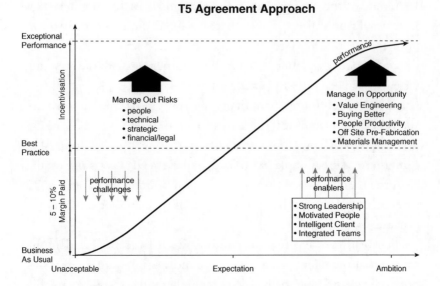

Figure 10.1 T5 Agreement approach.

The contract was based on a few simple principles. It manages cause not effect. It focuses on managing risk and really going after opportunities, and it was a contract that explicitly addressed organizational and cultural issues.

The approach to insurance and professional indemnity

To underpin this contract and allow BAA to manage this sort of risk, both professional indemnity (PI) and insurance policies were taken out. The professional indemnity was the first of its kind that allowed for 'collective negligence'; once a claim had been accepted it would be paid out on a 'no fault basis'. The insurance policy covered about 50 % of the value of T5 with a maximum of £500 million for any single item – for T5 that would have been the main terminal building – against fire or damage to the facility. What was a leap forward was that the financial institutions were also prepared to be open-minded to a different approach. Negotiating both had taken over two years, working with key players, but in December 2001 the details were finalized.

The legal contract, supported by the PI and insurance cover, was now very much seen as a bridge or enabler to deliver improved performance.

Step 2: Understanding and managing supplier motivations

It is fair to say that on T5 it was not until nearly halfway through the project that the senior BAA team really started to step back and think about the different motivations of different parts of the supply chain and think through what that meant for leadership, the contractual arrangements in some instances, and how the supply chain would be motivated to work in integrated teams. During the first half of the project the supply chain had 10–15 key suppliers or consultants who were in the main BAA framework suppliers, so they had a long history with BAA and many had as much to lose or gain on the back of T5. So these suppliers had more 'skin in the game' than the amount they would earn on T5. Moving to the second half, the supply chain landscape started to look quite different, with more suppliers on site, many of them wanting to work in a much more traditional, short-term, transactional way.

The idea of mapping suppliers and trying to understand their motivations and drivers was critical. Riley mapped the motivations of different suppliers and then overlaid the different suppliers on T5 (see Figure 10.2). The result was used to work with different suppliers in different ways; once people's motivations were understood then trying to get the best from them and manage their fears is more achievable.

As the T5 Programme moved into the second half in 2005, the T5 directors spent time at Templeton College exploring the prisoner's dilemma. This is an old theory from Merrill Flood and Melvin Dresher working at RAND in 1950, which Albert Tucker formalized in 1992, and is a gaming theory that looks at whether two prisoners will cooperate to minimize total loss of liberty, or whether one of them, trusting the other to cooperate, will betray him so as to go free. It is a type of nonzero-sum game, where the rational choice

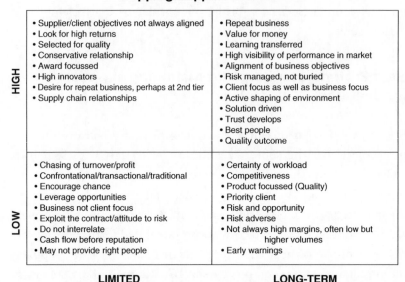

Figure 10.2   Mapping suppliers' motivations.

leads both to defect, even though each player's individual reward would be greater if they both cooperated. When looking at this theory, what became apparent about T5 was that those suppliers with whom BAA had long-term relationships were more likely to see the big picture and trust the other to cooperate, whereas for smaller suppliers the psychology did not stack up, signalling that a more vigilant approach was required. By this stage the T5 Programme report with key performance indicators for all subprojects was well embedded, the cost verification team was up and running, and probably most importantly the leaders were now much more experienced and confident leading such a big programme of work.

Step 3: Partnering to create value

The idea of tendering every time you needed to lay more runway or put in another link bridge was seen as value destroying in an airport environment that is complex and hence took time to learn how to operate in. When it came to T5, the idea of building it with an untested supply chain was an unnecessary and counterintuitive risk to take. Egan was clear that given the long-term spend on construction, BAA needed to find the best suppliers, and work with them to try to develop best-in-class approaches to buying and building so that both organizations could create more value together over time. Given the maturity and track record of the industry at the time and the inexperience of building multibillion-pound projects in the UK, a different role for the client also started to be carved out, a more hands-on, intelligent, facilitating role.

From 1993 BAA had the first generation of framework suppliers, selected partners who were employed to work on shell and core fit-out across BAA when work was required. This started to change the tone of the relationship and also deliver time and cost benefits. In the lifetime of T5 a second-generation framework arrangement was put in place in 2 000, confirming 750 first-tier relationships across BAA, including T5, at the same time as the T5 Agreement was signed.

A rigorous tender process picked up a supplier's quality of service, value management, predictability track record and HSE performance. Once a supplier had been selected to work with BAA, annual 'MOT' reviews would take place, and in the case of those on T5 quarterly key performance indicator reviews looking at performance against very explicit targets that changed over the duration of the project. Some of the suppliers will now have been working with BAA in this way for 10 years and are just about to sign up third-generation supplier framework agreements.

As the T5 supply chain started to assemble, it included over 150 first-tier suppliers that BAA had a contractual relationship with, 60 of significance, 500 second tier, 2 000 third tier, 5 000 fourth tier and 15 000 fifth tier.

Step 4: Supplier performance management

Key performance indicators were measured and given a red, amber, green or purple status. Red represented below par, amber industry average, green best practice and purple exceptional performance. In quarterly supply chain reviews the appropriate project leader and the supplier would sit down and review performance. Monthly subsets of this data were consolidated and shared with the 10–15 key suppliers and reviewed at the monthly principal contractor meetings. The power of peer-group pressure was significant on a project where the reputational impact, with peers both internally and externally, of being seen to let the side down was probably more important than a contract.

For those suppliers who, for one reason or another, didn't deliver to the agreed standard, several lines of action followed. Improvement plans and timeframes were put in place; individuals were coached or ultimately moved off the project if they were not the right people to deliver for their company in the integrated team; and suppliers could be removed. In practical terms suppliers did get paid profit if work was done badly first time; the second time they redid the work and received no profit; and finally they were to redo the work at no cost. No job ever got to stage three. During T5 two first-tier suppliers and about 12 subcontractors were removed from the project.

The approach to incentive on T5 was project team based, encouraging suppliers to support each other to ensure that the overall objectives were delivered. The approach to incentives changed during the journey on T5, as the initial set-up that paid 25% of the bonus when you finished the job and exceeded the targets and 75% at the end of the T5 Programme meant for some that payment could be three years later. BAA needed to create early examples of incentive payouts to build a belief that beating targets was financially in suppliers' interests. In 2003 a new approach was put in place that meant that if exceptional performance was delivered, one third of the incentive went to the supplier, one third to BAA and the final third was held as contingency for the programme. This was paid as each supplier completed their package.

Step 5: Disputes or issues resolution process

Most contracts do not outline how parties are expected to behave when things don't go to plan, except to reach for their lawyer. BAA explained that disputes needed to be viewed as issues, with the objective to have the team resolve their own disputes. If that failed, a meeting of the 'star chamber' was called bringing together the appropriate senior players, from BAA and the supply chain, to resolve matters; if that failed, an independent third-party mediator would be brought in; and only if that failed would matters go to adjudication. All were clear on this being the way in which issues or disputes would be managed. To date when the star chamber has sat it has managed to come to a resolution, and Riley is confident that the final few issues will be resolved without bringing the lawyers in. If that does happen, to spend £4.3 billion with 20 000 suppliers and not end up in any form of formal dispute will be a significant achievement.

Step 6: Accounts closure strategy and approach

BAA closes the final accounts with all of the 60 first-tier suppliers, who prior to sitting down with BAA need to have done the same with their subcontractors. The approach has been to do progressive final accounts and the ambition is that about three to six months after T5 is complete, all accounts will have been settled, with the bulk complete before opening. Given that most performance issues have been dealt with en route, there are few surprises in these meetings as the commercial teams sit down and review performance. Again, at this stage the conversations stay at the sum-of-the-parts level. Take an example conversation: 'Overall, in several work packages, we've spent £200 million with you, 95 % of which has hit all the targets. There are a few areas, however, that we need to talk about and do an appropriate commercial deal.' This pragmatic and mature approach builds on success and narrows the point of difference to a place at which most commercially minded players are comfortable to come to a deal.

THE CLIENT MANAGING AND MITIGATING RISK

Having decided to own most of the risk on the project, the client, BAA, needed to ensure that the right approach was put in place to manage and mitigate that risk, otherwise the commercial approach outlined above would prove flawed. In construction, risk is ordinarily held by the supplier and backed into the costs, hence as a client you pay regardless of whether these risks materialize. In addition, if you do end up in dispute, the normal approach of calling in the claims lawyers and surveyors to demonstrate scope change or some other unforeseen change means that the original contract terms no longer stand. Typically, the cost managers in projects spend their time focusing on 'provisioning for risk rather than preventing risk', explains Lee Stranders, head of risk on T5, and that philosophy works its way through the project.

If you own and hence pick up the bill for risk, you have a very clear motivation to manage and mitigate that risk, hence Stranders and others developed an alternative approach. Risk management was also a concern of the insurance community. Having insured £2.4 billion of T5 risks, they were also keen to make sure that T5 was managing the risks in the way it said it would when signing up the brokers. Dr Terry Mellors was appointed by the insurers and worked for several years on the project to ensure that was happening. During this time he was very challenging and rightly picked up areas in the early days where T5 needed to do better, but he was seen as a key stakeholder and kept very much 'inside the tent', having access to data and being used as a resource to help do the right things to improve risk management.

The early days were not perfect by any stretch of the imagination. The risk process, 'Con 26', was too complicated and the bespoke risk-capturing system, ORCA, was overwhelming. So early on risk was being managed 'despite some of the tools that were in place', remembers Mellors. Good work by Stranders and others put in place a much more straightforward risk process, CP7, moved to Excel risk registers and created a work-shopping approach to get a different engagement.

What is risk management?

Types of risk

There are different types of risks to manage: financial, business, reputation and prosecution risks. The T5 director team reflected on the famous Donald Rumsfeld quote about 'unknown unknowns' after the US and UK invasion of Iraq:

> We know, there are known knowns; there are things we know we know. We also know there are known unknowns; that is to say we know there are some things we do not know. But there are also unknown unknowns, the ones we don't know we don't know.

On T5 this categorization was actually quite helpful, as part of what we needed to do was to open our minds to risk, to think the unthinkable.

These were the sorts of questions the senior BAA players on T5 would review. Stranders facilitated risk workshops in the projects, looking at their risks using a framework that considered categories of risks that fell into 'oh well', which if it happened would be unfortunate but not devastating; 'oh dear', which was starting to get more serious and really did need management focus; and 'oh shit', big stuff that the right people needed to be doing something about if at all possible or be aware of the consequences if it were a risk out of their control. This was a great way to open everyone's minds. About once a year this type of session would be run at T5

Programme level to see if new risks were now understood. This really engaged people differently, and the detail could be built from this framework.

Process and accountabilities

The CP7 process was clear on accountabilities for risk management, the process and measures to deliver. Each team needed to have a risk-assessment plan, risk assessments, live risk registers, control action plans and risk and opportunity dashboards. These dashboards went through monthly dashboard reviews as part of the programme-management cycle.

Risk registers were very thorough and explicit, being clear on the owner, the root causes, inherent risk ratings, current controls or mitigating action in place so far, the residual risk, how the T5 team monitored the risk, the current control rating and additional actions planned. For thousands of risks this approach was mapped and brought to life through review processes and ultimately through people seeing it working. The control ratings were a trigger for escalation: 4 was inadequate control, 3 adequate, 2 optimal and 1 excessive. If a risk within a project was rated at 4 it would be cascaded upwards into the T5 Programme report.

On the ground, risk coordinators were embedded within the teams, and on a monthly basis Stranders brought this community together to ensure that they realized that the work they did was not only important in their projects, but was reviewed at a senior level.

Supported by senior leadership

Once again, the power of senior leaders getting involved, not just in the big picture but also in the detail, really set the tone. Tony Douglas, then T5 managing director, spent time with Stranders and Mellors listening to issues and making sure that all management knew that the risk was to be understood and managed or mitigated on T5. Mark Bullock as the programme assurance director was accountable at the top table for risk. His ability to signal this was important was by putting two-day sessions in the diaries with each of the project heads and their key players to go through their risk registers line by line. This left everyone in no doubt that they needed to be on top of risk management. Stranders also shared another example of where Bullock sat down with the Heathrow air traffic control team as they were getting ready to move the cab across the runway. The team had rated the control rating as 3, adequate. Bullock listened carefully to their plans and sent them away to come back with an optimal plan and stop CYA, 'covering your arse'. The team came back having made almost no changes to the plan, but they put their necks on the line and were committed that they had done all they could to move the control rating to optimal.

Joined-up risk-management plan

BAA had a joined-up approach to risk on T5. At different levels the key risks were understood, quantified, action taken to try to reduce the residual risk and the appropriate reviews and challenge were in place. At the 147 subprojects there were risk registers that rolled up to the 18 projects, which rolled up ultimately to the overall T5 Programme, and a few of these sat on the BAA risk register reviewed by the plc.

STRATEGIC FRAMEWORKS USED TO CREATE A SUCCESSFUL T5 ENVIRONMENT

Given that BAA had decided to be a hands-on client leading a new approach to partnering, it was important that some frameworks and ways of working were established. By mid-2004 most of these tools were in good shape, understood and being used well by most of the teams involved.

As BAA moved into the new millennium, some of the thinking from the T5 Agreement about the ingredients required not only to have a great idea, but to know how to implement successful strategies, really started to gather momentum in BAA. Hodgkinson,

Clasper, Priscilla Vascallin, HR director, and Tony Ward, services director, had created some very robust business frameworks that with modification could be used appropriately on T5.

Organizational effectiveness model

The organizational effectiveness model was a really simple and very systemic way for directors of T5 to look at what needed to be in place from a client perspective. With his Procter and Gamble background, Clasper was instrumental in ensuring that robust thinking was carried out, and there was a clear, if simple, line of sight between BAA corporate thinking and what was implemented. Although Anthony Morgan from PricewaterhouseCoopers said that 'clients often try and shoehorn corporate processes into projects', Clasper was challenging people to identify why T5 needed to be different from the rest of BAA, while at the same time being pragmatic and understanding of it being a different environment than an airport.

This framework looks at the different levers that have to be put in place and pulled appropriately to deliver success. The business strategy, processes, organizational structures, values and people were all included (see Figure 10.3). Most senior managers in BAA were quite able to think about T5 in this way, and hence were receptive to this way of working. The T5 organizational effectiveness team, the team that I led containing OD consultants, communications and HR professionals, worked closely with the key directors in helping facilitating many of the elements of this framework. The really critical point with this type of approach is working out not what needs to be done, but the most appropriate order to do it in.

Annual OGSM

OGSM, standing for objectives, goals, strategies and measures, was an annual process used in BAA to set the three-year direction and

Organisational Effectiveness Model

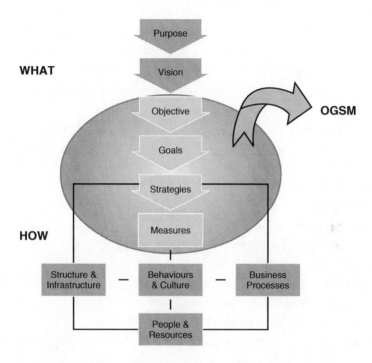

Figure 10.3   Organizational effectiveness model.

annual focus. Each year the measures and deliverables changed and a simple one-pager in layperson's language was made ready before Christmas, involving the top 20 key players in T5, and then rolled out in January of each year. The T5 Programme OGSM was the hook for each team to focus on what they then needed to do to deliver, and quarterly the T5 directors would take some time to review progress collectively.

Added to this, the monthly T5 Programme report and the strategic monthly deliverables meant that measures were visible and kept on track. The OGSM was shared with the senior supply chain and all the BAA teams' rewards and recognition directly related to the deliverables and measures it identified.

Structure and governance

Structurally, T5 was allowed to operate as a standalone business with the appropriate governance. This enabled it to break loose of corporate culture and find a new way to operate, while leveraging the resources and wisdom of the companies involved in a way that start-ups often don't benefit from.

Fundamentally the operating model for T5 was to have:

- A client role, led by Mike Forster, development and design director, ultimately becoming director, strategy, BAA.
- A build role, led by Wolstenholme, ultimately becoming director, capital projects, BAA.
- An operational readiness role, led by Bullock.

Douglas, then ensured that each part worked together to deliver the OGSM, and the support functions acted as a glue operating across the teams in a matrix structure (see Figure 10.4).

There were 300 BAA people at peak on T5 who played several roles, as well as the principal contractors with a shared accountability

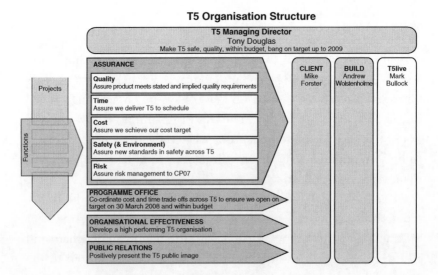

Figure 10.4   T5 Organization structure.

for safety on site, along with Laing O'Rourke, Mace, Balfour Beatty, Morgan Vinci and SPIE Matthew Hall, and team leader roles where most of the BAA people were embedded in teams working for or alongside team members from different companies. Some critics may say that this was a large client organization, but it is to be remembered that the client in this instance had multiple roles. BAA believed that this would allow it to identify and manage risks and opportunities at all levels of the programme, and it made it more difficult for bad news not to travel fast, so T5 could put the right resource on the job to fix a problem before it got out of hand.

At peak some 8 000 people were on T5 from all the different suppliers; 1 000 people joined and left each month as the terminal went through the different phases, so as a result at least once a year there would be a standback review of the objectives and structure. Once the macro approach was set with the key senior T5 players, the embedded performance consultants from the organizational effectiveness team worked with the key project and business leaders to reshape their teams to align with the next phase of the T5 Programme, or as was often the case, to try to reduce the costs of knowledge workers.

Governance and management forums

The management and governance forums were put in place, and again evolved once a year. Governance forums focused on the 'what issues': they took decisions on and about the brief, gathered stakeholder issues, signed off the budget and assured the delivery. Management forums took care of the 'how issues' or how the agreed scope would be delivered (see Figure 10.5).

Governance was simplified and cleaned up from the early days. Douglas's authority to spend was moved from £30 million to £500 million by the plc board. When the number of times the plc board would need to sit to sign off the amount of spend involved was reviewed, the number required was practically impossible at the

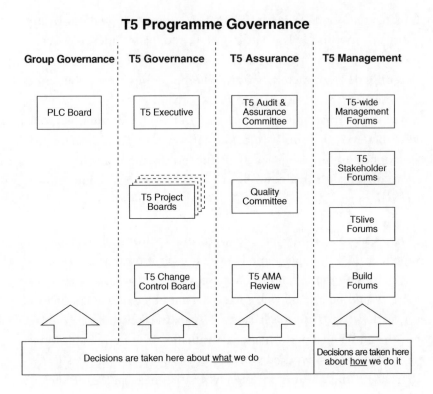

Figure 10.5   T5 Programme governance.

previous level. This was also a reflection of the strong relationship between Douglas and Clasper, described in Chapter 8. It was also the case that two plc board members, Clasper and Margaret Ewing, group finance director, sat on the T5 Executive to ensure the plc that the money as it was drawn down was spent wisely.

Initially the T5 executive could sanction up to £30 million spend, and each of the project boards, for example rail and tunnels or buildings, could sanction up to £1 million spend. The role of those involved in governance was not to manage, although this was always a tough discipline to instil. The development team, the client team lead by Forster, managed this process incredibly well for seven years.

The management forums were integrated forums, where key suppliers came together with BAA and reviewed performance against targets, discussed future delivery challenges and how they would work together to deliver. Wolstenholme and Douglas were outstanding at creating common agendas and getting the best out of the integrated supply chain. The contractors valued the openness and clear structure, and the fact that there were places where information would be shared and genuine debate could take place. The senior T5 team was very candid in these meetings about divulging key data that was shareholder sensitive, working on the basis that they needed the key contractors to share the challenges and work with them, which they did.

Clear individual accountabilities

As a leader Douglas strove for clarity and simplicity wherever possible and the determination he demonstrated on such a large programme typifies the focus with which he operated.

As the structure changed, accountabilities were reviewed and a very pointed approach to where the buck stopped was put in place for the top 20 BAA players, and again cascaded down within the integrated teams. The key questions for all key players were:

- What they were accountable for.
- Who would be held to account if something went wrong.

The key players found the structure straightforward and it left everyone very clear on what they had to deliver. The level of competence on T5 was high: at peak about 60% of the BAA resource, when not force ranked, hit a highly effective plus performance rating. With this much talent people needed clarity and were not worried that they wouldn't deliver. It is also the case that the strength of the team culture was sufficient and the environment genuinely supportive, so that when colleagues were faced with difficult challenges people went out of their way to help each other, rather than gloat if people were failing. This was an environment that if one failed, all failed, so sitting on a problem or not asking for help was a big issue.

Processes: The highway code

In the early days BAA had fallen victim to people who had nothing to do during planning permission apart from creating too many complicated processes. Prompted by the insurers' representative, Mellors and Forster led a team from across the project cleaning up all of the processes and creating 10 core processes that were user-friendly, supported by current management and rolled out with an attention-grabbing communication campaign across the T5 Programme. These were then held on the T5 intranet so that updates could be managed easily. Figures 10.6 and 10.7 give the details.

Culture and values: Teamwork, commitment and trust

The T5 Agreement was at the heart of the culture. This large document was digested and turned into a few simple pages, with teamwork, commitment and trust as the values all needed to live by. These were at the centre of the approach to integrated teams,

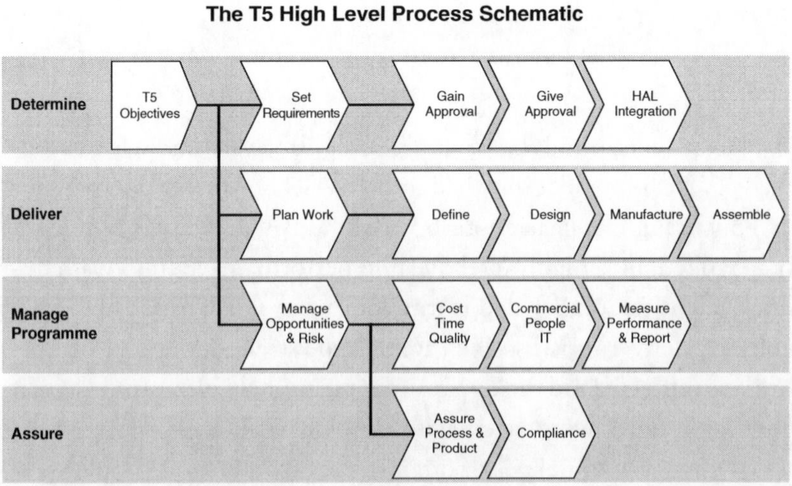

The T5 High Level Process Schematic

Figure 10.6 T5 high-level process schematic.

T5 Ten Core Processes

Determine		Project Approvals Process (CP01)
		Stage Approvals Process (CP02)
		Change Management Process (CP03)
Deliver		Execution Planning Process (CP04)
		H&S Responsabilities & Appointments (CP06)
Manage Programme		Commercial Management Process (CP05)
		Opportunity & Risk Management (CP07)
		Cost Management Process (CP08)
		Schedule Management Process (CP09)
		Performance Measurement Process (CP10)

Figure 10.7   T5 ten core processes.

underpinned the approach to contracting and were evident in most of the individuals, teams and suppliers who signed up. At the very big crunch points such as Heathrow air traffic control not going to plan, these were the core principles that governed the response.

People and resources

There are two people stories that need to be told. First, the employee engagement approach used to galvanize the 50 000-strong workforce to play their part in making T5 a success. This is picked up in Chapter 9 in detail. The second story is the approach to both BAA and other key knowledge workers that was a key to the success of the T5 Programme, and that will be explored here. The right team needed to be gathered and retained, and this integrated team, working in a market with a poor track record of attracting the best talent, needed some different nonconstruction ideas to be brought to the table.

At BAA the culture had been a job for life, and those employees who had done a good job on £10 million to £50 million projects were often given an opportunity to move up to multibillion-pound projects. In the early days this approach, while honourable, was misplaced, given that BAA had declared itself a hands-on client.

A robust approach to talent management for BAA and key players from its suppliers was put in place and once Douglas had been recruited, as the organizational effectiveness director I was able to go around the world and out of the industry to get the best in class into T5 to complement some of the world-class talent that was already there: multibillion-pound construction experience was found, heavy hitters from design and engineering, programme management experience from the car industry, commercial resource from the utilities, logistics experts from retail and the army, organizational development experts from the consultancies, among many. In total a 300-strong BAA team formed, all technically first rate and most importantly able to work in integrated teams collaboratively.

Senior recruits were assessed using the Bioss levels-of-capability tool, and their performance and potential were reviewed quarterly, ultimately with the key directors on T5. As the programme moved through the different stages, this resource was retained by continuing to develop their roles on T5, broadening the scope by working across other parts of Heathrow and BAA, and then coming back to T5 if they were needed.

The top 500 players for suppliers were just as important. The critical job roles at the suppliers needed to be filled by the best person, and it was important that suppliers used the highest talent. Once in place these people performed, and then left the project at a time that worked for both parties. An organizational effectiveness resource, using simplified BAA talent frameworks, identified key roles and talent and then rated that talent with line managers. In the early days I spent time in the key suppliers reviewing their talent with their HR directors, MDs and projects directors. These discussions were a real mark of the trust between organizations. I was always very sensitive that resource that wasn't right for T5 wasn't bad resource, just a poor fit for the T5 environment, and the key suppliers showed a huge commitment to work differently on something this sensitive. As the project progressed this process became embedded and the demobilization of key resource was managed against agreed principles. Laing O'Rourke in particular supplied more management resource than their core brief, Richard Rook in safety leadership, project leadership resource, logistics expertise and Andy Anderson in master planning, to name but a few. This was partly because they had some great people and also because their commitment to the success of T5 was second to none.

Message management

Both the external messages managed by the external communications team, led by Jon Phillips and latterly Ben Morton, and internal communication, for the first few years led by me, were powerful tools that the leadership team spent time reflecting on and were masters at deploying. Internal communications are reviewed in more detail in Chapter 9, but it is fair to say that all the 50 000 people on T5 knew that they were part of a history-making project and all had a sense of the size and shape of what they were involved in. More importantly, the message of being on time, to budget and delivering a quality programme safely ran through the buildings, the channels and all of the verbal messaging.

The external media were embraced, an issue that is again explored further in Chapter 9. Douglas, Forster, Wolstenholme and Bullock were well trained to deal with friendly and not-so-friendly press, and a programme of media interviews and site visits was managed against all of the key milestones. The key leaders were comfortable in front of the media, knew their subjects and were able to explain quite technical things in a big-picture way. Douglas in particular was the master of key statistics. The phrase 'If T5 delivered to industry standards it would be a year late, a billion over budget and kill two people' came from him, along with the idea of the 'project moving into the second half' and countless other ways of framing T5 in a way that took the internal or external audience on the journey.

One of the favourite press events has to be the topping-out ceremony to mark the roof raising being complete. Picture a building site with Alistair Darling, then at the Department for Transport, who has always been a good friend to the T5 Programme, Clasper and Douglas, all doing speeches in the main terminal building in front of about 1 000 construction workers, and to the right of the stage a full-size brass band bellowing away with all the players in high-visibility gear and hard hats. The handover of the twin rivers, the airside control tower plus other notable events, all were programmed in to gain the most positive coverage possible.

Reactive press management was always dealt with professionally and with comment. In the early days particularly as the team managed the employee relations challenges on T5, many of the suppliers wanted to revert to a 'no comment' position. This was discussed with them, and where they lacked resource or capability, the BAA communications team acted as their press team. Antonia Kimberly over the years proactively and reactively dealt with thousands of queries and planned hundreds of articles to ensure that the right message was put into the market.

As BAA and BA prepare to launch T5 there will be three openings: the official opening by the Queen that will take place close to but before the actual opening; the first day of operation, 27 March 2008; and a number of big events on Saturday 29 March, which currently look to include the Olympic torch passing through T5 and the National Lottery being broadcast from the terminal.

The senior team really understood the positive or negative reputational impact of managing the media and the internal motivation that came from a team being associated with a successful project. While Wembley Stadium got more press coverage for the wrong reasons, the media were always trying to get a negative angle on T5. Across the eight years of the project the communications team and the key leaders were always clear on the message and very able in their presentations to the press.

THE IMPACT OF THE T5 AGREEMENT

What was delivered by the client?

As an intelligent client BAA, under the guidance of its CEOs and ultimately the leadership of Douglas, Forster, Wolstenholme and Bullock, had the big idea that the T5 Agreement ultimately meant that with a 5% contingency risk they could deliver T5 on time and to budget. The safety record at T5 is industry beating, and the ultimate passenger experience has been delivered that will put the glamour back into flying in the UK and give a glimpse of what the new Heathrow could potentially look like.

It is impossible to prove that without the T5 Agreement the T5 Programme would not have been delivered successfully. BAA stands firm on the agreement being a critical ingredient and this is backed by industry experts such as Sir Michael Latham. Richard Williams, lead construction underwriter at Swiss Re, commented:

> Although it is difficult to measure the cost benefit of using the T5 agreement – that is, the actual cost of getting it right versus the hypothetical cost had it gone wrong – benchmarking against other projects of this size and nature strongly supports my belief that the investment in the T5 Agreement made by BAA has been more than repaid in full. The successful delivery of a T5, Heathrow is something that BAA and indeed the construction industry as a whole should be proud of.

What was different?

The ground-breaking contract

Fundamentally the T5 Agreement contract set a framework that tried to bring the best out of the client, the suppliers and the integrated teams, all of whom had a common objective and opportunities to succeed. The client had a clear role to manage risk and set up an environment that would enable the T5 Programme to be a success.

Suppliers received a fair reward for their efforts, as well as the opportunity to be associated with a successful mega project that proved lucrative for ongoing work with BAA and other clients. The teams of engineers and project managers were actually paid to do what their training had prepared them for, rather than always second guessing the commercial impact of decisions. That's why for so many of those involved this was one of their best and most rewarding jobs.

The lack of lawyers and litigation

T5 even at its peak had one lawyer, Fiona Hammond, who left in 2005 and was not replaced. To date there has been no external mediation required and Riley is optimistic that the project will be closed out without this.

Leaders taking risk management seriously

The approach to risk management is probably not matched in other environments. Insurers' representative Mellors was complementary: by the time he left he said, 'The risk process and its day-in, day-out implementation as a management tool to manage and mitigate risks was some of the best I had ever seen in my mega project experience around the world.' The client as the owner of risk genuinely engaged and got the integrated teams to assess risk and plan to mitigate it. In practical terms the decisions to do a dry-run study for the main terminal roof or the amount of off-site prefabrication were taken with risk considerations very much at the forefront of the thinking.

BAA was a hands-on client

A framework was created that enabled the developing UK construction industry to come together in integrated teams and perform. A different tone was set, whether through the approach to managing programme management, as discussed in Chapter 5, or the operating model, approach to governance, people and so on. BAA was in a situation in which failure could be reputationally devastating, and so it put its best team on the job and allowed them to do what was required to be successful.

Key learning

Getting the spirit of the T5 Agreement to penetrate to subcontractors took longer than was anticipated. Initially BAA worked with the 60 first-tier suppliers and left them to engage with their subcontractors. As time moved on and the basics were in place with the key players, the BAA team started to engage with the subcontractors directly and realized that they were not being managed as had been expected. A standard subcontractor contract was created by BAA and key players, partly for assurance and partly to manage risk, as some of these subcontractors were involved in areas critical to the success of T5. The subcontractors also found that this made them feel part of the T5 experience, so for example for Corus, which was involved in providing steel to 34 different sub-projects worth up to £150 million, or for Babcock, which built the mechanical and electrical modules, BAA ensured that sufficient time was spent with them and others.

Those at T5 ultimately learnt to balance collaboration with tough commercial decisions. At the beginning there were myths that you couldn't have tough conversations within the T5 Agreement. However, through phrases such as 'tough love', vigilant trust' or even 'it's our money so we will make sure it's being spent wisely', with the right BAA team and a focus on performance management, a good balance was reached.

As BAA looks forward to Heathrow East, the UK construction industry has matured and the key suppliers who have worked with BAA for over 10 years have now, with guidance or personally, developed more structured and innovative ways of operating. As BAA goes forward with its third generation of suppliers, the client role will get smaller and 13 complex-build integrators will step forward. Names such as Laing O'Rourke, Balfour Beatty and Mace will now take on more responsibility and a first-tier supply chain across BAA of 750 companies will reduce to 90, including consultants. BAA's approach to contracting will focus on commodity items and complex or large projects. For the next large project, Heathrow East, BAA will hold the complex risk, but not all of the risk. Time will tell how this unfolds.

SUMMARY

Most of those involved would acknowledge that BAA has been an intelligent client over the years. The ability to stand back and look at industry trends and think through how to develop a contract such as the T5 Agreement, and to be able to use that contract to facilitate a successful outcome with stakeholders and an integrated team on something so large and complex, is to be commended.

With the commercial contract in place, which drives problem solving not litigious behaviour, BAA then set out to put the right approach to organization, processes, people and governance in place. It has been ready to challenge industry thinking on these matters, but flexible and open-minded enough to adapt, or even start again, when looking at items such as risk management or financial reporting in order to get an approach that works in the T5 context.

CHAPTER 11

INTEGRATING TEAMS TO DELIVER EXCEPTIONAL PERFORMANCE

At times it felt like we were a band of brothers ... all for one and one for all ... as we tried to meet our targets.

Peter Emerson, chief operating officer, Severfield-Rowen

The focus for much of the leadership and client focus was putting everything in place to enable the integrated team to have the environment and tools to be able to do the best work they could. Working in integrated teams was one of the cornerstones of the T5 Agreement, and was a fundamental ingredient to the success of T5. Consultants and suppliers, in return for a guaranteed margin and access to an incentive scheme, committed to working in integrated teams alongside BAA. This approach extended beyond the design and build phase of T5, and included BAA in conjunction with BA working in a similar way all the way through.

Integrated teams are not the normal way of doing business for those familiar with the world of fixed-price and lump-sum arrangements. Outside T5 many clients, consultants and suppliers typically form different teams and deliver their own work package using resources from that company only. When companies did need to work together to deliver for example design and construction, individuals work in separate teams and come together at key times for meetings to manage handovers.

Integrated teams aren't the only way of operating, but on something as large, complex and running for so many years as T5, the idea of teams not working in this way seemed almost impossible to coordinate and deliver successfully. It was also seen on many occasions that individual companies just did not have sufficient resources, or even skills, to tackle some of the scale of the challenge or at times some of the technical expertise, and if left to operate under normal arrangements delivery would have been suboptimal.

The values outlined in the T5 Agreement of 'teamwork, commitment and trust' were easy words, but at times extremely testing in their delivery. There were some teams who never made the full transition to working that way, and for others significant management time was put into getting the team to be integrated and work effectively. At the simplest level there were three types of team set-up on T5, which delivered with quite different levels of effort and probably success:

- Traditional teams, with just one company working in them. For those work packages that could be delivered in a more traditional manner, the philosophy was to let people do what comes more naturally.

■ Inter-team working looked at teams coming together to deliver against a specific project, for example the twin rivers project or T5 satellite. During the phases of set-up, ongoing and close-out, this team type worked as a tight-knit unit regardless of the companies its members were drawn from.

■ Intra-team were the points where interdependencies overlap, such as the interchange plaza, where the surface access routes meet the terminal, rail and substructure, and multiple team elements had to come together to deliver. Within the T5 matrix structure, teams like the commercial team or the development team worked across teams, along with systems that as a team interfaced across all projects. These teams worked both centrally and deployed in projects. The not-invented-here syndrome made this type of team working much more difficult.

In 2004 when the T5 organizational effectiveness team did one of its annual employee surveys across the total site, 61% of people said that they could not rely on other people to deliver on time, while 76% trusted their own team members. This didn't surprise us: it's pretty much human nature that most people like to be in control of their own destiny and not be dependent on others. Many of the 300 BAA people involved on T5 found themselves facilitating either inter-team forming, norming, storming or performing; enabling interfaces between teams; or deploying T5-wide expertise. The organizational effectiveness team did employ performance consultants, typically with a background in consulting from PricewaterhouseCoopers, Accenture or PA, who would come and be embedded within teams where they would be used by senior project players either to assist in the establishment of teams or, if teams got into trouble and needed some help, to enable better cooperative work. The T5 team developed a 'winning teams' toolkit and along with the commercial team would try to educate and support people on the 'what' and 'how' of working together.

Half way through the project as the integrated team working became more challenging, in particular looking at the interfaces between buildings and systems a step change was required to gain momentum. Over a six month period over 150 of critical team players took over a week out to look at the task in hand and how there could be a 'breakthrough' in teamwork, to deliver a break through in performance. A very talent facilitator Miki Walleczek was brought in to work with the team. One of the great phrases that came from these sessions was about 'are you on the pitch or in the stands'. As there had been a real sense that some players were not engaging. It's always difficult to really assess the impact of interventions. There was however a real management belief that they needed this type of intervention, they were actively involved in the identification of a partner and were committed to the approach. In the mix it was another example of understanding the team issues and taking quality time out, as integrated teams, to discuss how to work together to deliver 'breakthrough'.

One of the more intriguing aspects of working in integrated teams was that most of the time, apart from the people you knew well, you were never completely sure what company the person you were talking to came from. Quite often you would hear companies talking about their people 'going native' and even having to retrain them in the more traditional contracting ways after their collaborative days on T5.

CO-LOCATING, THE 'BEST MAN FOR THE JOB', PROBLEM SOLVING AND INNOVATION

In practical terms the integrated teams approach included co-locating teams, and ensuring that they had the 'best man for the job'. This meant having people work in the spirit of problem solving, not protecting their company interests, as they try to deliver, at a minimum, industry best practice while striving to achieve exceptional performance. The commercial terms set out in the T5 Agreement, with BAA holding the risk and incentivizing team performance, enabled this way of working to operate

The plan required different companies to co-locate either at Longford House, the headquarters for T5, or out on site in one of the seven or eight compounds that housed all of the teams for the six years of construction. At times some of the designers or functions were not fully on board with idea of going out to work on site, parking the car and then getting on one of the buses that moved 8000 people around the site most days. However, once embedded in their specific team, many of these players found that they were more connected to the team challenges and actually enjoyed the experience. We saw this with designers on projects such as the roof or the airside road tunnel, where they started to comprehend the challenges faced by the team and deliver their design solutions with an understanding of cost, time, safety or quality needs.

'Best man for the job' meant just that: the person who had the best leadership or technical skills to deliver the project objectives. Whether the project required commercial, risk or programme management resource, this would be provided from those companies, or BAA, best positioned to provide the highest-calibre or experienced people, thus avoiding organizations making do with what they had. Getting companies to deploy their best resource on T5 at first was counterintuitive. Typically in the industry, suppliers put their best resource on projects that are losing money. T5 became such a rich experience that suppliers rotated their best players in to get the experience. Noel Gaffney from Mace talked of 'the best and brightest graduates being put on T5 to allow them to experience the unique environment and then take that learning to other parts of the industry'.

This resulted in companies like Laing O'Rourke providing production leadership for projects like the roof or T5 satellite, even though this was not core to their delivery. Often at first relationships would be a little strained, but as people worked on their objectives and put together their delivery plans, differences would pass and the focus would go into the task at hand. The performance of the key 500 supplier roles was reviewed by BAA twice a year, more regularly if there was a problem. Douglas, Wolstenhome, Forster, Bullock and I would review the data and take action. The project heads or managers from BAA would oversee team selection, at times being very hands on.

Moving people on if after support they didn't make the grade was a reality. Also, when certain gaps or opportunities arose, we looked outside to gain access to that experience, such as in the rail environment where BAA brought in EC Harris, and with some of the central programme management functions to get extra focus on commercial and process improvement opportunities. In the main, companies that needed to provide resource to support other parts of the programme stepped up, and those companies who either asked for specific resource, or who found themselves in conversations about company skill gaps, took advice in the spirit in which it was intended. T5 became quite a competitive environment: teams didn't want to fail against their time, cost, quality and safety objectives. Hence if helping hands were needed at specific times, that was a small price to pay in order not to hold up another team because you were late, and companies took the resources that were offered.

Co-locating and 'best man for the job', supported by the T5 agreement and all the other enabling mechanisms that BAA put in place, then set the scene for people to solve problems or see different opportunities that would allow their work to be industry best practice or exceptional. Mike Knowles from SPIE Matthew Hall explained:

Things go wrong on big projects and what BAA was able to do working with the suppliers was create an environment where in the main people tried to do the right thing for the success of the overall T5 Programme. If there were scope gaps between teams, people worked together.

WHAT DID THE TEAM STRUCTURE LOOK LIKE?

The operating model for T5 was to have one T5 Programme, led by Tony Douglas, T5 managing director, who ultimately became Heathrow CEO. Then there were three core parts to that programme:

- An expert client role, led by Mike Forster.
- A build role, led by Andrew Wolstenholme.
- An operational readiness role, led by Mark Bullock.

Functions worked across the core parts and were also embedded within each area.

The build in detail included:

- Infrastructure, led by Rob Stewart.
- Rail and tunnels, led by Ian Fugeman.
- Buildings, led by Russel Batchelor, who handed over to John Milford.
- Systems, led by Nick Gaines.
- Baggage, led by Jonathan Adams.

The 18 projects listed in Chapter 5 sat beneath the four project heads, and there were 147 subprojects, ranging from £2 million to £300 million, that sat beneath the projects. The overall structure is outlined in Figure 11.1.

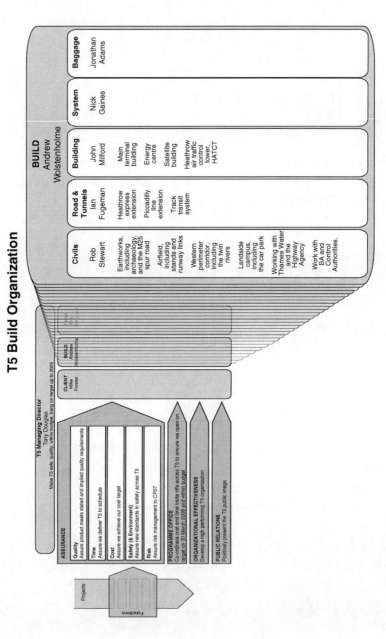

Figure 11.1   T5 build organization structure.

TEAM TESTIMONIES

Every team on T5 has a unique story and in different ways all have played their part in delivering the terminal. There are some that are worth highlighting as they signal the way teams of people from many different organizations did come together to deliver and on many occasions had to get back on track when things didn't go to plan.

Twin rivers

The western perimeter corridor, or the 'twin rivers' as it became commonly known, was perhaps one of the more controversial projects on T5. It was part of the infrastructure group of projects led by Rob Stewart. This set of projects included all of the airfield work comprising 700 000 square metres of high-technology concrete pavement; 62 new aircraft stands; earthworks that included managing all earth being dug for substructures and earth used for backfill; archaeological clearance; compounds; site roads; building the 4000-capacity car park with looping access ramps; landscaping; and the twin rivers, which also included redirecting the western perimeter road.

The Longford and Duke of Northumberland rivers originally ran between the main terminal area and the satellite building. Both rivers have a long history. The Longford River, which is owned by the Crown, was built in 1638 by Charles I to feed the fountains at Bushy Park and also to take water to Hampton Court. The Duke of Northumberland river, which is owned by the Environment Agency, was extended by Henry VIII in the 1540s to divert water from the river Colne to feed the river Crane and royal residences at Syon House.

The twin rivers project included diverting these two rivers to the west of the main terminal building and diverting the western perimeter road east, while keeping it open, to make way for the rivers, which would now end up on the western boundary of Heathrow. Each river diversion was 3000 metres long, most of which was open channel – that is, not in pipes – with approximately 60% of the length requiring concrete walls, the remainder being grassy banks. This had to be an environmentally responsible diversion, delivering an 'equivalent or better habitat' for wildlife, if it were to meet planning permission parameters.

Key players

The project involved from BAA Phil Wilbraham, Steve Bridgen from Laing O'Rourke, production leader Black and Veatch, designers KBR, landscape company HED, Environment Agency, Royal Parks Agency, river owners and consenting authorities. This was a co-located, integrated team, including key stakeholders.

Key risks

One of the last issues to be resolved in the T5 planning inquiry was the twin rivers diversion. While getting permission was probably inevitable, for those involved at the time it didn't feel that way. As time ticked by, the risk to a March 2008 opening was always in the balance, as moving the twin rivers was on the critical path and had to be completed by 4 May 2004.

There were three designs for the twin rivers, including the final solution, which worked out how the rivers that ran north to south on the site, between the locations for the main terminal building and the satellite, could be moved. Initially a very cost-effective solution of building pipelines for the two rivers under the proposed development and allowing them pretty much to continue on their original line was rejected. This was replaced with the idea of moving the two rivers to the location they sit in today, but in a single channel. As the team investigated further, it became apparent that the ecological impact of a single channel was not feasible, as one river was higher than the other. Finally, the western perimeter corridor solution was settled on by all parties, but with two separate channels. All of these design decisions were completed while eating into the time on the project's critical path.

The key relationships with both the Royal Parks Agency and the Environment Agency formed an ongoing risk that needed to be carefully managed. While BAA had earned the right to move forward, there were more than 20 consents en route that had to be signed, and all of the time the team had to show the agencies that the fine words and promises were a reality. All through the design process the team worked closely with the agencies informally; there were also formal monthly meetings that were minuted to give the agencies assurance that issues logged did not get lost and were moved forward.

Twin rivers deliverables

The deadline when they started the project was 4 May 2004 and the team delivered two weeks ahead of programme.

The western perimeter corridor, including the roads, and a number of other small projects resulted in a cost of £84 million, so the team was £4 million under budget. This was due to the team sticking rigidly to their plan, prefabrication of concrete off site, a drive on construction efficiency and value-management activities.

The quality of the twin rivers solution can be seen as people today walk on the banks of the rivers watching the ecology thrive. The Environment Agency now holds this up as an exemplar project. More tangibly, during the twin rivers project there was wasn't a leak anywhere, something even Wilbraham was surprised by.

The team worked 1.8 million manhours and suffered 5 reportable accidents and 143 minor accidents.

What was different

For many nonaviation or construction enthusiasts, perhaps the most interesting part of T5 is the environment story. While BAA had some success with moving the river Mole at Gatwick, that paled into insignificance against this challenge. Once the team understood that the brief included delivering an 'equivalent or better habitat' for wildlife, they entered into the spirit of the challenge. Wildlife at the start, during and at the end of the project was a top priority. Chub, dace, roach, bream, bleak, minnow, gudgeon, bullhead, pike, perch and eel had to be moved to the nearby river Colne before the twin river diversions began. The construction of the channels for the water was carefully planned; the rivers were constructed out of a mix of concrete walls and grassy banks. Hundreds of gabions were then placed in the rivers to force them to meander from side to side, and large branches and tree roots were also anchored in the river to provide a habitat for river fauna. The central access track, separating the two rivers, was then seeded with native wildflowers. More than 8000 square metres of coir matting, pre-seeded with 37 different plant species native to the Colne Valley, such as lesser pond sedge and great yellow cress, were laid on the riverbanks to enhance the ecological value of the rivers. The transferred fish stock, riverbed silt, gravels, shrimp, nymphs, snails, 1200 duck mussels and dwan mussels and a colony of 60 water voles from the old rivers were translocated into the new riverbeds to help kick-start the ecology.

A co-located team of people from a variety of companies, who in the main stayed working on the project from start to finish, had clear goals and with the right mix of challenge and support made the difference. Wilbraham has spent over 11 years involved in T5, initially on the twin rivers then moving to close-out design, with time in buildings before finally being the last construction leader standing on the project. He typifies the very best of leadership, drive, stakeholder management and enabling integrated teams.

Always understated, he talks about walking the twin rivers site in 2003 with some tough characters from his team who said that they weren't going to achieve their goals if they didn't double their efforts. Wilbraham had the leadership qualities to listen to those words and then work with the team to deliver within the environment constraints. The very good, trusting relationship he built with the agencies meant that the key players knew he was a man of integrity, and at times quiet words were had behind closed doors to ensure that progress continued while allowing some environment challenges to be managed in a slightly different way to that agreed.

Key learning

Wilbraham was quite up front that going into the project he was sceptical that so much of the concrete river could be pre-fabricated off site. In the end 75% of it was, and this is yet another example showing where off-site prefabrication and assembly were embraced by the T5 team and proved critical to the final success.

Doing anything at the world's busiest international airport is a challenge, but by the end of the project the team's appreciation of crane constraints and how to keep a road open, so that there was no negative impact on the volume of traffic going around Heathrow, sharpened their focus and was an exemplar to all.

The team followed the earthworks team and held its members completely to account. Any slippage or poor workmanship would mean that a key handover date might be missed. Wilbraham was always ahead of his team's needs, having good or difficult conversations with other teams to make sure that he could keep on plan. Clearly, the spirit of the T5 Agreement allowed this type of working to operate.

A more controversial lesson might be whether the decision to move the twin rivers at all was actually the right one. While it is a remarkable example of care for the environment, should the rivers have been left to run their natural course in pipes under the building and the £30 million or so saved invested in environment issues elsewhere?

Airside road tunnel

In total there were nine tunnels on T5, two for the Heathrow Express extension, two for the Piccadilly line extension, two for the airside road tunnel (ART), one for drainage and the pollution-control system and two short service tunnels. All were successfully designed, built and commissioned under the leadership of Ian Fugeman. For the insurers tunnelling was one of the most significant risks to the programme, given various incidents around the world and the memories of the Heathrow Express tunnel collapse in 1994. There remained a major concern regarding the risk resulting from the construction of 13.5 kilometres of new bored tunnels beneath the world's busiest international airport. As we come to the end of T5, the rail and tunnels record is impeccable and perhaps one of the finest examples of integrated teamworking is ART.

ART included the design and construction of an all-weather transport link between Heathrow's existing remote stands, and ultimately between T5 and the Heathrow central terminal area. This link would allow coaches to transport airside passengers in transit and the movement of goods and baggage. The 1.3-kilometre twin-bore tunnel, with an 8.1-metre internal diameter, was the longest road tunnel to be completed in the UK since the Dartford Tunnel in 1960. The team tunnelled from T5 towards T3 twice. In simple terms there were three core aspects of the work: the boring of the two tunnels lined with 12 000 concrete lining segments; the completion of entrances at either end of the twin tunnel; and the mechanical and electrical works for the plant rooms, two drainage systems, lights, ventilation, communications and CCTV.

Key players

For BAA Ian Williams; Selby Thacker from Morgan Vinci JV, tunnel constructor; Laing O'Rourke, civil constructor; SPIE Matthew Hall, mechanical and electrical design and installation; and Mott Macdonald, tunnel, civil and ventilation design and mechanical and electrical concept design. The management team consisted of members from all the companies selected on their ability rather than company allegiance. In addition, the manufacturer Herrenknecht worked alongside the team to develop a tunnel-boring machine (TBM).

Key risks

Work on ART was up and running in 2000, two years before the commencement of T5 construction, and consequently before many of the T5 procedures and processes had been created. In many ways ART blazed a trail that brought with it risks and challenges. The same was the case with a new code of practice for the risk management of tunnel works being jointly produced by the Association of British Insurers and the British Tunnelling Society. Dr Terry Mellors was joint chairman of the team writing the code, and subsequently was employed by the insurers on T5 as their site representative. The code of practice was published in September 2003 and the T5 rail and tunnels team worked closely with Mellors to ensure that its full application on the remaining T5 tunnels was to the satisfaction of the insurers.

There were significant technical risks with tunnelling underneath the world's busiest international airport, including the risk of some ground movement. The first challenge for the ART project was the T5 side entrance to the tunnel that was directly above the Piccadilly line. BAA challenges were added to by the changes that were taking place at London Underground with the creation of the shadow infracos or infrastructure companies to take control of its assets, and subsequently the award of the public–private partnerships contract to Tube Lines. That meant understanding the protocols that were required with the new organization and took extra stakeholder management. Secondly, the tunnels also passed over Heathrow Express twice with only a 3-metre clearance. Finally, there was the challenge of making sure the 8.1-metre diameter tunnel, which ran in places less than 6 metres below Heathrow's taxiways, did not cause damage to the very sensitive fuel mains, fire pipelines or the profile of the taxiway surface. This was the sort of technical challenge the insurers worried about, and all passed without any disruption to Heathrow or incidents.

There were a number of months, as the team worked on the second tunnel, during which the civil engineering, mechanical and electrical and rail trades all working together posed a potential employee relations risk. All of these trades were on separate rates and in other circumstances may have chosen to hold the project to ransom, given the time challenges by that stage.

ART deliverables

ART involved many challenges, none less than that the first tunnel had taken slightly longer than expected. This had been due to new machinery, a new site set-up and a new team all coming together. The tunnel-boring machine had been built in Germany by Herrenknecht and as the team began using the machine, it took about three to four weeks to get the right optimum process in place to tunnel, remove the spoil and erect the concrete lining segments. As the team prepared for the second tunnel, there were standback meetings with all the key players to understand how the schedule could be got back on track. This included not taking the TBM apart, as originally planned, but rather finding the vehicles and processes to be able to transport it back to T5 in one piece, and increasing productivity by having multiple trades working underground together and looking to improve their production rates. At this stage Ralph Abbot, an assistant BAA project leader, was brought into the team nine months from the end of the project, to start the process of asset handover, which included working through ever more detailed steps for testing, commissioning and handover to Heathrow. Given that this was one of the early and most significant handovers there were many pitfalls that could have created delays, but instead the team ended up actually handing ART over to Heathrow one month ahead of schedule in February 2005.

Commercially the project ended up £6 million below budget at £141 million. It had not been straightforward, as some of the labour-shortage risks hadn't been built into the original costs and given that ART was so early on, not all the logistics infrastructure was in place yet in the T5 Programme, so the team had the challenges of those costs.

Quality is always seen with the test of time, but one of the most notable deliverables was that in both tunnels the expected damage of the concrete lining was less than 3%. In fact at the end of the project only about 50 out of about 15 000 concrete-lining segments ended up damaged.

Tunnel construction can be a dangerous activity, due to personnel working in a confined space and often with only one direction for escape. The history books have far too many cases of injuries and accidents in tunnels. ART, and indeed the rest of the rail and tunnels work, passed without any fatalities and with very few injuries, due to extensive planning and risk management. But most of all it was helped by the T5 Agreement, which did not place the risk of time on the suppliers, so all parties could come together with a common focus and commitment to ensure that the risks were effectively managed to ensure the safest working environment. 1.6 million manhours were worked on ART and there were 12 reportable accidents and 174 minor accidents.

What was different?

The commercial environment created allowed people to work together to deliver the project objectives. There were critical points in the project when there were time and cost challenges, but the team focused on the task at hand and worked together. A senior player from one of the suppliers involved said to Williams, 'This is the first time I've been allowed to do the job of an engineer for which I am trained and qualified rather than having to focus on contractual claims.' The team spirit was good, helped by co-locating and a spirit of 'best man for the job' regardless of who the employer was. The key players bought into this way of working given the trust that had been built up and the open-book nature of the T5 contract. This collaborative working extended to the early involvement of TBM manufacturer Herrenknecht.

Williams and Thacker worked and led the team well. Selby had been on the project for more than a year prior to Williams joining, but once the two had spent a few months understanding each other's way of operating, both supported one another and the team through the many people and technical challenges that the project encountered. Williams talked about 'leading from behind', supporting the team, clearing the way to allow Selby and others to deliver.

Key learning

The right team of people were brought together and then given clear accountabilities, the right amount of governance and the autonomy to deliver. Key players owned the time, cost, quality and safety targets and worked together as one team to deliver ahead of the targets and jointly to resolve the challenges as they emerged. The biggest unforeseen event was the terrible terrorist attack in New York on 9/11. The immediate downturn in air travel worldwide meant that BAA imposed an immediate embargo on all projects. At that time the 800-tonne TBM was being shipped in parts from the factory in Germany by sea to England. The shipment was stopped and the lorries returned to Germany, where it was stored while BAA reassessed its strategy and project requirements. Eventually the ART got the go-ahead, but the cancellation of other Heathrow projects meant that the east portal had to be redesigned and the project reprogrammed to accommodate access one year later than originally planned. All this occurred with the team totally focused on creating the optimum programme to mitigate the delay, without showing the traditional behaviours associated with claims and individual suppliers maximizing their position. Without the T5 Agreement this adult approach would not have occurred.

Across the rail and tunnels scope of works, it was always recognized that management of stakeholders was critical to achieving a successful outcome. In the early days of the ART project, a BAA engineer was engaged solely to work with Heathrow's airside operations, the engineering maintenance teams, the fuel companies and the airlines to ensure that the works did not affect their daily operations.

But stakeholder management is much more that just having good relations with your neighbours. The statutory authorities in the form of Her Majesty's Railway Inspectorate and the London Fire and Emergency Planning Authority are responsible for the ultimate approval of all railways and subsurface stations. The processes established on delivery of the original Heathrow Express project, which led to its early opening in May 1998, were continued in rail and tunnels at T5, with regular meetings to ensure compliance and no surprises. The other key stakeholders were the various operators comprising Heathrow Express, London Underground and Network Rail. The interface with these organizations required experienced managers, with the right competencies to ensure that the new works did not present a risk to their existing operations, as well as seeking their support to meet the objectives of the T5 Programme.

The T5 main building roof

The T5 main building roof team was part of the buildings team, led by John Milford, and was part of a bundle of work worth over £1.5 billion including all three buildings, the control tower and the energy centre. The roof team designed and built the fourth and final Rogers Stirk Harbour + Partners and Arup roof design, or the 'wavy roof' as it is affectionately known. While this is viewed by some as too expensive at £85 million, the public inquiry was very clear that if the Queen could see T5 from Windsor, she needed to look at an attractive piece of architecture, so the design of the roof was very important. One can't help but think that decisions would be very different today, but the end result is a stunning piece of architecture that will no doubt end up being award winning.

The roof team had the challenge of covering a space of 176 metres wide by 400 metres long by 40 metres high, providing a bold architectural statement as a gateway to the UK, giving internal flexibility and saving time in the construction programme. Ultimately this required the lift of six roof modules and erection of 22 abutments, which in total allowed for more than 17 000 tonnes of steel and 5000 tonnes of roof cladding to be used on the T5 main building.

Key players

For BAA Mark Cowison; Bill Frankland from Laing O'Rourke, production leader, civil constructor and chief engineer; SPIE Matthew Hall, mechanical and electrical services; Hathaways, roof cladding; Watsons, steel erectors; Arup, structural engineer; Rogers Stirk Harbour + Partners, design.

Key risks

The technical risks around the roof lifts were significant. Each of the six roof lifts involved building the 2000-tonne roof module at ground level and erecting the abutments on either side, ready to receive the roof module once it was strand-jacked into position. Before the roof module could be lifted, its four rafters were pre-stressed to over 3000 tonnes to form a bowstring girder that was capable of supporting its own weight during the lift. The roof module was now strand-jacked from ground level to 30 metres high, where the roof module was connected to the abutments; at this point the strand-jacks were disconnected and temporary supports removed, so that the roof structure could take up its final position. Following this infills between lifts were added together with final installation of the roof cladding. The temporary works supports for the abutments were then pushed along the ground slab and used again for each roof module lift.

While it was easy to appreciate that lifting 2000 tonnes of roof module could indeed be catastrophic if there was either system or structural integrity failure, it should be realized that these type of operations have been around since the mid-1970s, over which time the lifting arrangements have become very sophisticated and made fail-safe. What were therefore considered more of a hazard were the simple things that could go wrong, and indeed potentially make the team look very foolish. In this respect the assembly of the roof module on the ground-floor slab was singled out for special treatment. The ground slab, by itself, was not capable of taking the weight of the cranes used to build the roof module, and had to be supported by special bridging beams where one small slip would see cranes falls through five levels of basement, a fate that could not be contemplated. In a similar way, the periphery of the building was crossed by many tunnels, which had not been designed to take the weight of the huge 400-tonne crawler cranes operating around the building. The method of controlling these hazards was simple: all the control measures, rules and regulations, safety criteria and no-go areas were captured on two drawings, one for the ground slab and the other for the periphery of the building. Constructors were also briefed in their use, so that they knew through the presentation of simplified rules just how to operate in these hazardous areas.

The time, cost, quality and safety risks that this level of complexity involves required the project team and BAA to be completely transparent on method statements, procedures and assembly manuals for the tasks, and the assurance and audit protocols had to be second to none. The team talked very openly about welcoming 'interrogators' in to help them see potential pitfalls. These interrogators were very much built into the team preparation process and included the roof team's own internal checks; an external review carried out by the T5 chief engineer, Neil Kitchener, who acted as a second pair of eyes; a special HAZOP (hazardous operation) and HAZAN (hazard analysis) review of structural integrity and safety; and BAA's risk and quality assurance checks. Wolstenholme commissioned his own audit team to report directly to him to ensure full compliance and that no shortcuts had been taken. Finally, the roof and interfacing teams signed off the assembly manual, to ensure lifting readiness, before the principal contractor's representative gave the go-ahead for the lift.

Given that there were six roof lifts, each lasting seven to nine weeks, one of the very real risks the team faced was key players dealing with the births, deaths and marriages that normal life throws at us all. For a period a key group of people needed to work together and it needed to be clear who deputized for them if anything happened. There is a great story of how before the first lift, Wolstenholme went down to site to review all the final preparations. He spent the first few hours with the A team, going through every step of the process, and the team felt somewhat relieved that they had known all the answers to all the questions. Wolstenholme then said, 'Great, can you all leave the room and can you send in the B team, I'd like to go over exactly the same drill with them.' Bill Frankland said that this really sharpened him up to the idea of deputies. This obvious but useful lesson had come from Wolstenholme's days on the Heathrow Express tunnel collapse.

T5 main building deliverables

The roof team had a 15-month schedule that ran from October 2003 to the end of January 2005. There were key interfaces with substructure, earthworks, internal structure, façades, rail box, car park and mechanical and electrical, all of whom required the roof team to deliver on time to allow them to continue on time. The team delivered ahead of schedule, with some of the time lost in the early lifts retrieved as the roof-lift cycle time reduced from nine to seven weeks.

Commercially the team delivered the £85 million project on budget.

It was a quality assembly. Realistic tolerances were agreed between structural engineer Arup and steelwork fabricator/erector Severfield-Rowen at every stage during the development of the roof design. This is an issue that constantly hampers steelwork construction: fabricators are required to pursue ridiculous and non-practical tolerances, resulting in considerable expense where the fabricator makes components to watch-like tolerances when far more generous and cost-effective tolerances would suffice. Under the T5 Agreement the fabricator was able to convince the structural engineer that wider tolerances on certain nonsensitive fabrications would deliver real value.

Safety was the life-blood of the team and was taken very seriously, not only because special HAZAN studies were done. This was a particular aspect of the abutment first-run study where issues were found that would not have been identified until too late, like the absence of hand railing in key areas, and confined-space protection when working in the boxes. Also one of the simplest things the first-run study found was that by attaching the 3.8 metre-deep slice plate to a simple hinge, the workforce could simply swing this into position when making the connection some 30 metres in the air. The team won the high 5 award because they were so conscientious, willing to please and to sort out difficult and dangerous practices. Unfortunately the roof team was a subproject so it was not possible easily to get its final health and safety statistics.

What was different?

The most significant difference on the roof was how client, designers and the build team worked together to find solutions to deliver an architecturally bold statement that could be built and operated safely, while managing the employee relations challenge found with a steel workforce. Having spent time reviewing the roof case study, with all key players involved, it was clear the early ideas put forward, where men weld in baskets 40 metres in the air, were going to prove structurally, and from an employee relations point of view, tough to deliver. Peter Emerson from Severfield-Rowen was clear that an integrated team way of working had made the difference. BAA, RSH+P and Arup listened to his concerns, and he likewise understood the design statement that needed to be made. In a close working relationship over several months, a solution was delivered that met all the objectives. Site welding was avoided by making the roof-field assembly totally bolted.

BAA invested £4 million in an off-site first-run study that took place in Yorkshire. All of the key players on each roof lift went to Yorkshire and over 12 weeks ran a trial carnage assembly of the abutment and a section of the roof rafters. From a business case this dry run at one level was a leap of faith, but the strategic decision to manage a huge risk to the time and cost of the programme paid off tenfold. Over 125 areas of improvement were found and it was estimated over 100 days would have been lost on site if this hadn't taken place, which would have probably resulted in time and cost failure on T5.

Frankland, a seasoned professional who worked on big projects such as Hong Kong airport and is now on the Olympics, described T5 as the 'height of his career'. The team chemistry worked, showing that the environment created by the T5 Agreement allowed people to problem solve proactively when things went wrong. For example on lift four out of the six, there was a problem with a bearing plate that was not at the right orientation. A problem that could have taken many days to fix was resolved and operationally back on track in two days. The integrated team stepped back quickly to understand what the problem was, in an environment without blame, and identified a solution that required a new machined part for the bearing assembly. Severfield–Rowen, which had all the way along been part of the team and involved in the test run in Yorkshire, pulled out all the stops, made a new part in 48 hours and got it to the site to allow the team on the ground to get back on track.

Key learning

Luck plays a huge part in building a successful team in the construction world. Frankland, who was an outstanding leader, returned from Hong Kong and bumped into Norman Haste, who sent him to see Wolstenholme, who then brought him on board, and not before too long he found himself leading the roof team with Watsons. All ended up fielding players who had worked together previously.

Prior to this Watsons had merged with Severfield-Rowen, which enabled Watsons to be engaged as part of the structural steelwork framework agreement, bringing their expertise from Hong Kong airport and combining it with Severfield-Rowen's experience from Stansted, to form one of the most powerful steel fabricators for airports in the UK and in the process making interface issues much easier to manage.

The assembly manuals, otherwise known as the 'comprehensive assembly bible', put together to deliver the T5 roof are now being used on other projects by Watsons. The discipline of understanding risk and its root cause, and the opportunities for process improvement required in the T5 Agreement, forced a much greater level of documentation than had previously been required.

Heathrow air traffic control tower

There are four distinct parts of the Heathrow air traffic control tower (HATCT) project. The cab at the top, the size of a six storey building, weighing 600 tonnes and providing a 360 degree line of vision, which would enable its operators to see every aspect of the airport whilst housing all the appropriate mechanical and electrical services, computers, power cables, ducting, communications, equipment cabinets and air conditioning systems. The plant rooms at the base and below the cab that dual fed, power, water, telecoms, all backed up with a standby generator and water storage tank to ensure adequate contingency in any eventuality. The mast was made of a 12 metres pieces of steel ultimately containing a spiral staircase on the inside and an exterior lift built to withstand all weathers and wind of up to 60 knots. Finally, the 100 metres link bridge connecting the HATCT at its base to T3.

Standing at 87 metres, the new HATCT has changed the landscape of Heathrow. Located airside at the end of Pier 7 at T3, it is the new home for National Air Traffic Services (NATS), from where 473 000 aircraft movements per year are now managed. It replaced the old tower, as with T5 coming it was clearly too low, too small and in the wrong place to meet the changing needs of Heathrow. The team had to construct HATCT with a slender mast of just 4.8 metres at the base and a cab of 15 metres at the top, weighing 900 tonnes with a centre of gravity two-thirds of the way up. They needed to move it one and a half miles across a runway to the other side of the airport, and then jack it vertically a further 60 metres, while building the mast in 12-metre increments, all the time being careful not to disrupt the world's busiest airport.

The HATCT project was the first significant project not to go to plan early in T5. For 24 hours after the failure was identified, both BAA and the suppliers involved nearly reverted to normal contracting behaviours, looking at whom to blame and calling in the lawyers, but having committed to the T5 Agreement the BAA team held their nerve. This defining moment ultimately became an example of the client and the suppliers working differently in a failing moment.

Key players

For BAA Nick Featherstone, handing over to Carl Devlin; Peter Czwartos from Mace, production leader; Richard Mathews of Arup and Stephen Barrett of RSH+P, design; Tony Whitten of Severfield-Rowen, steel fabricators and erectors; Schmidlin, glazing and cladding; Laing O'Rourke, substructures; Warings, fit-out and finishing; Schindler, lifts; SPIE Matthew Hall, mechanical and electrical engineering; and NATS, end user.

Key risks

The planning constraints meant that the HATCT mast had to be suitably slender to reduce its visual impact, which ultimately led to the solution of a slender steel 'cable-stayed' mast. Traditionally concrete would have been used and that would have been thicker and technically less challenging, but given the constraints this wasn't an option. This ultimately proved to be a technical risk: the first attempt didn't deliver a workable solution and over a three-month period the team had to go back to the drawing board.

A second technical risk related to the ongoing operational performance of HATCT. The equipment required to oversee aircraft movements has to have a level of resilience that guarantees no more than two hours outage over a 10-year period. The studies and independent reviews of each stage of the process, while not without error, brought together some of the best technical minds in the world to deliver this result.

The final risk was disrupting Heathrow. HATCT was built between three live aircraft stands that seriously constrained the approach to design and construction. The cab or top section was assembled remotely at T4, to simplify the construction and reduce high-risk construction activities at height. The top section was moved across the airport to its planned location, using specialist lifting technology capable of lifting and placing this weight accurately within 1 mm. Once the top section had been moved, the temporary works that would enable a mast to be jacked up were put in place. Although this could raise the mast the required height for each lift in a day, the process demanded so much preparation that it took about three weeks to add each section. The mast was supported throughout this process with the use of temporary cables, and high-tech computer equipment stabilized the mast throughout the jacking operation. On completion, the temporary cables were individually replaced with permanent more ridged cables, which had been designed to increase the stiffness of the structure and minimize movement of the air traffic controllers' workplace. Through the exceptional planning of these challenging operations no significant disruption was incurred by Heathrow operations.

HATCT deliverables

Work started on site near T4 in July 2003 and, despite the technical challenges two weeks into construction requiring the mast team to stop, the team handed the project over to NATS on 13 March 2006 as planned. The HATCT team was faced with an eight-month delay at the height of the technical challenges, and was able to halve that time by working successfully with NATS to absorb the residual delay through reprioritizing, releasing critical areas of the building earlier to enable NATS to commence their works to programme and using up some contingency.

More traditional contracts and styles of leadership would have resulted in unnecessary time being wasted, trying to apportion blame and responsibility for the issues caused by the delays due to the mast manufacture redesign. The decision by Wolstenholme to accept the aborted costs of the work already carried out allowed the team to keep moving forward, focusing on the task. In fact, the team would have lost more time than it eventually recovered endeavouring to protect itself against contractual recourse. Instead, its members remained highly productive and solution focused throughout, safe in the understanding that the T5 agreement was designed for such an eventuality, appointing risk evenly and fairly between all parties including the client. So although the costs were significant, they were substantially less than they could have been, and the control was delivered to the original programme.

A £47 million project did end up costing £52 million. The difference in part was offset by contingency and also an insurance claim drawn down against 'collective professional negligence'. In the context of a £4.3 billion project, with most projects on or below budget and an insurance policy in place, this was managed within programme budget and some would say that it was £5 million best spent to convince all the key players that BAA was serious about a different way of working and managing risk.

While the team cannot claim a right–first–time record on overall quality, the ultimate engineering achievement shouldn't be underestimated. Projects of this nature will always be challenging, given the very degree of complexity and specialism. If the right environment and behaviours are created, the team will become high performing. Featherstone commented:

> As we started out to fix the technical problem, I was confident that I had the best individuals in the country working with me. The challenge was how to get them to

interact in order to unlock the ultimate team performance necessary to overcome these inevitable tough challenges.

The health and safety culture was impeccable throughout. Everybody understood how important the project was and the risks associated with it going wrong. Everyone felt included and important, whether they were sweeping the floors to avoid falling objects within the cab ahead of the move, or just providing the site guys with great food to set them up for a decent day's work. 0.2 million manhours were worked on HATCT and there was one reportable accident and 27 minor accidents.

In April 2007 HATCT became operational without any disruption to the airport. While there was a significant need for airline, NATS and Civil Aviation Authority stakeholder management, the first significant part of T5 was handed over quietly.

What was different?

It is easier to be a great team or a good leader when things are going your way, but when you get into hot water that's when you are really tested. On a £4.3 billion programme these sorts of moments do happen. Risk-mitigation processes try to unearth and deal with these challenges before they strike, but when they do, different action is required. There was a deep intake of breath during the first few weeks after the mast work was stopped, due to a review in manufacturing that showed that the final seam welding was causing a distortion. Would the T5 Agreement work when tested? Would BAA go on the hunt for someone to blame?

The HATCT had been the first significant and very public project that hadn't gone to plan and the directors of T5 knew that the way this was dealt with would set the tone and belief in the T5 Agreement. Matt Riley, BAA commercial director, clearly understood that and with other key directors worked with the supply chain to get the team back on track and give the suppliers confidence that BAA would stand by its commitments even when things went wrong. Emerson talked about Wolstenholme getting him and Mitchell together for a bacon butty and saying, 'We have a problem. I'm not interested in blaming people, but it does need to be fixed, so whatever is needed to fix it, you've got it.' This sort of leadership and different way of working were what set T5 apart.

Featherstone recalled that while the situation was very tense, 'I did fully supported by senior management on T5,' who were there to give advice and review but allowed the experts to get on with the job. Richard Matthews from Arup, who led the design, had the best team put around him to make sure that he overcame the manufacturing challenges quickly. 'This was all about going slow to get ready to go fast,' explained Featherstone. The team devised new methodology to fabricate the mast sections in smaller sections, which were built in special jigs and then heat treated to ensure that they were free from stress and torsion, which would force the steel out of tolerance.

Key learning

Emerson said that the success of the roof had perhaps lulled some of those who had been involved into a 'false sense of security'. Originally the mast had been circular, with a spiral staircase inside and both lifts outside. But there was a risk of certain wind speeds rendering the external lifts periodically inoperable, and fire regulations required that at least one lift together with the access stairs remained available for a means of escape at all times.

By changing the cross-sectional shape of the mast to accommodate one of the lifts, the manufacturing process for the mast sections had inadvertently become exponentially more difficult. Although the team had overcome one substantial challenge, it had unknowingly created a greater problem. Often change control is seen as a means of varying or revising the financial budget on a project rather than fully evaluating the implications of the design. It is also vital that all of the right parties are consulted, at the right time, to ensure a balanced perspective and understanding of each party's specialism. This learning point dramatically changed the team's attitude and behaviour for the rest of the project, which ensured inclusion and improved communication, in turn fostering a much greater sense of ownership and responsibility. As Featherstone said: 'At that point we had solved one problem but the team hadn't gone through as thorough a change control process as required, given the complexity of the task.'

While it was a significant setback, the modular approach to the HATCT meant that only the mast-jacking part of the role completely stopped. Those involved in substructures and the cab were able to continue. The 'mast challenge team', as it was known, was able to step back without stopping the whole job.

From day one the integrated team had not had all the right people in it. While technically everyone passed the test, behaviourally at times not everyone pulled in the same direction. After the technical challenge was unearthed there was a standback review and a few team members were replaced. It was clear that everybody 'either pulled in the same direction or was asked to move on', and senior suppliers and BAA worked on this very collaboratively, all understanding the implications. The effort to support the team and create a high-performing unit was then tripled, and over a three-month period a team of people under huge pressure, but in a supportive environment, delivered a solution to the problem without fear of blame or retribution. The T5 Agreement had been tested and it had passed.

Baggage system

There was a real appreciation that baggage was one of the areas that could stop T5 from opening on time, or at least dampen the passenger experience if men in trucks had to move their luggage around in the background, rather than using the state-of-the-art baggage system that had been promised. There are many examples of airports that have had system challenges, time and cost challenges, end-user operational challenges or combinations of all three. Denver is one that is often quoted, causing the airport to open a year late due to significant mechanical and software problems as a result of poor planning and continual changes to requirements. The baggage system at Denver continued to be a maintenance challenge and in 2005 was finally terminated. BAA did an extensive review of projects around the world identifying key learning that came from each project. This learning generally focused on protecting the commissioning period and on system integration and network communication testing. Invariably when problems had manifested at previous mega projects, they had been due in significant part to the softer issues like training and induction of the operational team, as well as a lack of robust testing of operational processes with the systems.

The BAA, BA and Vanderlande Industries team designed the baggage system, 400 000 hours of software development followed to get the manufacturers in the Netherlands, Germany and the US to prepare the kit for assembly to start in March 2005 on T5. System testing and commissioning needed to be substantially completed by 28 September 2007 to then move into intensive proving trials, as part of operational readiness.

The new baggage system can process up to 12 000 bags per hour through the tilt tray sorter, provided by Beumer in Germany. At any point in time there will be 18 000 metres of conveyors being used for bags entering the system, normally from the check-in or transfer process. Passengers who are late will have their bags moved around on the 8000-metre, high-speed baggage rail link; those who want to get to T5 early to enjoy the views and great food and shopping will have their bags held in a 4000-bag capacity store. Every bag entering the system is individually bar coded before being screened and routed to its destination.

Key players

For BAA Martin Johnson, handing over to Jonathan Adams; Henk van Helmond from Vanderlande Industries, project director; L3 Communications, baggage screening; Viastore, bag-store cranes; Beumer, sorter; EIWHS and Inviron, installation; IBM, software controls; BA, end user.

Key risks

The baggage system vision was ambitious, but all concerned were committed to using tried-and-tested technology to mitigate this risk, although as often was the case on T5, the scale was the new challenge. That set the installation of the system in a less than perfect environment that wasn't weather tight or correctly lit when the team first started, and meant that time, cost, quality and safety risks all had to be managed. Van Helmond was clear that installing baggage systems is not a glamorous job. He recounted how on Fridays Adams would turn up with a big box of doughnuts and chat to the team; although a small gesture, this was symbolic of the fact that the client cared enough to take time to do this.

Perhaps the most significant risk in baggage handling is the systems integration that involves data from BA and BAA starting to flow between both companies as the team tests the resilience of the system. Detailed bag messages are sent from the departures control system at Heathrow for BA to identify where each bag is to fly to and when. The effective transmission of data over the Heathrow and T5 communications network, and its receipt and understanding by the baggage system, are core to the testing and management of the overall baggage product. This interaction was tested extensively off site at factory acceptance tests, then extensively on site at site acceptance tests and proving trials.

The baggage system was released on 28 September 2007 to allow BA and BAA to start weekly proving trials, and the challenges of having systems, processes and now people starting to interact are beginning to be understood and managed. From recent press coverage there is clearly an opportunity for improved performance in baggage and the new environment, systems and processes give BA the chance to make a real step-change, if it can take the people with it.

Baggage deliverables

As the team got ready to hand over to the operational readiness team on 28 September 2007 to allow proving trials to start, what was most surprising was that this date had been set four and a half years previously and stuck to. The baggage system, although fraught with 'unknown unknowns', has followed a tightly managed schedule on the critical path that had to be and was delivered on time.

With a budget of £250 million, all in the team delivered to cost by careful gains made in the early stages of manufacturing, through the use of efficient logistics to mitigate some of the underestimations in installation and testing at the back end of the project. The drive from day one to focus on efficiencies to mitigate future risks paid off.

Baggage systems are perhaps the most complicated pieces of equipment in airports. The quality of the craftsmanship overseen by Vanderlande Industries is to be commended, but the real test will come five or even ten years down the line as the maintenance record is understood and the lost baggage trends materialize. While the quality of the manufactured elements is key to long-term performance and reliability, the T5 team also focused on software quality control. Independent software assurance was carried out by Vanderlande and IBM.

Safety on baggage, like on the rest of T5, is a core value. Adams was candid that in the early days there were one or two near misses, the most serious involving a conveyor falling over as a result of a mistake made by a few of the workers. After that Adams and van Helmond stopped the site and jointly got 240 people together to discuss openly what had happened and how the team needed to work together to keep each other safe. Van Helmond said that this 'was a turning point in the relationship'. It was apparent to him that he and Adams would stand shoulder to shoulder. The baggage team worked 1.3 million manhours and had two reportable accidents and 100 minor accidents. Vanderlande Industries had not been exposed to the incident and injury-free culture before but it is now firmly part of the company's way of operating.

Predictable and consistent operational performance has been the ultimate goal for the team. With a connect time of 45 minutes for a bag to passenger or aircraft, and a 10 in a 1000 loss rate for bags moving down to 1 in 1000, this would put the system among the best in the world. The European hubs operate at between 20–30 lost bags in each 1000, similar to the current statistics at Heathrow.

What was different?

BAA understood the risk profile of the baggage system. Figure 11.2 shows a typical baggage risk profile and how BAA managed these risks early. It worked with BA from day one, investing in and hence putting in place computer modelling simulations and emulations that combine simulation hardware with real data, ultimately leading to robust baggage proving trials.

BAA and BA understood the critically of the baggage system from the very early stages. After all, airports ultimately have three functions: to move passengers, aircrafts and bags efficiently. The team jointly reviewed airport successes and failures from around the world and went into the project with realistic expectations. They wanted tried-and-tested systems, they know it would be a combination of systems, processes and people that would deliver success, and over 10 years both have worked together through joint meetings and governance forums to deliver that success.

Figure 11.2   Managing the risk in baggage.

The baggage system has been designed conceptually, to be very resilient to unexpected events or incidents. Most areas of the system are duplicated, so that operations can virtually always be protected. For example, there are not one but two independent baggage-sorting machines, which can operate independently. Together these sorters are 1.7 kilometres in length. The whole check-in and screening capability is mirrored at the north and south ends of the main building, and there are two separate tunnels connecting the baggage system into the satellite building at both the southern and the northern ends of the buildings

On the relationship between BAA, Adams and Vanderlande Industries, van Helmond was completely complimentary. His understanding of baggage systems was world class, having been the project director on among other projects Hong Kong, and Adams' prime reason for being there was to clear the way for Vanderlande Industries to allow a good company to do their best work. Prior to critical handover points Adams would go and work with SPIE Matthew Hall, Mace or others, getting extra support if needed to make sure that the baggage team and programme could always keep moving forward as planned. Both men had very different personalities but were well respected within their own companies and the industry, and they were a powerful double act that behaved with honour and trust during their time working together.

Key learning

Adams is convinced that it was the combination of the T5 Agreement, clear immovable goals, and the right integrated team of people with leaders who set an example that allowed the team to deliver a highly complicated baggage system to plan.

A rigorous testing and commissioning programme and then robust proving trials meant that the likelihood of surprises on day one has been minimized. By January 2008 15 000 bag trials had occurred in the baggage system. Since October 2007 these bags moving around have been joined by workers and pretend passengers to ensure that all processes are tested and workers are familiar and trained for all eventualities.

BA and BAA

At times BAA and BA appear from press reports to be two companies that don't see eye to eye. The reality is that Heathrow is BA's hub, it desperately needs upgraded facilities and BA represents 40% of Heathrow's business, so both companies' futures are very much dependent on the other's success. Over the years whether in construction or airport operations, the relationship has been tested but sustained on a positive footing.

BAA started to think about T5 and share its ideas with the airport operator community from the late 1980s. Countless conversations finally resulted in the agreement in the mid-1990s that BA would be the airline that would move into T5. Since then a BAA and BA co-located team has worked with other consultants and suppliers to create a T5 concept design, passenger experience, flow and CIP lounge that signal the future of Heathrow. BAA's £4.3 billion spend was influenced by BA; BA's £330 million CIP spend was actually delivered by BAA under the T5 Agreement.

The integrated team also spent a significant time together working on the processes, systems and approach to people that will finally be deployed on T5, a terminal built to manage 30 million passengers.

Key players

Through the different phases of the T5 Programme the names and faces representing both organizations changed. In the early days of planning permission and concept design, Gwilym Rees-Jones at BA was the counterpart to Ian Badger in BAA. BA handed the projects director role over to Colin Clarkson, who worked with the T5 managing directors, Eryl Smith, then John Stent and then Tony Douglas from BAA. Finally, in the run-up to opening BA handed the baton over first to Geoff Want and then to David Noyes, who is working closely with Mark Bullock from BAA as both get ready for 4 a.m. on 27 March 2008.

Some of the more critical junior people have talked about the senior disagreements that did take place, and that their role was to get together with their counterparts, understand the real issue and find a way through. Remarkably along the way, though moments have been tense, in the main common sense prevailed.

In the early days Liz Southern worked on design, who handed over to Chris Elliot from BAA with Roger Gibson and then Trisha Corstin-James from BA. On operational readiness matters Paul Fox, who handed over to Debbie Younger, worked with Paul Burton from BA. Both teams have spent years in small and large meetings trying to get alignment and ways forward.

Key risks/key challenges

For both companies the risk of not opening T5 on time was 'company shattering'. An outsider may find it interesting to watch some of the gaming that has gone on to get to a place were both parties have committed the T5 opening date publicly. For BAA the idea that BA might not be ready for opening, and in some way pull out suggesting construction reasons, was always a risk that lurked in the background. For BA once it was committed to the opening date, business and reputation damage would be devastating if the deadlines were not delivered or an unknown unknown risk materialized. Common sense and good leadership on the part of Willie Walsh, CEO BA, and Stephen Nelson, CEO BAA, ultimately enabled the right decision to be taken. For both companies T5 must and can be a good news story, but as with many important decisions and opportunities an element of judgement and bravery must ultimately prevail.

Clarkson was clear that the decision-making authority given to Douglas, his counterpart in BAA, was understandably greater, and this at times helped unblock impasses. The most significant decision that was needed, and took longer than expected, was getting BA to agree that BAA would build its CIP lounge. For BAA the risk of BA, a relatively inexperienced construction client, not delivering this work on time was a real worry; at the same time the BAA team would quite happily have not taken on the challenge of an additional £330 million building. The last responsible moment to make the decision had passed, and the different views in BA about entering a T5 Agreement contract were not coming to a point of resolution. As is often the case in these types of situations Douglas, working very closely with Clarkson, got together with about 30 different BA people and helped them understand the T5 environment and the challenges they would face with a construction project of this size. However, Douglas was very firm, 'Sign up as the client to own the risk or BAA walks away. Oh, by the way, you've got until Friday to make the decision otherwise you start to eat into my critical path.' Clarkson found this clarity incredibly helpful internally, and BA did commission BAA to do the work and for the months and years that followed. When those in BA wavered on that decision, he would remind them of that meeting that they had all attended and what they had agreed.

Along the way there have been countless disagreements between the two organizations, from single-terminal occupancy at the strategic level, right down to the positioning of some of the information desks at a tactical level. Again, the environment created by both has enabled appropriate debates and disagreements to take place, but ultimately sensible ways through were found.

BAA and BA deliverables

Talking to Walsh in October 2007, there was nothing that would stand in the way of BA and BAA opening T5 successfully. This had been signed off by the BA executive at a go/no-go meeting in September 2007 attended by BAA, and it signalled a fundamental commitment by both to move forward together. To have a demanding customer whose business future depends on you delivering cannot be underestimated. Contrast that with Wembley Stadium, where tickets were sold for the FA cup final and then the venue had to be moved to Cardiff. That trust as ever on this occasion was hard won. At the go/no-go meeting with the BA senior executive Wolstenholme shared the achievements so far, the challenges that were still being worked through and the plans for delivery. BA T5 team members were able to challenge him and equally to give their verdict on the next steps he proposed. The decision was taken, and Walsh said, 'I for some time had been confident, when I looked into the whites of the eyes of the people delivering I could see that they would.'

For commercial reasons neither BA nor BAA are candid about the commercial benefits of moving into T5. For BA, moving T1 and T4 into one terminal provided an opportunity to transform the business, normally shorthand for making it more efficient. Walsh talked of a 10% plus efficiency gain that had been dampened now that BA needed to spill into T3. For both organizations the chance to be working together to review processes and systems within their own teams, and also at points of opportunity to share tasks, was beneficial. For example, the current 'fit to fly' trial taking place at New York JFK will be adopted at T5, with BA passengers no longer receiving a final compliance check at the gate but this being done by existing BAA staff on the pre-security ticket-presentation desk as part of their other duties.

For both businesses the opportunity to deliver a passenger experience never seen in the UK, and some might say in many parts of the rest of the world, is perhaps the most fundamental deliverable for those involved. There is an iconic look and feel as passengers approach the terminal and enter a modern spacious building with flows that have a moving forward effect through waves of processing areas, starting with self-service check-in, fast bag drops through to security desks. Commercially important passengers have the choice of going straight through to the lounge or taking the opportunity to spend time in some of the world's signature brand stores such as Prada, Paul Smith and Harrods, or even to have a well-timed bite to eat in Gordon Ramsey's restaurant. All of this is done within a state-of-the-art infrastructure, with breathtaking views, and by staff who are excited about their new home and have been trained for months to give world class service.

One BA/BAA objective that wasn't delivered was the idea of having one front door for all employee inductions, 'Inside 5'. From the start there had been agreement that in the same way as the 50 000 construction workers had all gone through one induction and heard one message on T5 – that T5 would be delivered on time, to budget, safely and as a quality product – the same principle would continue with the operational teams. As an integrated team there was the will to do this, but in the end the different requirements and the desire for both companies to own their people was too great. At one level this does not matter, as the commonly agreed messages will work with both approaches. However, at another level it will be a missed opportunity to take the idea that as passengers travel through an airport, they receive a seamless service experience passing from airline to airport operator to other third parties, and vice versa with a symbolic 'one front door'. The chance has been lost for all to hear a T5-wide message that is reinforced by different teams working on the ground.

What was different?

Both businesses entered into the construction of T5 with a real sense of partnership, new beginnings and opportunities. Walsh was clear that he takes pride in the fact that his company's 'new home' is a UK construction success story. Perhaps a bigger challenge was to get the T5 operation to embrace and build on the partnering spirit that its construction had started. Fox remembers in 2003 starting to work with the BA team to create a joint operational vision, an opportunity for landlord and tenant to work on end-to-end processes that would make for a better passenger experience.

From the early conversations real company commitments have developed. The BA/BAA 'one team, one service' vision was signed off by Rod Eddington, CEO BA, and Mike Clasper, CEO BAA, in summer 2006. Walsh and Nelson, the new CEOs, have ratified these words and confirmed that the position holds (see Figures 11.3 and 11.4). As the teams start to move into T5 they are looking practically at how the new technologies being deployed allow both companies to use information that could allow each other's staff to give better service. Fox gave a very simple example: when a passenger makes a fast bag drop, the BA member of staff says, 'Madam, you'll find your passage quicker if you go through the southern security desks

BA/BAA T5 Purpose:
To enable the responsible and profitable growth of air travel
through passenger delight

T5 Goals:

A one team, one service vision approach based on common values

Staff
We will work as one team in a safe, secure, quality environment with inspirational behaviours and fulfilling roles. We will understand customer needs and have the skills, attitude and support to consistently deliver excellent customer service of which we will be proud.

**that enable staff to consistently deliver a
quality seamless passenger experience**

Passenger
A world class facility underpinned by operational excellence and great service consistently exceeding passenger expectations.

optimising commercial benefit to both organisations.

Figure 11.3   Joint BAA and BA purpose.

Joint BAA & BA Objectives

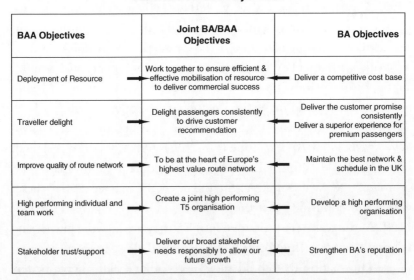

BAA Objectives	Joint BA/BAA Objectives	BA Objectives
Deployment of Resource	Work together to ensure efficient & effective mobilisation of resource to deliver commercial success	Deliver a competitive cost base
Traveller delight	Delight passengers consistently to drive customer recommendation	Deliver the customer promise consistently Deliver a superior experience for premium passengers
Improve quality of route network	To be at the heart of Europe's highest value route network	Maintain the best network & schedule in the UK
High performing individual and team work	Create a joint high performing T5 organisation	Develop a high performing organisation
Stakeholder trust/support	Deliver our broad stakeholder needs responsibly to allow our future growth	Strengthen BA's reputation

Figure 11.4   Joint BAA and BA objectives.

rather than the northern.' This is the operational team starting to measure and share data on queuing, not only at security but also at check-in and the gate. There are many ideas on sharing information or proximity of working, such as both control rooms being close to each other, shared office and canteen space, all creating a different way of delighting the passenger.

Although it may be challenging working with the end-user airline for a new terminal, BA and BAA would agree that it makes for a better experience for businesses and passengers alike. The more traditional model used by BAA in T4, or by other airport operators, is to build or nearly build a terminal, and then allocate an airline or airlines to the space. While this approach saves time at the front end of the process, by the time you get close to opening you start to experience the pain. There were occasions in the early days when BAA nearly pulled away from this integrated approach to working with BA, as it became too difficult to be inclusive and move forward with all the decisions that were needed, but the strong sense of stakeholder management prevailed and as opening approaches, both parties would say that it has been a winning formula.

As Fox set up the operational readiness for the T5live team, as a seasoned airport operator he had the experience of the impact of the commercial negotiations that both BA and BAA need to go through every five years. For every five years you could say 18 months of collaborative work in the operation is damaged, as CEOs from airlines make negative, and often unfounded, press statements, to try to get the regulator to think twice when confirming the final financial settlement. Fox with Stephen Wilkinson, BAA commercial director, ensured that Wilkinson's team dealt with all commercial matters, while airport operational issues were worked through with Fox and the T5live players.

Key learning

In hindsight, the norming, forming, storming and performing stages that BA and BAA tried to work through in the early part of the T5 project was founded on unrealistic expectations. A relationship that progressed to one of trying to deliver a joint commercial business case for Clarkson was just a step too far, and ultimately settled into a relationship of very constructive and challenging partnering to achieve a step–change in the Heathrow experience. As both companies evolved and became clearer on their own imperatives, partnering and commercial realities became more balanced.

Creating a way of working between airport operator and airline can only benefit the passenger, and using tangible data and clear protocols around who works with whom can make a marked difference.

SUMMARY

Working in integrated teams was one of the cornerstones of the T5 Agreement, and was a fundamental ingredient in the success of T5. Consultants and suppliers, in return for a guaranteed margin and access to an incentive scheme, committed to working to the principle of integrated teams alongside BAA. This principle extended beyond the design and build part of T5, and included BAA in conjunction with BA working in a similar way all the way through, including operational readiness.

Teams are where the work gets done – the roof gets lifted, the twin rivers get put in place, the control tower built. The leadership and client focus on T5 was to enable these and many other teams to ensure that they had the best people working as part of those groups, that they had the frameworks and tools they needed to do their best work, and when things went wrong that focus and energy would be put into fixing the problem, not blaming others or calling the lawyers in.

T5 by no means got it right all the time in every team. What is important is that leaders and the client understood that it was important to do everything possible to try to get teams working together and delivering.

Twin Rivers – Sections Of The 3,000 Metres Diversion At Start And Completion

Air Side Road Tunnel – Views Of Sections Of The 13.5km Of Road Tunnels

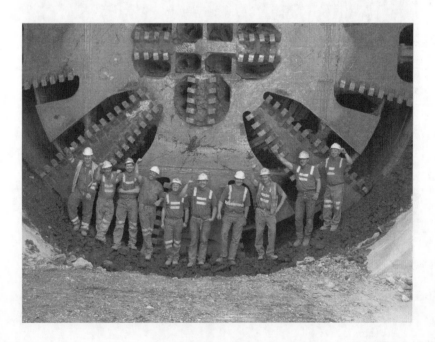

Roof Dry Run Study In Yorkshire Identified 125 Improvements

Raising The 40 Metre High Roof At Heathrow

Roof Team At Work

87 Metres High Heathrow Air Traffic Control Tower

Baggage – 12,000 Bags Processed In An Hour On 11 Carrousels, 2 For Domestic And 9 For International

PART 4

THE FINAL VERDICT

In the beginning there was a sludge farm on a site the size of Hyde Park that took years, countless conversations by Tony Powers, a BAA project manager, and a £300 million spend to clear. At the end there is a world-class airport that 30 million passengers will use each year. In between there have been 22 years of trials and tribulations, that the leaders, the client and the integrated team have worked together on to deliver T5 on time, to budget, safely and with care to the environment as a quality passenger experience.

Some of the characters have been involved in T5 for nearly all that time. Mike Davies, Liz Southern, Phil Wilbraham, Powers and others have been there for a moment in time and played their part in making history.

To compete this round-up on the T5 story and the reasons that in the main it has been a successful UK project, the final chapter reviews:

Heathrow's Terminal 5: History in the Making   S. Doherty
© 2008 John Wiley & Sons, Ltd

- What could still go wrong before opening.
- The verdict on the planning inquiry, design, construction and operational readiness.

T5 will open officially at 4 a.m. on 27 March 2008. The world's press will be watching, critically exploring what hasn't quite gone to plan. The first flight will arrive from Charles De Gaulle at 4.30 a.m. and the first real passengers will be quizzed by all involved for their impressions; potentially many of the press will be those passengers. There will be those who love T5 and those who will be indifferent or who focus on getting the rest of Heathrow up to the same standard. If everything goes to plan it will be interesting if there is a moment when the critics say, 'T5 has been a UK success story of how to design, build and open an airport that gets it right for passengers.'

CHAPTER 12

TWENTY-TWO YEARS IN THE MAKING: HOW WILL IT END?

T5 opened on time and to budget, the passengers think it looks good and works even better,
and both airline and airport operator are on
track to meet their T5 operating profits after the
first year.

Press report 27 March 2009 (or at least the one
BAA and BA are trying to deliver!)

When the dust settles on T5, many different views
will have been expressed, ranging from 'It has been a rare UK
mega project success story' to 'It was actually a well-managed PR
campaign' or, depending on the opening experience, there is still
room for 'It was a complete fiasco'. This book on T5 goes to print a
few months before a critical milestone, the actual terminal opening,
so we shall explore what hurdles still await those involved in the

Heathrow's Terminal 5: History in the Making   S. Doherty
© 2008 John Wiley & Sons, Ltd

T5 Programme, consider the pre-opening and post-opening criteria that are likely to be reviewed, look at the broader verdict of the impact on the aviation, construction and retail industries and finally provide a round-up of likely stakeholder comments.

In conversation with Andrew Wolstenholme, now capital projects director, BAA, he commented:

> There should be another book written about the last 2% of the T5 Programme. It may be the last few percentage, but it has taken 20% of the effort. For me T5 has been like climbing Mount Everest. On 17 September 2006 the team had reached the Southeast Ridge at 27 700 feet, as we handed T5 over to the T5live team. The reality has been we still had the South Summit and the Cornice Traverse to navigate, before we got to the final Hilary Step at 28 750 feet. Many climbers fail at these late stages and the team have had to dig deep to make sure that wasn't T5's legacy.

Mark Bullock, now managing director, Heathrow, BAA, is keeping a sharp focus on T5, partly as between now and opening the proving trials will identify things that don't work or need to be improved before the opening day. He says:

> I have a good team with the right detailed plan between now and opening which means we and BA are in good shape. There is no room for complacency in opening T5 or in the start of the planned moves for another 54 airlines that start as BA moves out of T1 and T4. As we open T5, we pretty much go into a busy Easter and that will be a test for the facility, the team working there, but also for the rest of Heathrow as they become accustomed to having a fifth terminal.

Willie Walsh, CEO BA, was clear: 'I've looked in the eyes of the BAA team and my own and there is nothing that will stop T5 opening, not just on time, but it will be an experience that wows our passengers from day one.'

WHAT COULD STOP T5 OPENING ON TIME?

In the spirit of good risk management and mitigation to the end, the T5 and increasingly Heathrow management team will be reviewing the risks that they face in the run-up to opening and making sure they don't occur. However, plans will be being developed to understand what contingency plans need to be in place in case the unthinkable did happen.

The big risks are a fire at T5, systems failure, employee relations issues and terrorism.

Fire

There are two elements to fire that continue to be a risk for the project: not having a fully integrated fire-alarm system and the potential for a fire during the fit-out process. For the insurers of T5 there is a step-change in the risk profile in the run-up to T5 opening, but for Grant Levy, T5 head of systems and technical leader for fire systems, all is in hand.

The integrated fire-alarm and public announcement system is probably the largest system in the world serving the four main buildings. The good news is that the satellite building has already been approved, and the other three are on track to be completed at the end of January.

The size of the task should not be underestimated, though. The fire system is a business-critical system that is fully integrated across all the other utility systems and into the BSI (bitstream integrated) graphical headend or distribution system. If a fire alarm goes off in the main terminal building, there are potentially 1700 interfaces that need to be shown to work, ranging from door release to damper operations, fans starting and fans stopping. After the T5 systems assurance team has reviewed the fire systems, the building control and fire brigade will then give the final witness signoff.

In preparation for approval, the team involved is currently scenario planning each eventuality and testing that the system works in those circumstances.

As the 4000 'men in white vans' move in and out of T5, the building, in an unfamiliar environment with a potential for introducing combustible materials, T5 is at its highest risk of a fire. As it stands there are fire systems in operation, including the sprinkler system, that would allow people to escape from the building safely. Operationally, considerable effort has been made to limit this potential exposure through awareness training as a part of the incident and injury-free approach and strict control of hot works and waste-management activities.

After Christmas, the risk of extensive damage to the building prior to opening will be significantly mitigated as the active fire systems go live; however, there is still an inherent risk of serious damage. As this book goes to print this has been managed.

Unknown unknowns with systems

On such big, complex projects there are always things that could have been overlooked. Having spent over £150 million on different systems, excluding baggage, there is a lot to work on from day one. The track record of Hong Kong and Denver airports is of systems failures at opening and afterwards they are stark reminders of what could have been.

It is impossible to know how everything will actually work under the pressure of tens of thousands of passengers. The T5 team has, however, studied previous airport failures, and put in all the right steps to mitigate this type of risk.

The systems construction and operational readiness strategy outlined in Chapter 6 was designed to make sure that a systems failure didn't happen. Being very cautious with technology innovations, the off-site systems-testing facility has been in operation since early 2004, testing every system before going to site individually as well as with its interfaces and during operational readiness.

Finally, the early start of operational readiness, working with the airline from day one, guarding the six-month window for the 72 trials across landside, terminal and airside processes, including BAA,

BA and all other third parties, have all been in part about testing systems.

Employee relations challenges

Both BA and BAA have over the last few years been on long journeys with their workforces and trade unions in preparation for T5. In principle, both have agreed, or at least gained acceptance of, most of the significant changes before employees move into T5. Both organizations have worked hard to build direct relationships with their workforce as well as the appropriate relationships with the trade unions to be ready for this change.

Strategically Unite which represents both BAA and BA workers, the largest union at Heathrow, representing check-in, security, engineering and baggage staff, has been supportive of Heathrow expansion, as it creates more jobs and more members for them.

The huge risk Heathrow faced that there would be industrial action in the run up to opening T5 has been avoided. However, in September 2007 BAA announced its intention to close the final salary pension scheme. The fight to reverse this decision has been the top priority for the trade unions since that time. Strike action was only narrowly avoided in January 2008 and discussions were continuing, with the scheme still open to new employees, as this book went to print. This means that whilst there is no immediate threat of industrial action directly related to the opening and operation of T5, BAA face the risk of a company wide dispute very soon after the new terminal opens.

Add to this backdrop the operational pressures which will be caused by employees experiencing changes of rosters, working practices and place of work, some of whom will not like what is going on.

Terrorism

T5 has always been a potential terrorist target, as a high-profile construction site and then an operational airport, part of Heathrow airport. At one level that is the same for the rest of Heathrow and all major airports, but there will be extra focus around opening and in the early weeks and months because T5 is an iconic building.

It must be remembered that a few month after Madrid's Barajas airport opened, a bomb went off in the car park killing two people and injuring 26. ETA, the Basque nationalist organization, claimed responsibility for the explosion.

The police and security at Heathrow are first rate and both work well together. Those teams have done and will continue to do what is required to manage this risk. This section has been purposely been left vague for security reasons.

The impact of a poor T5 opening

There would be a big difference for BAA between a terrorist attack on the day of opening or the baggage system breaking down on day one. While neither would be welcome, any management failing would have a huge reputational impact. Also the press would swoop on any issues as the shape of things to come for both BAA and BA, and any glitch on the big opening day would put their relationship under significant pressure. A final hitch with T5 opening is improbable but not impossible.

PRE-OPENING VERDICT

Planning

The longest ever planning inquiry will go down in history, but unfortunately for all the wrong reasons. While meaningful checks and balances do need to be in place, there have been reforms in the approach to planning permission from the painful lessons learnt on T5. BAA, in the shape of Heathrow East, has already benefited from those changes.

Verdict: Heathrow and the passengers using the facilities have suffered more than they might have due to the long planning inquiry. The strain that the travelling public have felt has intensified since 2000 as a 45-million-capacity airport has dealt with the steady climb to 68 million passengers in 2006 and additional security measures. With a more prompt inquiry Heathrow could now be on track not only to have opened T5 in early 2000, but also to be near completing Heathrow East and upgrading the rest of the airport. Some judgements were made that have had significant consequences for the public, the airlines, BAA and potentially the reputation of the UK.

Design

For the design consultants and in-house BAA design team, there would be great pride in T5 winning one of the big design awards such as the Stirling prize. However, of much more importance and a test for the team will be the passenger reaction. Whether the main terminal building delivers the 'wow' impact will be a key indicator of a shift in the experience of Heathrow. Everyone who comes out impressed with what the future looks like for the airport will give real credence to the claim of Heathrow transformation.

T5 has changed the skyline of Heathrow and as such will no doubt be a contender for design prizes. The BAA team is braced for some criticism from the external design community, as there are a number of areas in the building that the team know could have been improved, noted in Chapter 4.

Within the budget available, to achieve the best passenger experience substance has at times prevailed over form. For example, some may say that the large way-finding beacons distract from the form of the building, but they increase the ease with which passengers will move through the terminal. If it is as good as the design team have suggested, T5 may not win the best-looking airport in the world, but it could be the one passengers enjoy using most, an accolade that on balance the design team would prefer.

There are many examples of design success. The design team has set a clear vision for T5 and guarded that concept under pressure. There have been great examples of integrated teamworking between design, construction and end user, who have jointly developed safe and cost-effective design solutions. There will equally be some questioning over whether finishing and freezing design took longer than it should have and whether a more disciplined regime of milestone management should have been put in place to manage production design earlier.

Verdict: Lessons have been learnt about the design discipline required on mega projects and are already being put to good use on Heathrow East. The proof will be in the pudding, as they say, when it comes to design. The prediction is that the travelling public will enjoy using T5, because it looks good but works even better. It may even pick up a prestigious award or two!

Construction

As long as there are no final hitches, there can be no doubt that the time dimension has been delivered. In 2001 the 30 March 2008 deadline was set and through hard-nosed milestone planning and delivery, the project will actually open ahead of time on 27 March 2008.

There will be more critics on cost. Scope changes and outturn costs do make it difficult for the outside world on any mega project to see absolute transparency on costs. That ambiguity will fuel speculation, but if closing of final accounts goes to plan, the £4.3 billion target set in 2003 will be delivered.

There will also be those who are critical that T5 just cost too much, even if it was on budget. Some of the design is too elaborate, the T5 Agreement paid over the odds for risk management, too much was spent on the people and logistics agendas and there were too many BAA people involved in micro-managing what suppliers should have been left to do. But as Andrew Wolstenholme commented, 'Project management seems too expensive unless something goes wrong. T5 went well because we put in place the right contract, leaders, approach to teams and invested in an environment that gave them the tools they needed to deliver.'

At one level these are all valid challenges. At another, it is important to remember what could have been and some of the reasons. On industry predictions a year late and a billion over budget was the risk that BAA faced as it started T5, and in Chapter 2 there are few examples of multibillion-pound construction success stories. BAA going into T5 only had a 5 % risk pot, significantly smaller than most projects, and yet with an approach to managing and mitigating risk that got integrated teams to perform differently, it seems to have paid off. Much of the design look and feel were stipulated by planning permission consent. Finally, most of the innovation and discipline that were established on T5 in some shape or form had a BAA person setting an objective, facilitating an outcome or doing a job that in other projects a supplier would be doing, but with a different set of skills or focus to come up with new ideas.

Safety on T5 did set a new tone for the building-construction industry. The approach to behavioural safety saved lives and changed the attitude of all who were involved; most importantly, the major players on T5 now have it as part of how they operate.

Verdict: The T5 Agreement was a courageous approach to contracting that not all in BAA or its suppliers fully embraced. However, there was enough support for it to act as a philosophy that enabled integrated teams to deliver in good times and when things went wrong and settled £4.3 billion of final accounts without the lawyers, as things stand going to print. BAA's third-generation framework supplier agreement demonstrates that Heathrow East is likely to take advantage of the T5 learning.

Operational readiness

The approach to operational readiness has been fairly textbook, BAA has learned from others and started early on working with the end user, BA. There may be critics who say that BAA has been too cautious and hence spent too much money on this activity, but the alternative of scrimping on testing in such a complex and integrated environment as Heathrow is easy for those without accountability for it to suggest.

Verdict: This approach to opening and integrating T5 has created certainty and more transparency in the run-up to opening. Operational readiness has developed into Heathrow integration and the tools and methodologies are now part of how any new project or process is deployed across the airport. The prediction is that T5 will open on 27 March 2008 and that the meticulous regime of testing will have paid off.

POST-OPENING VERDICT

Political

What might those in government say and learn?

Provided that T5 opens on time and is a success, it will be symbolic, along with St Pancras, of what the best of British design and engineering can deliver. While Heathrow continues to be upgraded, T5 and the Virgin T3 experience, along with other refurbishments, will be tangible examples of what international business people using London can expect in part now and across most of Heathrow by 2012.

In the corridors of government there is, however, some scepticism about BAA's approach at T5. With respect to the T5 Agreement and partnering, while the government is interested in this concept, there remain naysayers who will talk about T5 as goldplated or having a soft attitude to suppliers. At the heart of this thinking is government's understanding of risk management. Take the financial markets as another example. Government securitized risk, reduced it to small packages, dispersed it across the system on the assumption that it would be readily absorbed. When problems arose, government was surprised that it did not know where the risk was and could not price it.

There is a long way to go for the deeper understanding of risk, and for contracts that drive collaborative behaviour and why this should be best practice for both private and public-sector investment. There is a real question for government about how the public is best served when it comes to spending public funds on capital investment. The need to be seen to be fair and transparent drives a culture of re-tendering and yet as the likes of Tesco, housing associations, Thames Water, BAA and many others would confirm, in Wolstenholme's words, 'Partnering if you build one project is not a definite recipe for success. Build 100 and it's the only option to drive out waste and deliver value to the client.'

Impact of T5 on the rest of Heathrow

'Whether T5 is the making or breaking of Heathrow, that's the real question.' The question was posed by Mick Temple, managing director, Heathrow until 2006. The T5 opening presents an opportunity for Heathrow to start the climb back to being a world-class airport and as long as the Heathrow East project goes ahead together with the upgrade promised in T4, then the competitive equivalence debate, while simmering in the background, will not get out of hand. All the key stakeholders in the airline community, Virgin and the alliances will have or see their new home being built or upgraded.

If the regulatory settlement makes some of those plans impossible or less ambitious for one airline or grouping than another, then some of the emotions that can run high within the community will be difficult to manage for today, but more importantly for joint and collaborative working for Heathrow's future.

Economic

Numbers of passengers using T5

It is highly unlikely that T5 as part of Heathrow will ever find itself with the challenge of not having enough passengers. Flybbjerg *et al.* (2003) are not only critical of design and construction overruns, but also conclude that 'future traffic forecasts are not to be trusted', citing Calcutta metro, in India, which delivered 5 % of the actual predicted traffic predicted in year one, to the Channel Tunnel, 18 %; Paris Nord, TGV, 25 %; Denver Airport, 55 %. Even the successful design and construction project St Pancras is suffering from 'overoptimistic forecasting by the consortium that took on the project, they had expected 21 million passengers in year one and it looks more like eight million (Radio 4, 2007; *Times*, 4 November 2007).

T5 is predicted to be a 30 million passenger terminal when the second satellite is complete in 2010. Year one with one satellite is predicted to deliver 28 million passengers, even if they are already using the airport. There is something unique about T5 and Heathrow in comparison with most of the projects reviewed by Flybbjerg; that is, the scarcity of capacity and the limited choice mean that it is highly likely T5 will fulfil its passenger forecasts.

Efficiency gains

Both BAA and BA have been guarded about what they say about the cost efficiencies and revenue-generating opportunities that T5 presents. The party line for BA is that it will benefit from a 10 % plus people efficiency gain as a result of moving the T1 and T4 operation in T5, a figure that could have been more, but with the airline now also going into T3 that is not the case. There is also an ambition that the improved passenger experience of T5 will make BA an airline of choice, a position Virgin will be working hard to defend with its newly refurbished T3 service.

BAA has been quiet on the operating efficiencies that T5 will deliver. According to Bullock, new security technology, while creating a more efficient security process, will not be seen as an opportunity to cut staff but rather to build in more resilience. It is also the case that for at least another year after opening BAA will be oper-ating five terminals not four, with the same number of passengers, so that the benefit of new facilities will take some time to wash through.

Revenue gains

For retail, the position is that a 10 % uplift in income per passenger will be achieved. As passengers enjoy the T5 ambience, getting through security more easily and then being faced with the choice of great views and great shopping there may be more opportunities.

Environment

BAA is on target to reduce its own CO_2 emissions from energy by 15 % below 1990 levels by 2010. This is in excess of the UK's targets under the Kyoto treaty and is despite a predicted growth in passenger numbers of 70 % during this period. BAA has recently set a new target to further reduce CO_2 emissions from energy use in buildings by 30 % by 2020. T5 is part of this big-picture improvement for Heathrow.

Construction has laid some strong foundations about working with the Environment Agency and taking the environment agenda seriously. During T5 construction 97 % of waste was recycled, and the twin rivers were moved successfully with a mandate to create an 'equivalent or better habitat' for the wildlife, which was achieved.

In the operational airport, T5 will have significantly reduced the consumption of potable water up to the target of 70 %, and has a target of recycling or composting 40 % of its waste by 2010. By 2020, 70 % of the waste will be recycled. Landscaping and the design of the building have taken into account noise control.

THE FINAL WORD

Familiarity, fascinating facts and impossible challenges overcome by human endeavour that can be learnt from – that is what has made T5, over 20 years in the making, a story that needed to be told.

68 million passengers a year use Heathrow, 28 million of those will from 27 March 2008 start to use T5, and with T5 online Heathrow's capacity can increase to 90 million. Love or loathe

Heathrow, it is difficult to ignore. It is an economic powerhouse for the UK, contributing to employment, competitiveness and tourism. It is in the country's interest for Heathrow to be a world-class gateway, and T5 is one of the many steps to deliver a new Heathrow for London on a journey to 2012, taking in the building of Heathrow East and significant refurbishments across the rest of the campus.

A year late, a billion pound over budget was the T5 risk that would have broken BAA if it had not been mitigated. The BAA executives had that as a challenge with a backdrop of a UK construction industry that had failed to deliver on mega projects such as the Jubilee line, the British Library and, coming up to date, Wembley Stadium and Holyrood. T5 had to buck the trend or it would break BAA.

T5 has been the largest construction site in Europe and if all goes to plan, it will be delivered ahead of a date agreed with the BAA executive in 2001 and be bang on budget, as agreed by the BAA executive in 2003. The environment has been taken seriously from the beginning, and whether building to accommodate archaeology, working with the Environment Agency on the twin rivers or taking care in the materials that have been used, BAA has had the environment at front of mind. The new approach to safety, incident and injury free, is a behavioural safety programme that has been acknowledged by suppliers, trade unions, industry awards and the workers on site as ground breaking. Sadly, despite a relentless commitment to safety, two men still lost their lives on T5.

Time will tell if the operating profits, retail spend and workforce efficiencies are actually delivered. But what stands the test of time will be the passenger experience. Promised to look good and work even better, T5 is an iconic building and setting that was designed by Rogers Stirk Harbour + Partners, built and opened by an integrated team led by the client BAA, which will set a new UK and maybe even world benchmark in some aspects.

Many things went wrong along the way. The planning inquiry lasted longer than anyone had ever imagined. The scheme design had to be changed three times, partly due to planning recommendations, but also due to the sheer time it had been in inquiry and world events happening around it, which required new specifications and, in turn, new designs. The first winter of construction was harsh and put the team on a late, not early, production curve, which meant that from day one, time was in short supply. Cost challenges were unearthed in the early days and the challenge of getting back on plan was again an uphill struggle every day to exploit opportunities, buying better, having fewer knowledge workers, looking at stopping or driving costs out of design. Projects didn't go to plan, most notably in the case of the technical challenges on HATCT; fraud was detected; suppliers were asked to leave; there was a strike; and there were probably more births, deaths, marriages and divorces than anyone would care to remember.

But failure was never an option for T5. Fundamentally, that was due to the key leaders, working with an intelligent client, BAA, to get an integrated team to deliver. The leaders saw the big picture, were driven and were able to trust differently when working with stakeholders and teams. The client, BAA, fundamentally set the tone with the T5 Agreement, a commercial contract in which the client owned most of the risk. With new rules of engagement the integrated supply team, made up of 20 000 different suppliers, felt able to focus on the work, solving problems and innovation, rather than worrying about bringing in the lawyers.

T5's legacy to BAA is a well-managed risk that unlocks the regeneration of Heathrow. BA has a new home and the rest of the campus is on plan for improvement. This is all good for the travelling public. For the construction industry, 50 000 people experienced T5 and take that with them to their next jobs. We hear great examples of workers demanding the T5 safety culture as they move onto other sites, some of the ideas, frameworks and, probably most significantly, people moving to important projects like the Olympics. Sadly though, the ideas of the ground-breaking contract, the T5 Agreement, haven't made the impact that some would have hoped for. Clients and their approach to risk management are on a very slow journey towards partnering. Ray O'Rourke from Laing O'Rourke commented, 'The industry needed five T5s to really make the transformation we are all looking to try and achieve.' That is unlikely.

Heathrow's Terminal 5: History in the Making is for those in the industry, those interested in modern history or those keen to explore details of how large-scale transformation was delivered. It is also for the 50 000 people who played their part in *making history*.

TIPS AND QUESTIONS WHEN STARTING A MEGA PROJECT

The BAA way isn't the only right answer, but BAA has been an intelligent client for over 20 years now and has pioneered different thinking and a track record of doing what they said they would do.

Sir Michael Latham, industry expert

When the team started on T5, one of the commonly used phrases was: 'There isn't a book on the shelf that will tell you how to do deliver T5.' That was true for the T5 team, though they did learn from successes and failures from around the world and from the industry by going to see and listen to others, commissioning many reports along the way.

Heathrow's Terminal 5: History in the Making   S. Doherty
© 2008 John Wiley & Sons, Ltd

To deliver T5 a team of people with some experience of big projects, looking at other industries and plenty of experimentation, created a set of ideas, frameworks and ways of working that to differing degrees are captured in the previous chapters. However, a summary of the right questions to ask and the key tips from the experience is given below. This will not quite be the book on the shelf that gives the answer, as no two projects are ever the same, but it is hopefully an easy read and helpful starting point.

In keeping with the critical success factors of the book, this appendix will look at questions from the perspectives of:

- The leaders
- The client during planning, design, construction and operational readiness
- The integrated teams

For those clients who choose to not be 'hands on', these questions may still give some clues as to what your representatives should be doing. The appendix finishes with a checklist of strategies, frameworks and systems that the client and contractors need to think about having in place.

TIPS AND GOOD QUESTIONS TO ASK

Leadership and people

- What is the size of the leadership challenge? A sufficient number of leaders should have an understanding of the size of the challenge, be able to create a comprehensible, joined-up plan and lead the team to deliver against it, and then be adept at navigating the stakeholder environment.
- Different leaders will be needed for different phases of the project. Plan for this in advance and influence suppliers to make sure that they do the same.

- Treat site workers with respect, taking their needs seriously, as it is then likely that they will be more productive and less likely to strike.

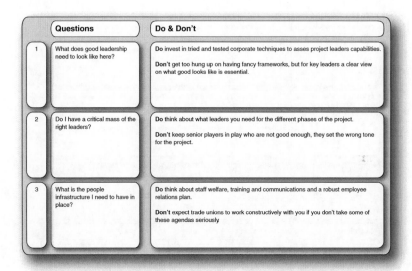

	Questions	Do & Don't
1	What does good leadership need to look like here?	**Do** invest in tried and tested corporate techniques to asses project leaders capabilities. **Don't** get too hung up on having fancy frameworks, but for key leaders a clear view on what good looks like is essential.
2	Do I have a critical mass of the right leaders?	**Do** think about what leaders you need for the different phases of the project. **Don't** keep senior players in play who are not good enough, they set the wrong tone for the project.
3	What is the people infrastructure I need to have in place?	**Do** think about staff welfare, training and communications and a robust employee relations plan. **Don't** expect trade unions to work constructively with you if you don't take some of these agendas seriously

Client

- Understand, manage and mitigate the risks and opportunities.
- Know what you want to deliver: the brief, time, cost, quality, safety and environment targets.
- Set the targets and then programme-manage time, cost, quality, safety and environment deliverables, putting in place transparent reporting and effective governance.

	Questions	Do & Don't
4	What are the risks & how do I best manage them?	**Do** debate what complex risk is and differentiate between cause and effect versus work that can be ring fenced. **Don't** think you can give away complex risk at no cost.
5	What does success look like in design, cost, quality, safety and environment?	**Do** understand who are the stakeholders in this decision and then be clear with them about what they are getting at what cost. **Don't** keep changing your mind and not expect it to impact the time and cost.
6	As a client what role do I need to play and do I have the capability in-house to deliver?	**Do** be hands o if you have a supply chain that you know and trust, and that has a track record of delivery. **Don't** be hands on if you don't have the capability to deliver. A clear and realistic business case needs to be in place, with a focus not just on build costs, but also a view on ongoing maintenance costs.

	Questions	Do & Don't
7	What are the challenges during each phase & what infrastructure needs to be in place to enable?	**Do** map out at a high level the different phases, get the right numbers and capability of team in early enough to make the difference. Ensure you or your principal contractor/s sets the team up for success. Remember silo working can make it difficult to drive out waste. **Don't** get obsessed with the bits of paper being filled out at the expense of the leadership culture taking and being seen to take risk seriously.
8	How am I going to know the ongoing targets are being delivered?	**Do** put in place in place accurate programme management and governance processes. **Don't** rely on reports only, get out and talk to the people the project leaders don't want you to talk to.
9	How do I manage stakeholders?	**Do** have a proactive plan of engagement and have the right personalities to get personal relationships. **Don't** be a victim even if some of the relationships are complicated and difficult to manage, think about using last responsible moment, LRM, to be clear about what they need to do by when to contribute to the success of the project.
10	How am I going to manage the message?	**Do** have a communication strategy and plan to take your message continually to the press and stakeholders. **Don't** say no comment.

Client in planning

	Questions	Do & Don't
11	Have I tested my proposal against national, regional and local policy before submission?	**Do** adapt your proposal if it doesn't comply with policy, not doing so will prove costly and delay your start date. **Don't** assume you will get consent if you don't comply, only 20% of those who contest decisions win their case.
12	Have I talked to all the key stakeholders before submission, persuading them in line with policy and if there are differences taking mitigating action?	**Do** really listen and understand, in your submission use their phrases and raise the issues they have raised with mitigating actions proposed. **Don't** pay lip service to your stakeholders, they will end up feeling patronised.
13	Have I got the proper professional help from advisors, e.g. noise assessments, ecology reports etc?	**Do** give a clear brief to the experts. **Don't** go with the cheapest, they need to be advisors you trust and will be credible.

Client in design

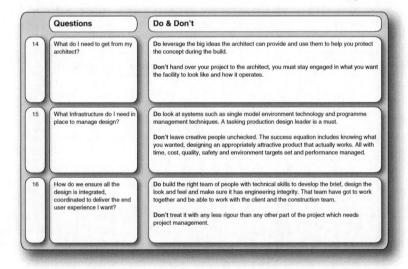

	Questions	Do & Don't
14	What do I need to get from my architect?	**Do** leverage the big ideas the architect can provide and use them to help you protect the concept during the build. **Don't** hand over your project to the architect, you must stay engaged in what you want the facility to look like and how it operates.
15	What Infrastructure do I need in place to manage design?	**Do** look at systems such as single model environment technology and programme management techniques. A tasking production design leader is a must. **Don't** leave creative people unchecked. The success equation includes knowing what you wanted, designing an appropriately attractive product that actually works. All with time, cost, quality, safety and environment targets set and performance managed.
16	How do we ensure all the design is integrated, coordinated to deliver the end user experience I want?	**Do** build the right team of people with technical skills to develop the brief, design the look and feel and make sure it has engineering integrity. That team have got to work together and be able to work with the client and the construction team. **Don't** treat it with any less rigour than any other part of the project which needs project management.

Client in construction

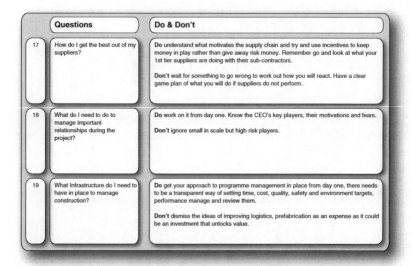

Questions	Do & Don't
17 How do I get the best out of my suppliers?	**Do** understand what motivates the supply chain and try and use incentives to keep money in play rather than give away risk money. Remember go and look at what your 1st tier suppliers are doing with their sub-contractors. **Don't** wait for something to go wrong to work out how you will react. Have a clear game plan of what you will do if suppliers do not perform.
18 What do I need to do to manage important relationships during the project?	**Do** work on it from day one. Know the CEO's key players, their motivations and fears. **Don't** ignore small in scale but high risk players.
19 What Infrastructure do I need to have in place to manage construction?	**Do** get your approach to programme management in place from day one, there needs to be a transparent way of setting time, cost, quality, safety and environment targets, performance manage and review them. **Don't** dismiss the ideas of improving logistics, prefabrication as an expense as it could be an investment that unlocks value.

Client in operational readiness

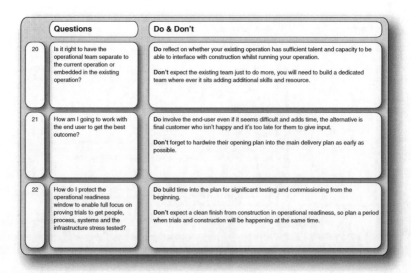

Questions	Do & Don't
20 Is it right to have the operational team separate to the current operation or embedded in the existing operation?	**Do** reflect on whether your existing operation has sufficient talent and capacity to be able to interface with construction whilst running your operation. **Don't** expect the existing team just to do more, you will need to build a dedicated team where ever it sits adding additional skills and resource.
21 How am I going to work with the end user to get the best outcome?	**Do** involve the end-user even if it seems difficult and adds time, the alternative is final customer who isn't happy and it's too late for them to give input. **Don't** forget to hardwire their opening plan into the main delivery plan as early as possible.
22 How do I protect the operational readiness window to enable full focus on proving trials to get people, process, systems and the infrastructure stress tested?	**Do** build time into the plan for significant testing and commissioning from the beginning. **Don't** expect a clean finish from construction in operational readiness, so plan a period when trials and construction will be happening at the same time.

Integrated teams

- A commercial contract was put in place, the T5 Agreement, which encouraged the right behaviours.
- Client, designers, suppliers and end users worked together to common, visible goals.
- Success was celebrated. Failures were quickly rounded on and support given to solve the problem and get back on track, as well as learning from it.

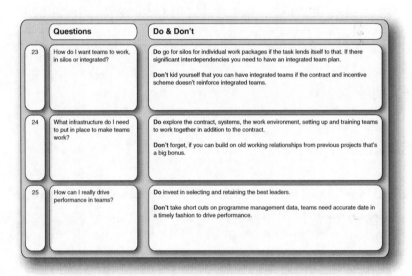

	Questions	Do & Don't
23	How do I want teams to work, in silos or integrated?	**Do** go for silos for individual work packages if the task lends itself to that. If there significant interdependencies you need to have an integrated team plan. **Don't** kid yourself that you can have integrated teams if the contract and incentive scheme doesn't reinforce integrated teams.
24	What infrastructure do I need to put in place to make teams work?	**Do** explore the contract, systems, the work environment, setting up and training teams to work together in addition to the contract. **Don't** forget, if you can build on old working relationships from previous projects that's a big bonus.
25	How can I really drive performance in teams?	**Do** invest in selecting and retaining the best leaders. **Don't** take short cuts on programme management data, teams need accurate date in a timely fashion to drive performance.

MUST-HAVE STRATEGIES, FRAMEWORKS AND SYSTEMS

Strategies and plans

- Commercial
- Design
- Construction, including logistics

- Operational readiness
- People and employee relations
- Communication
- Stakeholders

Frameworks

- Objectives setting
- Governance
- Programme management, time, cost, quality, safety, environment and risk management, in all phases of the T5 Programme
- User-friendly processes
- Risk management
- Supplier review
- People review

Systems

- Intranet – to manage communication generally and a go-to place for all the other systems
- Single-model environment and Documentum – to manage design
- Artemis – to manage time and cost
- People tracking that links to logistics

SUMMARY

Hopefully the combination of reading all of this book and reflecting on the key questions to ask will assist in preparation for the different stages of leading projects.

Quite often projects sit for a while in the planning inquiry stage and time is lost in getting ready for detailed design, construction and opening. This time isn't best used to actually make sure that everyone is ready to get a good start on a project. Try to get on to the early stages of a project quickly, having all the suppliers in place and organized, with processes and systems set up to manage time, cost, quality, safety and environment requirements through all phases of the project.

THE T5 INTEGRATED TEAM

Over 20 000 organizations have been involved in T5 over the years. Obviously these included BAA and key stakeholders such as BA, the control authorities, retailers and many others, but the vast majority were:

- Designers
- Suppliers with greater than £5 million spend
- Cost and commercial consultants

Heathrow's Terminal 5: History in the Making   S. Doherty
© 2008 John Wiley & Sons, Ltd

Designers

Who	What they did
Rogers Stirk Harbour + Partners	Lead architect
Arup	Building superstructures designers, main terminal building t-out, mechanical electrical services designers, building acoustic consultants, communications, IT and Security designers, security consultant
HOK International Ltd	T5 station interchange design, terminal planning and production support architects
Pascall & Watson Ltd	T5 buildings scheme and production design architects
Mott Macdonald	Building substructures designers
Hyland Edgar Driver	Landscape architects
DSSR	Mechanical electrical services concept designers
DIN Associates	Fit-out design consultants
Priestman Goode	Product design consultants
Stantec	Wayfinding consultants
BUA	Energy centre architects
Gebler Tooth	Baggage systems designers
TPS	Landside and Airfield Designers
Speirs and Major Associates	Lighting architects
Chapman Taylor	Retail architects
YRM	British Airways' architects
WSP	T5 satellite building, MSCP5, landside campus services production designers, British Airways services concept designers, British Airways structural designers
Davies and Baron	British Airways' commercially important passenger areas concept designers
3DReid	Production design for British Airways airfield projects

Suppliers of £5 million plus spend

Who	What they did
Laing O'Rourke Civil Engineering Ltd	General civil engineering & concrete structures
Spie Matthew Hall, was Amec group limited	Mechanical and electrical installation & aircraft pavements
Sever eld – Rowens Ltd	Structural steelwork
Vanderlande Industries UK	Baggage installation
MACE Ltd	Fit-out and project management
Morgan Vinci JV	Bored tunnels
Crown House, was Carillion Construction Ltd	Mechanical and electrical installation
NTL Group Ltd	Systems
Balfour Beatty Ltd	Rail and station fit-out
Honeywalls, was Novar	Fire alarms & business management systems
Hathaway Roofing Ltd	Roofing
Ultra Electronics, was Ferranti	Systems
Bombardier Transportation, Holdings, USA inc	Track transit system
Seele, Austria GmbH	Glazed screens
Kone PLC	Escalators and lifts
ThyssenKrupp Airport Systems	Air bridges and xed links
Permasteelisa	Internal glazed walls
CMF Limited	Architectural metalwork
Network Rail	Signalling for HEX
Lindner Schmidlin Facades	Facades
Swift Horsman	Doors
Project Security Moves	Security
Compass Services, UK Ltd	Catering
Barlows Group Limited	Desks
Vetters	Flooring
Grants of Shoreditch	Flooring

Key consultants

EC Harris Group Ltd	Cost and commercial management
Turner & Townsend Group Ltd	Cost and commercial management

REFERENCES

Quotes

Page 6, courtesy of BBC News Online (18 May 2004) – Flying squad foils £80 m robbery

Page 8, courtesy of BAA (July 1995) – Heathrow into the 21st Century

Page 13, courtesy of BAA (June 2005) – Heathrow Airport Interim Master Plan

Page 13, courtesy of Cushman & Wakefield Healey & Baker (2005) – European Cities Monitor

Page 13, courtesy of Oxford Economic Forecasting (2006) – The Economic Contribution of the Aviation Industry in the UK

Page 13, courtesy of BAA (June 2005) – Heathrow Airport Interim Master Plan

Page 18, courtesy of Oxford Economic Forecasting (2006) – The Economic Contribution of the Aviation Industry in the UK

Page 19, courtesy of Daily Mail Online (10 August 2007) – Our airports are a national disgrace

Page 23, courtesy of Civil Aviation Authority (November 2002) Competition Commission report on BAA London airports – Appendix 10.1

Page 24, courtesy of UN (2007) – The 2007 Revision Population Database

Page 25, courtesy of Asiaone Online (6 September 2007) – Riding the regional aviation boom

Page 26, courtesy of BAA Annual Report 2005–06

Page 27, courtesy of Times Online (19 June 2005) – Growth is the big challenge facing the aircraft industry

Page 30, courtesy of Construction Industry Task Force (1998) – Rethinking Construction

Page 31, courtesy of Department of Trade and Industry (2004) – Construction Report

Page 31, courtesy of Department of Trade and Industry (2006) – Construction Report

Page 33, courtesy of Flybbjerg, B., Bruzelius, N. & Rothengatter, W. (2003) – Megaprojects and Risk, Cambridge University Press

---

Heathrow's Terminal 5: History in the Making   S. Doherty
© 2008 John Wiley & Sons, Ltd

Page 34, courtesy of Economist Online (26 August 1999) – Bad landing

Page 35, courtesy of Wikipedia – Denver International Airport

Page 35, courtesy of BBC World News Online (8 July 1998) – Hong Kong airport honeymoon ends

Page 35, courtesy of CBC News Canada Online (24 May 2004) – New cracking noises heard in Paris terminal

Page 37, courtesy of Times Online (16 April 2003) – A scandal of monumental proportions

Page 38, courtesy of Times Online (1 April 2006) – Battle lines drawn in Wembley stadium saga

Page 38, courtesy of Times Online (26 May 2004) – Holyrood project a catalogue of failures, says QC

Page 41, courtesy of Sunday Times (4 November 2007) – St Pancreas

Page 47, courtesy of BAA (2007) – ICE Planning Report

Page 60, courtesy of BAA (Feb 2003) – The Future of Air Transport in the United Kingdom

Page 112, courtesy of HSE (2007) – Statistics for 2006/2007

Page 115, courtesy of BAA (2007) – Heathrow and Climate Change

Page 166, courtesy of Times Online (12th August 2007) – Heathrow hell puts BAA in firing line

Page 166, courtesy of Times Online (3rd May 2007) – Bmi chief accuses BAA of forcing passengers to shop

Page 331, courtesy of Flybbjerg, B., Bruzelius, N. & Rothengatter, W. (2003) – Megaprojects and Risk, Cambridge University Press

Page 332, courtesy of Radio 4 (13 June 2007) – Frontiers

Page 332, courtesy of Times Online (4th November 2007) – Lessons in building a railway

Photographs

All photographs courtesy of BAA except images on Page 43 and the following:

Page 43, Sydney Opera House courtesy of janestrachan2, www.Flickr.com, with kind permission of Sydney Opera House

Page 43, Paris Charles de Gaulle Airport courtesy of topher76, www.Flickr.com, with kind permission of Aéroports de Paris

Page 199, Mike Peasland, courtesy of Balfour Beatty

Page 199, Chris Hughes, courtesy of Morgan Vinci

Page 199, photograph of Mark Reynolds, courtesy of Mace

Page 199, photograph of Mike Robins, courtesy of Laing O'Rourke

Page 199, photograph of Grahame Ludlow, courtesy of Spie Matthew Hall

Page 200, photograph of Dervilla Mitchell, courtesy of Arup

Page 207, photograph of Steve Cork, courtesy of Laing O'Rourke

Page 207, photograph of Henk Van Helmond, courtesy of Vanderlande

Page 208, photograph of Willie Walsh, courtesy of BA

INDEX

Printed and bound in the UK by
CPI Antony Rowe, Eastbourne